The Cambridge Introduction to
Shakespeare's History Plays

Shakespeare's history plays, as fresh today as when they were written, are based upon the assumption that time is not simply a destroyer but a preserver, and that 'examples past' might enable us to understand the present and anticipate the future. This lively study examines the continuing tradition of Shakespeare's history plays in stage and film productions as well as giving an account of the critical debate on these plays. Following two introductory chapters giving essential background on the genre, the English history plays are discussed in turn, bringing out the distinctive characteristics of each play: the three early *Henry VI plays*; the perennial stage favourite *Richard III*; *King John*; *Richard II*; *Henry IV 1* and *2*, famous for the character of Falstaff; *Henry V*, which is treated very differently in the film versions by Olivier and Branagh; and *Henry VIII*. An invaluable introduction to these fascinating and complex plays.

Warren Chernaik is Visiting Professor at King's College London, and Emeritus Professor, University of London.

Cambridge Introductions to Literature

This series is designed to introduce students to key topics and authors. Accessible and lively, these introductions will also appeal to readers who want to broaden their understanding of the books and authors they enjoy.

- Ideal for students, teachers, and lecturers
- Concise, yet packed with essential information
- Key suggestions for further reading

The Cambridge Introduction to
Shakespeare's History Plays

WARREN CHERNAIK

CAMBRIDGE
UNIVERSITY PRESS

CAMBRIDGE UNIVERSITY PRESS
Cambridge, New York, Melbourne, Madrid, Cape Town, Singapore, São Paulo, Delhi

Cambridge University Press
The Edinburgh Building, Cambridge CB2 8RU, UK

Published in the United States of America by Cambridge University Press, New York

www.cambridge.org
Information on this title: www.cambridge.org/9780521671200

First published 2007

Printed in the United Kingdom at the University Press, Cambridge

A catalogue record for this publication is available from the British Library

Library of Congress Cataloging-in-Publication Data
Chernaik, Warren L.
The Cambridge introduction to Shakespeare's history plays / Warren Chernaik.
    p.   cm. – (Cambridge introductions to literature)
Includes bibliographical references (p.   ).
ISBN 978-0-521-85507-5 – ISBN 978-0-521-67120-0 (pbk.)
1. Shakespeare, William, 1564–1616 – Histories.   2. Historical drama, English – History
and criticism.   3. Great Britain – History – 1066–1687 – Historiography.   4. Literature
and history – Great Britain.   5. Kings and rulers in literature.   6. Middle Ages in
literature.   I. Title.   II. Series.
PR2982.C53   2007
822.3'3–dc22   2007033002

ISBN 978-0-521-85507-5 hardback
ISBN 978-0-521-67120-0 paperback

Contents

List of illustrations

Cover illustration: David Troughton as Henry IV, *Henry IV, Part 1*, Royal Shakespeare Company, Swan Theatre, Stratford, 2000, directed by Richard Attenborough. Photograph by Geraint Lewis.

Acknowledgements

Much of this book was written in the Humanities Reading Room of the British Library, and I am grateful for the helpfulness of the library staff there and in the Rare Books room, the Senate House Library, and the Maughan library of King's College London. For help with illustrations and with research into the stage and cinematic history of the plays, I owe a particular debt of gratitude to the library staff at the Shakespeare Centre Library, Stratford-upon-Avon, the Theatre Museum, and the British Film Institute. Among copyright holders of film versions of *Richard III* and *Henry V*, I am grateful for the assistance of Lisa Katselas, Photofest Inc., and the BFI.

Sarah Stanton not only commissioned the book, but has been an unfailing source of encouragement and gave me excellent advice on revision. Judith Chernaik, as well as attending endless productions, good and bad, with me, has carried on a running conversation about Shakespeare with me for many years, from which I have profited greatly. Friends and colleagues who have read chapters in draft form or have helped me to clarify my views in conversation include Janet Clare, Robyn Bolam, Gabriel Egan, F. J. Levy, Michael Hattaway, A. R. Braunmuller, Gordon McMullan, René Weis, Kate McLuskie, Sandra Clark, Sonia Massai, Ann Thompson, Richard Proudfoot, and Andrew Gurr. I am especially grateful to Sarah Hatchuel and Nathalie Vienne-Guerin for inviting me to give a paper comparing the Olivier and Branagh films of *Henry V* at the International Shakespeare Conference organized by the Shakespeare Institute in August 2006; that essay, a version of which appears in chapter 8, will be included in a forthcoming collection edited by them, *Shakespeare on Screen*. Sonia Massai invited me to give a paper on *Henry VI* (mostly about the relationship of different versions of *2* and *3 Henry VI*) at the London Shakespeare Seminar in 2005. And among the Shakespeare scholars from whom I have learned most, I must particularly thank Emrys Jones, Annabel Patterson, and Phyllis Rackin.

I have gained immeasurably from discussing Shakespeare's histories with my students at King's College London, the University of Southampton, and Queen Mary, University of London. But my main debt, other than to Shakespeare himself, is to the actors and directors who have made the history plays of Shakespeare come alive in productions.

Chapter 1

The uses of history

Renaissance ideas of history

Shakespeare and his contemporaries did not share the belief, widely held by historians and literary critics today, that there are essential differences between past and present more significant than any possible continuities. To the Shakespeare of *Julius Caesar* and *Henry V*, the past was by no means a foreign country, ruled by different ideological assumptions. The reading of history, according to the preface to Sir Thomas North's *Plutarch's Lives* (the source of Shakespeare's *Julius Caesar, Antony and Cleopatra,* and *Coriolanus*), makes the past present, in the way it 'setteth before our eyes things worthy of remembrance', preserving them from 'the death of forgetfulnes':

> For it is a certaine rule and instruction, which by examples past,
> teacheth us to judge of things present, and to foresee things to come: so
> as we may know what to like of, and what to follow, what to mislike, and
> what to eschue.[1]

History, in this view, teaches by examples, enabling us to understand the present by reflecting on past triumphs, disasters, and missed opportunities. The practical lessons history teaches are applicable to everyday life, by 'comparison and application' to our own circumstances.[2]

The Shakespearean history play is notoriously unconcerned with anachronisms: his ancient Romans and medieval noblemen are Elizabethans, thinly disguised. Cleopatra plays billiards, the conspirators in *Julius Caesar* wear hats and listen to the clock striking, medieval warriors shoot pistols and fire cannons long before they were in use. Samuel Johnson in the eighteenth century complains of Shakespeare:

> He had no regard to distinction of time and place, but gives to one age
> or nation, without scruple, the customs, institutions, and opinions of
> another, at the expense not only of likelihood, but of possibility.[3]

According to his fellow dramatist Thomas Heywood in *An Apology for Actors* (1612):

> If wee present a forreigne History, the subject is so intended, that in the lives of *Romans, Grecians,* or others, either the vertues of our Country-men are extolled, or their vices reproved . . . either animating men to noble attempts, or attacking the consciences of the spectators, finding themselves toucht in presenting the vices of others.[4]

Shakespeare's history plays are not naïvely didactic in the way Heywood suggests, nor, aside from the *Murder of Gonzago* in *Hamlet,* is the link between what is represented on stage and the world of the spectator ever this literal. But drama works, as Heywood recognized, by 'attacking the consciences of the spectators' in awakening their feelings – including, at times, patriotic sentiments and feelings of guilt.

> What English blood seeing the person of any bold English man presented and doth not hugge his fame . . . as if the Personator were the man Personated, so bewitching a thing is lively and well spirited action, that it hath power to new mold the harts of the spectators and fashion them to the shape of any noble and notable attempt. What coward to see his countryman valiant would not be ashamed of his own cowardice?
>
> (*Apology for Actors*, Sig. B4)

Dramatic representation has a magical quality, 'bewitching' the spectators and encouraging what Coleridge later called the willing suspension of disbelief: we watch the events unfold before our eyes, and experience them as happening at this moment.

In *Henry V*, cited by Heywood as an instance of the power of historical drama to 'new mold' and 'fashion' character, the warrior king by implication enrols generations to come in the 'band of brothers' fighting side by side. Memory, reinforced by the retelling of the story in dramatic performance, keeps alive what 'all-oblivious enmity' would destroy:

> This story shall the good man teach his son,
> And Crispin Crispian shall ne'er go by
> From this day to the ending of the world
> But we in it shall be remembered,
> We few, we happy few, we band of brothers.[5]

'Old men forget' (4.3.49), and it is the responsibility of historian and dramatist to counteract the natural tendency to forget or ignore anything beyond the immediate moment. As Ralegh writes:

> For as wee are content to forget our owne experience, and to counterfeit
> the ignorance of our owne knowledge, in all things that concerne our
> selves . . . so wee neither looke behind us what hath beene, nor before us
> what shall bee . . . Wee are compounded of earth, and wee inhabit it.
>
> (*History of the World*, p. 61)

The events of historical narrative and historical drama differ from those in other narratives and plays in that they are assumed to be true, with a separate existence outside the imagination of the author. Shakespeare's English and Roman history plays occupy a hinterland between fact and fiction, challenging the sharp distinction Aristotle in the *Poetics* and Sir Philip Sidney in *The Defence of Poesy* draw between the imaginative artist or poet and the historian who, as they see it, is limited to relating what 'has happened', the realm of verifiable fact. Sidney contrasts the 'golden' world of the poet, who can roam freely 'within the zodiac of his own wit', inventing entire universes, with the 'brazen world' ordinary people and historians are forced to live with.[6] But plays like *Henry V* and *Julius Caesar*, though based closely on historical sources and thus 'tied . . . to the particular truth of things', show that there is plenty of room for invention, interpretation, dramatic heightening within the parameters of given facts or events. The historian writing a narrative and the dramatist writing a play about Henry V needs to make certain formal decisions in shaping his material. Such a writer, as Hayden White has argued, 'confronts a veritable chaos of events *already constituted*, out of which he must choose the elements of the story he would tell'.[7]

The extent to which sixteenth-century historians felt a need to shape and select their material varied greatly, and it has been argued that attitudes towards the writing of history changed markedly during the course of the century. The chronicles of Holinshed and Hall, the main sources for Shakespeare's history plays, are organized 'on the principle of including as much as possible'. Yet this inclusiveness of apparently 'random information' can be seen as a strength rather than a weakness, in allowing for differing voices to be heard. Holinshed's *Chronicles* often juxtapose several accounts of the same events, refusing to select and edit, 'to give everie author leave to tell his owne tale':

> For my part, I have in things doubtful rather chosen to shew the
> diversitie of their writings, than by over-ruling them, and using a
> peremptorie censure, to frame them to agree to my liking: leaving it
> nevertheless to each mans judgement, to controll them as he seeth
> cause.[8]

The 'politic historians' of the later sixteenth century, strongly influenced by Tacitus and Machiavelli, placed a far greater emphasis on causation, on examining the motivations underlying action, often treated with a bracing scepticism. This scepticism, in writers like Ralegh, extended to the reliability and authenticity of the primary sources on which historians depended. As Ralegh wrote in 'a digression' on 'using conjecture in Histories':

> Informations are often false, records not alwaies true, and notorious actions commonly insufficient to discover the passions, which did set them first on foote . . . For the heart of man is unsearchable: and Princes . . . by their own close temper, or by some subtill miste . . . conceale the trueth from all reports.

Ralegh's remarks suggest that the historian's responsibility is to 'search into' the hidden springs of behaviour, hoping to discover 'the most likely motives' of any action, while remaining aware of the endless obstacles which may render his or her task impossible.[9]

In *2 Henry IV*, the King, sick and weary, cries out: 'O God, that one might read the book of fate!' The only lesson one learns from history is that nothing lasts, that 'the revolution of the times' will eventually 'Make mountains level, and the continent, / Weary of solid firmness, melt itself / Into the sea': we are powerless to avert the buffetings of 'chance's mocks / And changes' (3.1.45–9, 51–2). The book of fate is closed to us, and if we could read it, what it reveals would be unbearably painful to contemplate, extinguishing all hope:

> O, if this were seen,
> The happiest youth, viewing his progress through,
> What perils past, what crosses to ensue,
> Would shut his book and sit him down and die.
>
> (3.1.53–6)

The Earl of Warwick, seeking to counter the King's despair, in contrast finds a pattern in history, discernible both in the individual life and in the collective history of 'all men'. Time is not simply a destroyer, but a preserver, planting the seeds of new life in 'the times deceas'd'.

> There is a history in all men's lives
> Figuring the nature of the times deceas'd;
> The which observ'd, a man may prophesy,
> With a near aim, of the main chance of things
> As yet not come to life, who in their seeds
> And weak beginnings lie intreasured.
> Such things become the hatch and brood of time.
>
> (3.1.80–86)

Warwick's organic metaphor suggests that it is possible to learn from experience (the King ends the scene saying 'I will take your counsel'), recognizing recurrent patterns and, wherever possible, taking advantage of them: 'Let us meet them like necessities' (3.1.93, 106). History, Warwick maintains, is not a closed book, and it is not a mass of unconnected details, dead facts. A recognition of the shaping forces of history enables us to understand the past and to anticipate the future.

Two views of history widely held in later periods were far less common among Shakespeare and his contemporaries. Though antiquarian research, the investigation and collection of material remains from past civilizations – inscriptions, coins, place names, records 'hidden in old books hoarded up in corners' – became more and more popular during the sixteenth century, history tended to be identified with narrative. Even distinguished antiquarians like William Camden saw their own researches into 'small things' as falling below 'the Dignity of History', concerned 'to handle Businesses of great weight and Importance'.[10] The positivist conception of history, associated with Leopold von Ranke in the nineteenth century, that the historian, aiming at a scientist's objectivity, should limit himself to 'strict presentation of the facts', 'to let the things speake' and thus 'transmit what happened', avoiding any contamination by values or personality, was virtually unknown in Shakespeare's day.[11] The poststructuralist conception of history, which questions the very existence of objective 'fact', is equally at variance with Renaissance notions of history. In poststructuralist theory, historical facts are 'constituted' by the historian, who imposes a 'fraudulent outline' on his or her materials, making them fit a pre-existing template.[12] Renaissance historians looked for an overall coherence in the events they described, but considered this pattern to be implicit in the events themselves, rather than imposed by the historian. In the Renaissance, history was seen as exemplary, providing practical lessons for its readers. Holinshed, at the end of his first volume, urges his readers to 'imagine the matters which are so manie yeares past to be present, and applie the profit and commoditie of the same unto our selves'.[13]

If it was generally agreed in the Renaissance that a didactic element was prominent in historical narratives and history plays, there was considerable disagreement at the time as to what kind of lessons these works taught. One view, particularly emphasizing the appeal of dramatic performance to a wide popular audience (including the 'unlearned'), is expressed in Heywood's *Apology for Actors*. As we will see, such a view of the history play as fundamentally conservative and serving the interest of the English monarchy in preaching obedience has had considerable currency among twentieth-century Shakespeare critics:

> Plays have made the ignorant more apprehensive, taught the unlearned
> the knowledge of many famous histories, instructed such as can not read
> in the discovery of all our *English* Chronicles . . . Playes are writ with this
> ayme . . . to teach the subjects obedience to their King, to shew the
> people the untimely ends of such as have moved tumults, commotions,
> and insurrections, to present them with the flourishing estate of such as
> live in obedience, exhorting them to allegeance, dehorting them from all
> felonious stratagems. (*Apology for Actors*, Sig. F3, F3v)

According to E. M. W. Tillyard's enormously influential *Shakespeare's History
Plays* (published in 1944 and still in print), this is precisely the intention of
Shakespeare's histories: plays not only keep the past alive, but, by means of
vivid, memorable examples, they teach the audience the virtues of order and
degree, the evils of disorder and disobedience. As Tillyard points out, Edward
Hall's chronicle (1548), one of Shakespeare's principal sources, states as its
'general theme':

> What mischiefe hath insurged in realmes by intestine division, what
> depopulacion hath ensued in countries by civill discencion, what
> detestable murder hath been committed in citees by seperate faccions,
> and what calamitee hath ensued in famous regions by domestical
> discord & unnatural controversy: Rome hath felt, Italy can testifie,
> France can bear witnes . . . and especially this noble realme of Englande
> can apparantly declare and make demonstracion.[14]

Yet if we look at the Preface to Ralegh's *History of the World*, which includes
a brief survey of English history in the same period treated in Hall's chronicle,
the moral he draws and the 'patterne' he finds are very different:

> Oh by what plots, by what forswearings, betrayings, oppressions,
> imprisonments, tortures, poysonings, and under what reasons of State,
> and politique subteltie, have these forenamed Kings, both strangers, and
> of our owne Nation, pulled the vengeance of GOD upon them-selves,
> upon theirs, and upon their prudent ministers! and in the end have
> brought those things to passe for their enemies, and seene an effect so
> directly contrarie to all their owne counsaile and cruelties; as the one
> could never have hoped for. (*History of the World*, p. 61)

The pattern Ralegh describes is fundamentally ironic, or even tragic: as in *Hamlet*, 'purposes mistook / Fall'n on the inventor's heads' (*Hamlet*, 5.2.389–90).
Historical example does not demonstrate the benevolence of those in power
and the prudential wisdom of obedience, but presents a litany of oppressions
and disasters, perpetrated by those priding themselves on their 'politique sub-
teltie'. Though divine providence, as in Hall, is invoked ('But the judgements

of GOD are for ever unchangeable' (p. 50)), Ralegh's perspective, like Machiavelli's, is profoundly secular and without comforting illusions. His advice is being offered to princes rather than subjects, in full awareness that they are probably not going to listen.

Shakespeare's history plays

The *First Folio* (1623) bears the title *Mr William Shakespeares Comedies, Histories, & Tragedies*, dividing the plays into three generic categories, fourteen comedies, eleven tragedies, and ten histories. The arrangement of the plays in the *First Folio* reflects the chronology of the events treated in each play, beginning with *King John* (early thirteenth century) and ending with *Henry VIII*, rather than the order of composition.

Conventionally, the three *Henry VI* plays and *Richard III* are known as 'the first tetralogy', written and performed between 1589 and 1593, and the four plays *Richard II, 1* and *2 Henry IV*, and *Henry V*, written and performed between 1595 and 1599, 'the second tetralogy'. These eight plays treat a continuous slice of English history, beginning late in the reign of Richard II (1398) and ending with the death of Richard III in 1485. In each group of four plays the action is closely linked, with characters appearing in successive plays and explicit references in one play to events depicted in another. *3 Henry VI* begins 'I wonder how the King escaped our hands', a direct reference to the final scene of *2 Henry VI*, and both *Richard III* and *1 Henry IV* begin with tributes to peace succeeding the 'grim-visaged War' or 'civil butchery' presented in an earlier play.[15] A more complex instance of links between plays occurs in the confrontation between father and son in *1 Henry IV*, where the angry king likens his scapegrace son to the deposed Richard II:

> The skipping King, he ambled up and down
> . . .
> Mingled his royalty with cap'ring fools,
> Had his great name profaned with their scorns
> . . .
> And in that very line, Harry, standest thou;
> For thou has lost thy princely privilege
> With vile participation
> . . .
>   For all the world,
> As thou art to this hour was Richard then,
> When I from France set foot at Ravenspurgh.
>   (*1 Henry IV*, 3.2.60–4, 85–7, 93–5)

This scene serves several functions: it links the present action with antecedent action, reminding the audience of a play they may recently have seen, acted by the same company with a number of the same actors; it suggests the recurrence of certain patterns in history, the burden or legacy of the past; and it provides motivation for the action to follow, as Prince Hal strives to disprove his father's accusations and wash away his 'shame' on the battlefield (3.2.137).

Generic categories are not absolute. The term 'history' was used promiscuously in titles of plays during this period: quarto editions of Shakespeare's plays include *The True Chronicle History of King Lear*, *The Tragical History of Hamlet*, and *The Most Excellent History of the Merchant of Venice*, and titles and subtitles of plays by other authors include 'The Famous Chronicle historie', 'The Comicall Historie', and 'An English Tragical History'.[16] Quarto editions of *Richard II* and *Richard III* describe these plays as tragedies. As Paulina Kewes points out, plays by Elizabethan and Jacobean dramatists set in ancient Rome and contemporary or near-contemporary France, the Netherlands, Scotland, or Turkey share thematic concerns and formal characteristics with Shakespeare's English histories, and 'blur the boundaries between the native and the foreign'.[17]

Shakespeare's 'Roman plays', *Julius Caesar* (1599), *Antony and Cleopatra* (1606–7), and *Coriolanus* (1607–8), are classified as tragedies in the Folio, and generally accepted as such. These plays, based on events from Roman history, resemble Shakespeare's English histories in many respects. A play like *Julius Caesar*, first performed in the same year as *Henry V*, not only includes battle scenes staged in a similar manner, but performs a similar balancing act between fact and fiction, between fidelity to a historical source and the requirements of dramatic form. As David Daniell, its recent Arden editor, has said, the subject of *Julius Caesar* is 'the morality of rebellion', which, as in *Richard II* and nearly all of Shakespeare's English histories, is treated as deeply problematical, beset with uncertainties.[18] Bathing their hands in blood, the conspirators prophesy correctly that the present scene will in future years be staged over and over again in theatres like the Globe:

> CASSIUS
> Stoop, then, and wash. How many ages hence
> Shall this our lofty scene be acted over
> In states unknown and accents yet unknown?
>
> BRUTUS
> How many times shall Caesar bleed in sport
> That now on Pompey's basis lies along,
> No worthier than the dust?

CASSIUS
So oft as that shall be,
So often shall the knot of us be called
The men who gave their country liberty.
(*Julius Caesar*, 3.1.111–18)

What they fail to prophesy is that history may judge them differently – not as patriots and heroes of liberty, but as the bloodstained perpetrators of a 'foul deed', the unleashers of 'domestic fury and fierce civil strife' (3.1.263, 274). This kind of dramatic irony is equally characteristic of the English histories, where words are shown to be subject to violently opposed interpretations, and where characters, immersed in a struggle for power and the illusion of autonomy, bring about by their actions 'an effect . . . directly contrarie to all their own counsailes' and intention.[19] In all these plays, individuals are subject to historical forces beyond their understanding and control.

In this study, the primary emphasis will be on the ten plays categorized as histories in the First Folio, with comparisons, where relevant, to the Roman plays and to plays by Shakespeare's contemporaries and predecessors closely related to particular Shakespearean texts. Though *King Lear, Macbeth*, and *Cymbeline* concern themselves with 'the matter of Britain', they are plays of a very different kind. *Edward III* and *Sir Thomas More*, plays of multiple authorship with Shakespeare as a possible co-author, are generically similar to Shakespeare's history plays, but reasons of space do not permit any detailed treatment of these plays here.

The history play is a characteristically Elizabethan genre, prominent during the 1580s and 1590s and markedly declining as a popular dramatic genre after 1603, in the reign of James I. As a genre, the English history play was not invented by Shakespeare: according to Scott McMillin and Sally-Beth MacLean, the Queen's Men, the most prominent and successful theatrical company of the 1580s, specialized in plays based on recent English history. *The Famous Victories of Henry the Fifth* (1586?), probably 'the earliest of extant English history plays among the professional companies', and *The Troublesome Reign of King John* (1588?), both in the repertory of the Queen's Men, may have served as partial sources for Shakespeare.[20] Several other plays belonging to the genre are roughly contemporaneous with Shakespeare's English histories. Marlowe's *Edward II* (1592) and the anonymous *Woodstock* (1592?) are the best known of these, and two other plays, *Edward III* (1590?) and *Edmund Ironside* (1588–90), have, with varying degrees of plausibility, been attributed to Shakespeare, either as sole author or as collaborator.[21] History plays continued to appear on stage, in decreasing numbers, after the death of Elizabeth I. The prologue to John Ford's *Chronicle History of Perkin Warbeck* (1634), described by Levy as the only history play 'of any importance' after 1616, characterizes the genre as 'out of fashion'.[22] Though Shakespeare did not create the history play as a viable dramatic genre, he was more responsible than any other dramatist for establishing its contours and conventions, and his plays are the ones which have endured.[23]

Extremely popular in Shakespeare's lifetime, his English history plays continued to be performed frequently after his death, with a long stage history in the eighteenth, nineteenth, and twentieth centuries. *Richard III*, which provides a star part actors still love to play, is one of the three or four Shakespeare plays most frequently performed today: there are two famous films, with Laurence Olivier (1955) and Ian McKellen (1995) as Richard, as well as Al Pacino's tribute, *Looking for Richard* (1996). Early testimony to the popular success of *1 Henry VI* (a play much less familiar to modern audiences) is provided in Thomas Nashe's *Pierce Pennilesse His Supplication to the Divell* (1592), in praise of the history play as a genre by means of which 'our forefathers' can be 'raised from the Grave of Oblivion'. Like Heywood in *An Apology for Actors*, Nashe locates the moral efficacy of plays in their 'open presence' in live performance, the way they make historical figures immediately present, involving the spectators as participants, where otherwise these 'valiant acts' would lie 'buried' and inaccessible.[24] The example he gives is Talbot, the warrior hero who dominates the first four acts of *1 Henry VI*, dying nobly at the end of Act 4, to rise triumphantly from the grave in each performance, greeted by the tears of spectators.

> How would it have joyed brave *Talbot* (the terror of the French) to thinke that after he had lyne two hundred yeares in his Tombe, hee should triumphe againe on the Stage, and have his bones newe embalmed with the teares of ten thousand spectators at least (at severall times) who, in the Tragedian that represents his person, imagine they behold him fresh bleeding? . . . There is no immortalitie can be given a man on earth like unto Playes. (2.212)

Nashe's figure of 'ten thousand' may not be an exaggeration in indicating the large audiences the play drew in the 1590s. Henslowe's Diary records seventeen performances in 1592–3, and the Rose Theatre, where it was acted, could have held a thousand spectators at each performance.[25] Nashe singles out the death of Talbot as the scene that is most effective in stirring the emotions of the audience; paradoxically, it is presented as a moment of triumph, giving joy to the spectator and to Talbot himself, beyond the grave. As we will see, the patriotic element in Nashe's account of 'brave *Talbot* (the terror of the *French*)' is central not only to *1 Henry VI*, with its English and French armies confronting one another, but to the Shakespearean history play as a genre.

Queen Elizabeth I herself attests to the popularity of *Richard II*, in complaining in 1601 that a play she considered disrespectful to monarchy 'was played 40 times in open streets and houses'.[26] The Queen's disquiet about public performances of a play which modern critics have often seen as promulgating notions of divine right monarchy – the English monarch as 'the figure of God's majesty, / His captain, steward, deputy elect', in the Bishop of Carlisle's eloquent lines (*Richard II*, 4.1.126–7) – would suggest, at the very least, that the play creates certain problems of interpretation. Probably the most famous comment on the play is also attributed to Elizabeth I: 'I am Richard II. Know ye not that?' A reigning monarch sees in a past monarch a reflection of herself – and, perhaps, a commentary on the instability of worldly power. According to Tudor law, 'imagining the death of a king' is one definition of treason. As David Scott Kastan has argued, the representation of monarchy on stage 'undermines rather than confirms authority, denying its presumptive dignity by subjecting it to common view' in the playhouse. The absence of the deposition scene (4.1.154–317) from the first three Quartos (1597 and 1598) of *Richard II* suggests that the Elizabethan authorities recognized the potential for subversion in that play.[27]

The genre and its conventions

These examples of contemporary reaction to Shakespeare's history plays suggest a number of characteristics which might help define the genre and its conventions and assumptions.

1. The history play dramatizes events which purport (or pretend) to be historical fact. The alternative title for *Henry VIII* is *All Is True*, sharply contrasting with *As You Like It, What You Will, All's Well that Ends Well* – though, as we'll see, the claim that 'all is true' can be interpreted in a number of ways. In Shakespeare's English history plays, the materials are drawn from fairly recent British history – the fourteenth century in the first and second tetralogy. There are relatively few plays by Shakespeare and his contemporaries dramatizing historical events under the Tudor monarchs: *Henry VIII*, written and performed in 1613, long after his other history plays, is anomalous in other ways as well.

2. Shakespeare's sources, which he follows in detail, are prose chronicles of the sixteenth century, especially those by Holinshed (2nd edition, 1587) and Hall (1548). Many passages in the plays are close adaptations of passages in the chronicles. The relationship between dramatic text and source is very similar in the Roman plays, where many passages are virtual paraphrases of Sir Thomas

North's translation of *Plutarch's Lives* (1579). A famous example, often cited, is Enobarbus's description of Cleopatra, beginning 'The barge she sat in, like a burnished throne' (*Antony and Cleopatra*, 2.2.196–231). As with Holinshed and Hall, North's Plutarch provides Shakespeare with the general outlines of his plot and characterization, along with many incidental details.

3. In the English histories and in *Julius Caesar* and *Antony and Cleopatra* (though possibly not in *Coriolanus*), the materials of the play were familiar to Shakespeare's original audience.[28] Those coming to see the play knew the story in advance, just as, in all probability, would be the case today in a British audience encountering a play, film, or novel about the First World War or about the life of Queen Victoria (like the Pat Barker trilogy or the film *Mrs Brown*). This of course means certain constraints upon the author, who can't alter facts that are widely known – in a story about Queen Victoria, Prince Albert can't live to a ripe old age, and in a story about Richard II, he has to be deposed and replaced as king by Henry IV. But, within these limits, the dramatist is free to shape his or her materials, suggesting to the audience ways of interpreting the given facts, even at times demonstrating how 'fact', rather than being a stable category, is the product of interpretation.

4. In the Elizabethan history play, the author is not primarily interested in historical accuracy, as a modern historian would be. Shakespeare's plays adjust the facts of history in order to make a play more effective dramatically, emphasizing a pattern or bringing out conflicts of character. Hotspur and Prince Hal were not the same age, and Shakespeare's sources, Holinshed and Hall, do not present them as such. In fact, the historical Hotspur was about twenty years older than the Prince. Shakespeare deliberately makes them two young men for dramatic contrast, setting up their rivalry in the play's first scene. In *1 Henry IV*, he also simplifies and rearranges history in other ways – for example, combining two men named Edmund Mortimer into a single figure. There are accounts of Richard III that do not present him as villainous, do not give him a hunchback and a withered arm. Shakespeare, in this case following his source – Sir Thomas More's *History of Richard III*, as embellished by Hall and Holinshed – makes Richard a deformed villain and tyrant, exulting in his wickedness, and that is the way he is remembered. The plays are thus full of minor inaccuracies and anachronisms which don't matter, as well as deliberate choices by the dramatist which help determine the way he presents his material. We can see historical forces at work through individuals.

5. In Shakespeare's English histories, there is frequently a patriotic element, which constitutes part of their appeal. The tributes of Heywood and Nashe ('What English blood . . .') stress this aspect of the plays, and so, two centuries later, does Coleridge in arguing that 'in order that a drama be properly

historical, it is necessary that it should be the history of the people to whom it is addressed'. The nationalistic or patriotic element is especially prominent in *Henry V*, captured powerfully in Olivier's 1944 film, dedicated to 'the Commandos and Airborne Troops of Great Britain, the spirit of whose ancestors it has been humbly attempted to recapture'.[29]

Yet, as critics have often pointed out, *Henry V* is a play that 'points in two opposite directions', and it has been interpreted in recent productions as anti-heroic and anti-war.[30] John of Gaunt's moving tribute to 'this blessed plot, this earth, this realm, this England' in *Richard II* is equally celebrated as a patriotic set-piece, but in its dramatic context, it emphasizes the sickness of the state ruled by a tyrannous and selfish king:

> That England that was wont to conquer others
> Hath made a shameful conquest of itself.
>
> (*Richard II*, 2.1.40–66)

The King, who should be the embodiment of England, has become a parasite, preying on and destroying England. Rather than projecting a simple, unproblematical patriotism, then, Shakespeare's English history plays subject to critical scrutiny such ethical and political concepts as honour, justice, loyalty, obedience, and the nation.

6. Shakespeare's history plays are a tract for the times, intended to have contemporary relevance. In writing about English history (and to an appreciable extent, in writing about Roman history), Shakespeare is indirectly writing about the England of Elizabeth I. The Queen recognized this in saying 'I am Richard II' and the supporters of the Earl of Essex recognized this in commissioning a performance of a play about the deposition of Richard II (probably Shakespeare's) on the eve of his planned *coup d'état*.[31] The extent to which the plays explicitly 'point at the present' through figures of the past has been much contested by critics. Lily B. Campbell in *Shakespeare's "Histories": Mirrors of Elizabethan Policy* (1947) argued in considerable detail that 'each of the Shakespeare histories serves a special purpose in elucidating a political problem of Elizabeth's day'. Thus, in her view, *King John* reflects 'the actual pattern of events in the long confrontation between Elizabeth and the Catholic church', and *Richard II* 'offers the follies of Richard II only as a background for the problem that was so often discussed during Elizabeth's reign, the problem of the deposition of a king'.[32] More recent critics have stressed the role of local, topical references to support readings of Shakespeare's histories as expressing the dominant ideology of the age, or, alternatively, as serving to undermine such doctrines. For a number of critics, *Coriolanus* is a play about grain shortages in Elizabethan or Jacobean England. Dollimore and Sinfield have argued

that Henry V's war against France stands in for 'the attempt to conquer Ireland' in a play about 'actual or threatened insurrection', promoting the doctrine that 'nothing is allowed to compete with the authority of the King'. For Leah Marcus, *1 Henry IV* 'brings into the open a set of suppressed cultural anxieties about the Virgin Queen, her identity, and her capacity to provide continuing stability for the nation' at a time of 'waning heroism' closely parallelled to 'the situation of England in the early nineties'.[33]

Yet if these plays, English and Roman, treat political issues of immediate concern to Elizabethan England, that relevance need not depend upon specific topical allusions. Indeed, the very nature of historical drama is that it seeks out analogies between the past and present, and these analogies are likely to be general as well as particular. Brecht's *Mother Courage and her Children* is a play about war and how ordinary people are caught up in it, not only about the Thirty Years' War in seventeenth-century Europe. Arthur Miller's *The Crucible*, which like Shakespeare's histories is closely based on historical documents (in this case mostly trial records), is a play about the Salem witch trials of the seventeenth century, which, as Miller says, 'straddles two very different worlds to make them one'. The play's occasion, widely recognized at the time of its first performances, was the anti-communist hysteria in America in the early 1950s, the activities of the House Un-American Activities Committee and Senator Joseph McCarthy. Yet, in later productions, removed from its initial circumstances, the play's central concerns came to be recognized more clearly: 'the power of human imagination inflamed', persecution and scapegoating, the intolerance of dissent in an authoritarian society. As Miller said nearly fifty years after the original production: 'it is part of the play's history . . . that to people in many parts of the world its story seems so like their own.' His 'Note on the Historical Accuracy of this Play' suggests a process of composition analogous to that in Shakespeare's English histories: occasional departures from the literal historical facts, in so far as they are ascertainable, but fidelity to 'the essential nature' of the materials.

> Dramatic purposes have sometimes required many characters to be fused into one . . . [Yet] the fate of each character is exactly that of his historical model, and there is no one in the drama who did not play a similar – and in some cases exactly the same – role in history.[34]

Chapter 2

The wars of the critics

Hall, Holinshed, and Tillyard

Edward Hall's 1548 chronicle, one of the two main sources for Shakespeare's English histories, has as its title *The Union of the two noble and illustre famelies of Lancastre and Yorke, beeyng long in continual discension for the croun of this noble realme*. His two key terms are union and discord: the benefits of 'union or agrement' can only be fully appreciated by comparison with 'the calamities, trobles & miseries' that disharmony brings.[1] E. M. W. Tillyard has characterized this view of history as 'the Tudor myth', by which a nation torn apart by civil strife, extending over many years, is restored to health with the accession of the Tudor line of monarchs.

Tillyard and Lily B. Campbell, writing in the 1940s, have argued that Shakespeare's view of English history was substantially identical with that in Hall, expressing an overarching 'comprehensible scheme of history: a scheme fundamentally religious, by which events evolve under a law of justice and under the ruling of God's Providence, and of which Elizabeth's England was the acknowledged outcome'. In treating Shakespeare's indebtedness to his two principal sources, Hall and Holinshed, Tillyard consistently favours Hall, minimizing the influence of Holinshed, because in his view Holinshed 'blurs the great Tudor myth', including material less in keeping with the overall moral pattern Tillyard finds in the plays.[2] Tillyard sees the two Shakespearean tetralogies as telling one continuous story, even though Shakespeare wrote the second half first – a story which ends with the triumphant accession of Henry VII, grandfather of the reigning Queen. The ideology of restored order, of 'smiling plenty, and fair, prosperous days', as contrasted with 'streams of blood', is neatly summarized in the couplets at the end of *Richard III*:

> Let them not live to test this land's increase
> That would with treason wound this fair land's peace.
> Now civil wounds are stopped, peace lives again.
> That she may long live here, God say 'Amen'.
>
> (*Richard III*, 5.7.34, 37–41)

Tillyard's argument is twofold. First of all, the plays are interpreted as explicitly didactic and as deeply conservative in their ideology. This view of Shakespeare as spokesman for Tudor orthodoxy found wide acceptance in the decades following the publication of Tillyard's book, and still may be said to be the received view of the plays.[3] A second strand in the Tillyard–Campbell argument has not met with as widespread acceptance: that the eight plays in the two tetralogies make up a single coherent pattern, illustrative of God's providence in exacting the penalty for the sin of disobedience. England's original sin, in this reading, is the usurpation of Henry IV in overthrowing his rightful monarch, to be punished not only in his own lifetime but for generations to come in the destructive civil wars during the reign of Henry VI.

Critics of the Tillyard–Campbell school regularly cite the Elizabethan *Homily against Disobedience and Wilful Rebellion* as evidence for a 'universally held' belief in the sinfulness of disobedience among Shakespeare's contemporaries. The Homily, occasioned by the Northern Rebellion of 1569 and the issuing of a Papal bull in the same year condemning Queen Elizabeth as a heretic, attempts to give a spiritual sanction to political doctrines, citing the Fall of Man as evidence that 'obedience is the principal virtue of all virtues, and indeed the very root of all virtues, and the cause of all felicity'. Satan is the father of rebellion, rebels are justly punished with 'shameful ends and deaths', and 'such subjects as are disobedient or rebellious against their Princes, disobey God, and procure their own damnation'.[4]

The perceived need of the Elizabethan authorities to issue this Homily and have it read aloud in church, as well as the arguments it advances, do not reflect the calm assurance of a widely accepted Elizabethan consensus, as Tillyard seems to claim, but deep anxiety. The official establishment in state and church warned against disobedience because they saw it around them all the time, because they were worried about challenges to their power by those they tried to keep in subjection. Not all Elizabethan wives, children, and servants in their daily conduct accepted the view that God 'ordained that, in families and households, the wife should be obedient unto her husband, the children unto their parents, the servants unto their masters' (p. 385). Where the Homily argues that 'it cometh neither of chance or fortune, as they term it, nor of the ambition of mortal men and women, climbing up of their own accord to dominion, that there be Kings, Queens, Princes, and other Governors over men' (p. 386), Shakespeare's history plays can be read as demonstrating the exact opposite. Every one of these plays shows strong-willed and ambitious men climbing to power, with varying success, and most of the plays raise the possibility that 'who's in, who's out' is the result of the lottery of chance or the wheel of fortune.

Shakespearean ambivalence: liberals and sceptics

Where conservative critics of the Tillyard school see the plays as 'cautionary tales', firmly rooted in religious belief, later critics, dissenting from Tillyard's reading, prefer, like Machiavelli in *The Prince* and *Discourses on Livy*, to explain 'history in terms of force, fortune, and practical politics'. John Wilders comments that *The Prince* reads like 'a manual of instruction studied by Shakespeare's politicians'.[5] Prince Hal's soliloquy in Act 1 of *1 Henry IV* ('I know you all . . .'), in which he announces his intention to 'throw off' Falstaff and his other companions, can be read as a practical illustration of Machiavelli's advice that it is more important for a prudent prince to appear to have virtues than actually to have them. Machiavelli's advice on how to gain and retain power can thus provide an illuminating gloss for the three *Henry VI* plays, *Richard III* (whose hero proclaims himself 'subtle, false, and treacherous' and akin to 'the murderous Machavil'), *King John*, and the four plays in the second tetralogy.[6]

Tillyard's conservative, providential reading was challenged by several critics in the next generation, notably Henry Kelly (1970), Robert Ornstein (1972), and John Wilders (1979). These critics argued that 'the supposedly orthodox view of Richard II' as a monarch whose deposition was a heinous sin was 'not the view of most Tudor and Elizabethan writers', could not be substantiated in Shakespeare's *Richard II*, and in fact was not consistently adhered to by Holinshed or Hall. Though Holinshed characterizes Richard II as 'a prince the most unthankfullie used of his subjects, of any one of whom ye shall lightlie read', he also presents him as guilty of 'insolent misgovernance' and of being 'prodigall, ambitious, and much given to the pleasure of the bodie'.[7] Hall similarly includes materials allowing for a balance of sympathies towards Richard II and the man who supplanted him. Other contemporary accounts, including the play *Woodstock*, depict Richard as a tyrant. Rather than a single 'Tudor myth', we can find among Tudor writers a 'Yorkist myth', favourable to Richard, and a 'Lancaster myth', according to which 'the corrupt reign of Richard II was providentially overthrown by Henry Bolingbroke, his cousin, who was next in line for the crown': 'each historian tended, naturally, to favour whichever monarch was in power at the time he wrote or on whose patronage he depended'.[8]

Where Tillyard, writing in wartime England, saw the plays as didactic in intent, the next generation of critics tended to emphasize ambiguity, irony, ambivalence. Echoing Keats's praise of Shakespeare's 'negative capability' and seeing Shakespeare, as Hazlitt did, as 'the least moral of all writers', whose works are characterized by a 'sympathy with human nature in all its shapes', A. P. Rossiter, in his essay 'Ambivalence: The Dialectic of the Histories' (1961), found in the history plays 'a constant Doubleness'. Shakespeare's approach to history and to dramatic construction, according to Rossiter, is dialectical: a 'juxtaposition of opposites, without submitting to urges . . . to obliterate or annihilate the one in the theoretical interests of the other'. Rather than the moralist's certainty, the plays present to the audience opposed points of view in which, one way or another, 'both are valid'. Truth is always double, never single.[9] In this view, rather than providing in *Richard II* an object lesson in the wickedness of usurpation, Shakespeare is careful to preserve a balance of sympathies between the rival claimants to the throne. No moral case can be made for Richard III, but here too the response of the audience is likely to be ambivalent, since he is presented as an attractive figure, full of comic energy, which encourages us to be 'on his side'.[10] Tillyard and other moral critics like J. Dover Wilson in *The Fortunes of Falstaff* (1943) tend to see Falstaff as an 'old white-bearded Satan' (*1 Henry IV*, 2.4.446), the embodiment of those temptations of the flesh which need to be resolutely resisted by an aspiring monarch. In contrast, critics of the next generation tend to find ambivalence, divided sympathies, a refusal to privilege one point of view over another.

Critics of this school pay particular attention to a play's dramatic structure or formal coherence, praising the 'carefully crafted unity' of *1 Henry IV*, with its interweaving of two plots, serious and comic, and its patterning of rival fathers and rival sons. The assumption underlying such criticism is that there is a 'directing intelligence at work' in the play, with its overall structure established at the outset in the King's comparison of Hotspur, 'a son who is the theme of honour's tongue', with the 'riot and dishonour' of his own young Harry (1.1.79–89).[11] Here again the critics tend to stress plurality of interpretations, critical disagreements not easily resolved. In 'The Structural Problem in Shakespeare's *Henry IV*' (1956), Harold Jenkins concludes that 'in the two parts of *Henry IV* there are not two princely reformations but two versions of a single reformation. And they are mutually exclusive.'[12] Norman Rabkin in *Shakespeare and the Problem of Meaning* (1981) finds in *Henry V* a play which 'points in two opposite directions, virtually daring us to choose one of the two opposed interpretations it requires of us'. According to Rabkin, 'no real compromise is possible' between these 'extreme readings', illustrating 'Shakespeare's habitual recognition of the irreducible complexity of things'.[13]

New Historicism and ideology

In the past two decades, the dominant school of criticism of the history plays has been New Historicism, as exemplified in two volumes of essays published in

1985, *Political Shakespeare* and *Alternative Shakespeares*, Stephen Greenblatt's *Shakespearean Negotiations* (1988), and a number of books by Graham Holderness. New Historicists, influenced by poststructuralist notions of history, reject the idea that a historian or critic 'can see the facts of history objectively', as they reject any distinction between literature and historical 'background', literary and non-literary texts. Literary and dramatic texts must be seen as historically specific, not as inhabiting some timeless realm, and as material products, dependent upon the 'material forces and relations of production'.[14]

New Historicists see the history plays as overwhelmingly concerned with power and subject the plays to an ideological critique – as Graham Bradshaw says acerbically, they alternate between presenting 'a repressively authoritarian Shakespeare' and 'a suppressed, subversive Shakespeare'. New Historicists accuse Tillyard and his school (and sometimes accuse Shakespeare) of legitimizing the dominant Elizabethan social order by projecting a 'world picture' which 'reinforces particular class and gender interests by presenting the existing social order as natural and God-given'. Greenblatt, the most subtle and illuminating of New Historicist critic, sees ideology as operating in more complex and unpredictable ways: 'Even those literary texts that sought most ardently to speak for a monolithic power could be shown to be the sites of institutional and ideological contestation.'[15] Among critics generally categorized as New Historicists there is a rough distinction between those who see Renaissance texts as 'univocal . . . shaped by the interests of the dominant classes' and those who prefer to treat the texts as polyphonic, giving expression to 'voices silenced by the repressions of the dominant discourse'.[16]

In his influential essay 'Invisible Bullets', Greenblatt analyses the complex relationship between Prince Hal and Falstaff as illustrative of the general proposition that, in the body politic as in the world of *1* and *2 Henry IV*, 'subversive voices are produced by and within the affirmations of order'. This is generally called the *containment* thesis, and is indebted to the theories of Michel Foucault about the operations of hegemonic power: 'Thus the subversiveness that is genuine and radical . . . is at the same time contained by the very power it would appear to threaten. Indeed the subversiveness is the very product of that power and furthers its ends.'[17] Like many critics, Greenblatt sees Falstaff as profoundly disruptive and anti-hierarchical, representing superabundant physical life and its energies, and as opening up the two plays to 'voices that seem to dwell outside the realms ruled by the potentates of the land' (p. 43). The rejection of Falstaff in *2 Henry IV*, he argues, is 'not an attractive sight but is perfectly consistent' (p. 57). What it is consistent with, in Greenblatt's dark and unsettling view of the play, is not the moulding of an ideal prince but Machiavellian statecraft, using force and fraud to secure its ends, 'squalid betrayals', 'acts of calculation, intimidation, and deceit' (pp. 52–3). Greenblatt thus finds in these plays an ambiguity of a different kind from that praised by Rossiter and Rabkin, 'radical instability tricked out as moral or aesthetic order', a dramatist's conjuring trick (p. 47).

A position similar in many ways is argued in Jonathan Dollimore and Alan Sinfield's 'History and Ideology: The Instance of *Henry V*', included in *Alternative Shakespeares*. In this essay, the focus is almost exclusively on ideology, presenting the play as a reflection of 'real historical conflict' and finding 'counterparts in Elizabethan England' to the action of the play and the issues it raises. The essay concludes belligerently that in Shakespeare 'the ideology which saturates his texts, and their location in history, are the most interesting things about them'.[18] Like Greenblatt, Dollimore and Sinfield see ideology as an attempt to contain possible resistance to hegemonic power, in texts which 'represent society as a spurious unity' and thus 'efface conflict and contradiction'. The role of 'materialist criticism' is to reveal what the literary text seeks to occlude.

> Ideology has always been challenged, not least by the exploited themselves, who have resisted its oppressive construction of them and its mystification of their disadvantaged social position. One concern of a materialist criticism is with the history of such resistance, with the attempt to recover the voices and cultures of the repressed and marginalized in history and writing. (p. 214)

Dollimore and Sinfield are less concerned with recovering the voices of the repressed than with demonstrating how *Henry V* subserves the 'Elizabethan state ideology' (p. 219) in colluding with such repression. Possible areas of resistance include the common soldiers fighting in the war against France, who might contest the myth of national unity. But Dollimore and Sinfield read the scene where the King in disguise encounters the common soldiers Williams, Bates, and Court not as a dialogue or debate, in which two contrasting views are juxtaposed, but as illustrative of 'strategies of containment' (p. 225). Their commentary on the scene (4.1) presents it entirely from the King's point of view, allowing only one voice to be heard. Williams's powerful lines challenging the statements of his disguised companion on the eve of the battle ('But if the cause be not good, the King himself hath a heavy reckoning to make . . .' (4.1.134–43)) go unmentioned. To Dollimore and Sinfield, the scene with the four quarrelling Captains Macmorris, Fluellen, Jamy, and Gower (3.2) illustrates 'the English domination of Wales, Scotland, and Ireland' (p. 221). Again we are given no opportunity to hear their individual voices.[19] It is an open question whether 'the drive for ideological coherence' (p. 222) is located in the critics or in the play they are discussing.

Other recent critics place greater emphasis on the 'subversive potential' in the plays, arguing that Shakespeare's dramatic method of 'polyphony' means that no one perspective is allowed to dominate. In *Stages of History*, Phyllis Rackin argues that the very fact of dramatic performance in itself subverts 'the written discourse of official history', allowing 'the voices silenced by the repressions of the dominant discourse' to 'be heard'. Falstaff's 'witty, irreverent prose', contrasted throughout with the blank verse associated with king and court, is 'the emblem of his freedom', resisting 'confinement to any single, defined place in the social hierarchy'.[20] Other critics, like Michael Bristol and Graham Holderness, see Falstaff as a Bakhtinian Carnival figure, of 'festive abundance', whose words and actions represent 'a comic uncrowning of authority'. Quick-witted, resilient, the embodiment of Bakhtin's 'material bodily principle', Falstaff is, as his recent Arden editor says, 'an unruly presence challenging the fundamental assumptions that motivate the political world'.[21]

'Plebeian men' and 'masterless women', as Rackin shows, are potentially subversive elements within the world of the history plays. If in Shakespeare's historical sources, concerned with 'authorizing present power in genealogical myths of patriarchal succession', women are denied a voice, in plays like *King John*, these disruptive, rebellious feminine voices 'will become more insistent'. *Engendering a Nation*, by Jean E. Howard and Phyllis Rackin, announced in its subtitle as 'a feminist account of Shakespeare's English histories', finds the plays 'as interesting for their contradictions, symptoms of conflict and unresolved struggle as for their coherence'.[22] As the title indicates, *Engendering a Nation* treats the relationship between the 'sense of national identity' the plays create and the development during the early modern period of an 'ideology of domesticity', in which woman's proper sphere was defined in terms of home and family (pp. 33, 39). In the first tetralogy and in *King John*, there are a number of prominent roles for women who exercise power in ways that threaten patriarchal authority. Joan La Pucelle and Margaret of Anjou in the *Henry VI* plays, demonic yet ambivalent figures, violate expected norms in every conceivable way – woman warriors stronger than the men surrounding them, active political figures and agents of disruption, associated with witchcraft and sexual licence.[23] In the second tetralogy, in contrast, 'women are strategically peripherized', occupying 'a space largely set aside from the world of public action' (p. 30), and are often treated as trophies won in arranged marriages, passive objects of exchange.

In this and other studies influenced by New Historicism, the emphasis on ideology has encouraged a revaluation of the plays (both familiar plays like *Henry V* and less familiar ones like *1* and *2 Henry VI*), allowing twenty-first-century readers and viewers to see these works in a new light. As we will see in the chapters that follow, stage productions at different times, as well as films reaching a wider audience, can also bring English and Roman history alive, refashioning the plays in accordance with changing conceptions of the relationship between past and present.

Chapter 3

The paper crown: *1, 2,* and *3 Henry VI*

Henry VI and the critics

Until recently, the three *Henry VI* plays were rarely performed and were gen-erally dismissed by critics as unworthy of the sacred name of Shakespeare. J. Dover Wilson, in his New Cambridge edition (1952), is briskly dismissive: the Henry VI plays are illustrative of the bad taste of the Elizabethan audience, they are hastily cobbled together, they are crude and clumsy, and in all probability they are not by Shakespeare. The received view of these plays at the time of Dover Wilson's edition was that rather than being the work of 'a single mind in the organization of material' in accordance with a 'central design', each of the plays was patchwork, 'poor poetry and poor drama', hastily put together by several dramatists, sometimes working at cross purposes.[1]

Tillyard in *Shakespeare's History Plays* (1944) mounted a strong argument in favour of the coherence of the plays and of their single authorship. But he was more interested in seeing the *Henry VI* plays as a sequence, with each one 'an organic part of a vast design' illustrating an overall moral pattern, than in their individual qualities.[2] To Tillyard, the sequence is 'a series of plays which in the execution are sometimes immature and ineffective', but given an overall coherence by 'the great lesson (implied always and rarely stated) that the present time must take warning from the past and utterly renounce all civil dissension' (pp. 150, 155).

Several critics in the generation after Tillyard rejected his providential, heav-ily didactic interpretation of the sequence, paying close attention to the dra-matic structure of each play and to the motivation of the characters, as well as to the dramatic effectiveness of individual scenes. For Philip Brockbank, writing in 1961, and for Emrys Jones in his excellent *The Origins of Shakespeare* (1977), the dominant pattern in the plays is not didactic, but tragic. Jones devotes par-ticular attention to two extended episodes, one in *2 Henry VI* and one in *3 Henry VI*, 'conceived as . . . brief tragedy'. The first of these is 'the fall and death of Duke Humphrey of Gloucester', the main action of Acts 1–3 of *2 Henry VI*.[3] Duke Humphrey is presented as a virtuous, unselfish servant of the commonwealth, an honest counsellor and repository of the traditional values of duty, loyalty, and integrity, surrounded by a cabal of unscrupulous intriguers plotting his downfall. As Jones shows in detail, the underlying pattern in the episode is the trial of Jesus, especially as it appears in the medieval mystery plays, with the isolated, innocent hero beset by malevolent, unrelenting accusers. A key figure in the scene in which Duke Humphrey is baited by his enemies is King Henry, who like Pilate in the biblical narrative, can 'find no fault' in the 'just man' before him.[4] Though the King is fully aware of Duke Humphrey's innocence and the malice of his enemies, he does not lift a finger to save him or to contest the charges.

It is only after Duke Humphrey is led off to his certain death that the King expresses his sorrow, bewailing 'with sad unhelpful tears' the sacrifice of an innocent man, borne like a calf to the 'bloody slaughterhouse' (3.1.210–12, 218). The tragedy of Humphrey is thus a central element in the larger tragedy of the weak but virtuous King Henry and the maimed commonwealth, as Humphrey himself recognizes in the last lines he speaks in the play, one of the many prophecies of disaster in Shakespeare's histories to be fulfilled afterwards:

> DUKE HUMPHREY
> Ah, thus King Henry throws away his crutch
> Before his legs be firm to bear his body.
> Thus is the shepherd beaten from thy side,
> And wolves are gnarling who shall gnaw thee first.
> Ah that my fear were false, ah that it were!
> For good King Henry, thy decay I fear.
>
> (3.1.189–94)

A second scene with biblical echoes, tragic in its conception and in its effect on audiences in production, is the humiliation and torture of the Duke of York, claimant to the throne, by his mocking enemies, led by Queen Margaret. A scene of 'unmitigated atrocity', prefiguring in many ways the blinding of Gloucester in *King Lear*, the episode, occurring early in *3 Henry VI*, is part of a cycle of vengeance and meaningless slaughter. York, 'that would be England's king', is crowned with a paper crown, made to stand upon a molehill, and tormented by being shown a napkin stained with the blood of his young son. In productions I have seen, Queen Margaret forcibly smears the blood over his face.[5] As Jones and Brockbank have pointed out, the scene, drawing on and expanding details in Holinshed, is both a mock-crucifixion and a mock-coronation. In the play, the ritual mocking of the helpless, wounded York is presented as a desecration of the ideals of chivalry, fatherhood, and kingship, as well as being overtly blasphemous.[6]

Stage history, 1963–2006

The most significant event in the critical rehabilitation of the *Henry VI* plays was
the Royal Shakespeare Company production of *The Wars of the Roses* in 1963,
adapted by John Barton and directed by Peter Hall and Barton. Acclaimed by
reviewers as 'a landmark and beacon in the postwar British theatre', *The Wars
of the Roses* received ecstatic notices.[7] Part of the excitement came from its
being virtually a 'new play' by Shakespeare, fashioned from three plays that
were almost never performed. Peggy Ashcroft, who played Queen Margaret,
said it was her favourite of all the parts she had played. Ashcroft's comments
suggest that she saw the character and the play as essentially tragic:

> What first attracted me to the idea of playing the part? The problem of
> presenting with credibility a woman who could carry her lover's severed
> head on the stage and play a scene holding it in her arms . . . She is one
> of the classic tragic characters in the sense that she is not the victim of
> circumstances but of her own nature.[8]

Reviews emphasized the tragic aspects of 'a spectacle full of awe and fear' in
Hall's production – and indeed, these are apparent in the video, filmed for the
BBC in 1965.[9]

   The Wars of the Roses consciously departed from traditional notions of Shakespeare productions as a vehicle for star performances, attempting 'to strip away
the romantic false accretions of centuries from Shakespeare' by creating an
ensemble production for an acting company working together over an extended
period. The 'house style' which Hall and his associates developed for the RSC
in the 1960s was anti-heroic, suspicious of 'artificial pageantry', accommodat-
ing the plays to a twentieth-century theatrical ideal of expressionist realism,
influenced by the theories of Brecht, Artaud, and Jan Kott's *Shakespeare Our
Contemporary*.[10]

   The Wars of the Roses did not present Shakespeare's text, but a radically
condensed and altered version in which three plays were turned into two.
Feeling that 'the *Henry VI* plays, immensely diffuse and uneven in quality, were
not viable as they stand', Barton reduced the 12,350 words of the Shakespearean
original to 7,450, of which slightly over 6,000 are from Shakespeare and 1,444
lines pseudo-Shakespearean pastiche by Barton.[11] The most extensive cuts,
rewriting and reordering of scenes occur in Parts 1 and 3, while Part 2 is
divided between the two plays, each designed to be 'as theatrically self-sufficient
as possible'.[12] Probably the most successful bit of transposition and rewriting
is the *coup de théâtre* that ends Barton's first play: the death of the Duke of
Suffolk, Queen Margaret's lover, is moved from Act 4 of *2 Henry VI*, to allow

for the dramatic entry of Queen Margaret cradling the head of her dead lover, providing a moving and violent climax, as well as motivating the character's later actions by 'the violence perpetrated on her lover'.[13] Here as elsewhere, Barton and Hall seek to bring out the tragic potential in the individual scene.

Several later productions follow the example of Barton and Hall in turning three plays into two. Adrian Noble's RSC production *The Plantagenets* (1988) was 'cut ruthlessly', with 'battle scenes jammed together . . . speeches broken up and reshuffled'. One critic commented that this version was closer to 'a loose chronicle form' than Shakespeare's *Henry VI* plays.[14] In many respects, *The Plantagenets* was a more traditional, less innovative production than *The Wars of the Roses*, with a great emphasis on medieval pageantry, brightly coloured costumes, and the 'visual splendours' of 'resonant stage-pictures'.[15] As in *The Wars of the Roses* and other productions, King Henry and Queen Margaret provided excellent parts for actors, as did Duke Humphrey and Richard Duke of York.

A far more radical production, also compressing three plays into two, was directed by Michael Bogdanov for the touring English Shakespeare Company, in 1987–9, a modern-dress production, done on a shoestring with minimal resources. Bogdanov's production was full of topical parallels: Jack Cade's rebels are football hooligans, National Fronters; Talbot, complete with eye-patch and clipped accent, is a figure from the imperial past; and Queen Margaret, in a superlatively nasty performance by June Watson (a far cry from the tragic or sympathetic figures portrayed by Peggy Ashcroft and Penny Downie), in appearance and voice resembled Margaret Thatcher. This was a strongly anti-war production, slanted towards satire, while bringing out moments of pathos effectively. Where other productions treated Henry VI as a tragic figure with moral stature, 'the ESC saw him as just one of many characters involved in a power struggle'.[16]

The most radically cut version of the *Henry VI* plays is *Rose Rage*, as directed by Edward Hall and adapted by Roger Warren for an all-male acting company of twelve actors in 2001–2. Here all pretence of human dignity or pathos vanishes in a rapidly moving, cartoon-like display of meaningless butchery. In a succession of very short scenes, the action of *1* and *2 Henry VI* is crammed into a single play, with the character of Joan of Arc eliminated altogether and Talbot's part reduced to one scene. Heads are lopped off, one after another, to indicate 'the increasing savagery'. The deaths of these more or less undifferentiated victims are represented in the production by actors in blood-soaked aprons wielding cleavers, flourishing bloody chunks of meat and ferociously chopping up red cabbages. Some reviewers praised the 'ritualistic horror' as 'absolutely chilling to watch', while others found the treatment of the play reductive.[17]

Productions of the three *Henry VI* plays, uncut, in 1977 and 2000, showed that the plays are theatrically viable in their original form. One great advantage of Terry Hands's 1977 production of the three plays for the RSC is that it allowed *2 Henry VI* to emerge as a self-contained, coherent play, whereas in the shortened versions the material of *2 Henry VI* was divided between two of the revised plays (or in *Rose Rage,* cut to the bare bones).[18] Michael Billington, reviewing the production in the *Guardian,* praised *2 Henry VI* as 'one of Shakespeare's major works', 'a hitherto unreclaimed masterwork'. Reviewers agreed that using 'the full text' of the plays, 'without any reshaping, without any tailoring, without any adapting', had inestimable advantages, enabling audiences to observe the ways characters developed from play to play in the actors' performances.[19]

The production of the three plays by Michael Boyd for the RSC in 2000, widely acclaimed by reviewers, again showed 'how effective and coherent these playhouse scripts can be, even without major revisions or additions'. The critics no longer treated the plays patronizingly as immature and second-rate: to Joyce McMillan, *Henry VI* 'stands revealed, in this . . . complete RSC production, as an underrated masterpiece . . . and one that could hardly speak more clearly to western audiences today'.[20] Far more than Terry Hands's 1977 production, Michael Boyd in 2000 and again in 2006 sought by striking visual symbolism in the staging 'to unify the stylistically variable plays'. In 'skilful use of repeated and echoed actions', characters reappeared in various guises, sometimes as ghosts overseeing the action. Duke Humphrey was brought back to preside over the death of his enemy Winchester, Talbot and his son returned again and again in other paired characters 'as representatives of martial virtue and patriotic feeling betrayed'. Battle scenes made imaginative use of the full resources of the Swan Theatre (and, in the 2006 restaging, the Courtyard), with actors swinging from ropes or ladders and dead bodies hoisted aloft, contributing to an 'evocation of a world turned to chaos'. In an ensemble production, Boyd and his actors were concerned throughout to bring out 'the plays' structure' and 'to exhibit the playing-out of conflicts and processes larger than any single figure caught up in them'.[21]

A new and original production of a play will always be a reinterpretation, and Boyd's version of the *Henry VI* plays differed greatly from both *The Wars of the Roses* and the Tillyardian view of Shakespeare as the conservative proponent of order and obedience. To one reviewer, the plays represented 'the young Shakespeare at his most radical, questioning the real value of all the conventional loyalties', whereas to another, the production 'clearly rejects the conservative notion that the history plays show England rescued by providence emerging from civil war into the sunlit securities of the Tudor monarchy'.[22] But if Boyd's production sees history as nightmare while *The Wars of the Roses* sees the pattern of history as akin to tragedy, they agree in presenting King Henry VI, the central figure of the plays, as a virtuous, ineffectual political innocent surrounded by wolves, raising the question of 'whether the exercise of power is always tainted'. King Henry VI, interpreted differently by the actors David Warner, Alan Howard, Ralph Fiennes, and David Oyelowo in these productions, is in each of them the moral centre of the plays, the 'tormented conscience of his entire reign', impotently watching it spiral towards destruction.[23]

1 Henry VI: brave Talbot and his adversaries

Structurally, *1 Henry VI* is the most straightforward of the three plays. Scenes of warfare, set in France, alternate with scenes of domestic quarrelling among powerful English courtiers. Talbot, an embodiment, like the dead Henry V, of traditional values of courage and integrity, is contrasted throughout the play with the selfishness, divisiveness, and arrogance of such courtiers as Winchester, York, Somerset, and Suffolk. In the English court, only Duke Humphrey, Lord Protector, exhibits any concern for the good of the commonwealth, rather than the pursuit of self-interest. The unity of the French, under the charismatic leadership of Joan La Pucelle, is contrasted with the crippling divisiveness among the English.

Talbot's death in Act 4 is directly brought about by the mutual animosity between the leaders of the Yorkist and Lancastrian factions, the Duke of York and the Duke of Somerset, prefiguring the destructive civil wars which erupt in Parts 2 and 3. York blames 'that villain Somerset' for not sending troops, and then refuses to send his own forces to aid Talbot, 'hemm'd round' by the French. Sir William Lucy, one of many choric figures representing traditional values, comments explicitly on the betrayal of Talbot by his supposed allies: 'his fame' is contrasted with 'their shame' (4.3.9, 47–52; 4.4.21, 46).

The cast of characters in *1 Henry VI* is different from that in the later two plays. Talbot and Joan, with the two largest roles, are dead before the end. Queen Margaret enters the play in Act 5 – significantly, at more or less the moment Joan, another disruptive Frenchwoman, leaves it. In Michael Boyd's 2000 and 2006 productions, the two parts were played by the same actress (with some rearrangement of lines to allow for a costume change), creating the impression that the two women are manifestations of the same subversive, destructive force.[24]

King Henry VI is a less central figure in Part 1 than in the later two plays. He does not appear until 3.1, where, protesting 'O, how this discord doth afflict my soul', he has little influence on the 'civil dissension' swirling around him, impotently calling for 'love and amity' among those who are disinclined to restrain their 'slaughtering hands' and 'keep the peace' (3.1.68, 72, 87, 106). Though he warns here of how divisiveness weakens the nation in time of war, later in this scene he shows political ineptitude in visibly preferring the red rose of Somerset to the white rose of York and then in giving the two bitter enemies joint command of the English forces in France.

One reason that Henry VI does not appear until Act 3 is that, in literal fact, he was a child during the events depicted in much of *1 Henry VI*. Shakespeare radically simplifies, compresses, and alters the facts of history in this play, re-arranging and transforming material derived from the chronicles of Holinshed and Hall far more than in *2* and *3 Henry VI*. Part 1 covers the events of thirty years, from 1422 to 1451, compressed into five acts with no indication of time passing, where Part 2 presents events which in Hall's chronicle take up only thirty pages. Talbot is given a prominence as English champion far more than in the chronicles – at times he seems to be fighting the French wars single-handed – and the symbolic opposition of Talbot and Joan La Pucelle is largely Shakespeare's invention. In historical fact (and in the chronicles), Joan was burned at the stake in 1431, where Talbot died in battle in 1453, and not as a result of the feuding of York and Somerset. The marriage of Henry VI and Margaret of Anjou occurred in 1444, and the battles depicted in Acts 1–4 took place over an extended period, twenty-five years and more. As Cairncross says, the overall effect is 'almost to annihilate historic time', reshaping history in order to bring out a dramatic pattern, in which ideals of heroic virtue and service are supplanted by a destructive ethos of selfishness.[25]

Talbot's death is properly heroic, showing not only stoical endurance ("Tis but the shortening of my life one day'), but a commendable concern for 'chivalry' and the continuity of tradition in the son for whom he has acted as 'tutor' in the ways of honour (4.5.2; 4.6.29, 37). Young John Talbot, dying by his father's side, can say to his father 'Is my name Talbot? And am I your son? / And shall I fly?' Death is thus fulfilment, the long-desired mistress, the inevitable end of a hero's life.

> Soldiers, adieu! I have what I would have,
> Now my old arms are young John Talbot's grave.
>
> (4.5.12–13; 4.7.31–2)

At his death, Talbot is given the traditional obsequies by Sir William Lucy, who recites, over nine lines, a list of the titles 'that designate his patriarchal lineage and heroic achievement' ('Great Earl of Washford, Waterford, and Valence . . .'). Joan's mordant comment suggests an alternative set of values: anti-heroic, reductive in its insistence on the physicality of the decaying corpse, anticipating in its comic realism Falstaff's battlefield soliloquy on honour:

> PUC.
> Here is a silly-stately style indeed!
> The Turk, that two and fifty kingdoms hath,
> Writes not so tedious a style as this.
> Him that thou magnifiest with all these titles,
> Stinking and fly-blown lies here at our feet.
>
> (4.8.63, 72–6)[26]

Joan La Pucelle is an ambivalent figure. One frequently expressed view is that the treatment of Joan is 'crude slander', chauvinist and misogynist, appealing to the prejudices of the Elizabethan audience. Yet the prowess demonstrated on stage of a female warrior, 'strong beyond the conventional expectations of her sex', makes the Joan of *1 Henry VI* a complex figure ideologically.[27] There are two perspectives on Joan within the play, French and English, and they are completely opposite. In her first appearance in the French camp, on a mission to 'free my country from calamity', she is challenged to single combat and immediately overcomes the Dauphin. She is equally formidable in her first encounter with Talbot, again in single combat. The stage direction presents her as 'driving Englishmen before her', to Talbot's dismay: 'Where is my strength, my valour, and my force?' (1.5.1). To the English, her powers are unnatural, repeatedly stigmatized as derived from witchcraft: they hurl insults at her, calling her 'strumpet', 'trull', 'damned sorceress', agent of 'hellish mischief', 'vile fiend' and 'shameless courtezan'. To the French, she is 'divinest creature, Astraea's daughter' and 'France's saint', a 'sweet virgin' who displays a mastery of 'stratagem' along with undaunted courage and patriotism. Holinshed's account of Joan shows a similar ambivalence, speaking of her in one passage as 'of person stronglie made and manlie, of courage great . . . an understander of counsels', and in another castigating her 'execrable abhominations', including 'conversation with wicked spirits'.[28]

In Joan's last appearance in the play, the English perspective seems to win out, as she calls on evil spirits to aid her (the stage direction is 'Enter Fiends', who then 'shake their heads' and 'depart', deserting her) and then, after being captured by the English, pleads for her life by claiming to be pregnant. The degradation of Joan in the final scenes can be seen as a way of neutralizing the threat that she represents. Stripped of her demonic allies, she is revealed as a mere woman after all, and is punished for stepping out of line.[29] Yet in every performance I have seen, Joan is presented as a sympathetic, attractive figure, and, as staged, her death comes across not as the triumph of English virtue over perfidious France, but as cruel, unmerited suffering.

2 Henry VI: 'Thou art not king'

At the end of the first scene of *2 Henry VI*, the Duke of York is left on stage to soliloquize. Any soliloquy creates a degree of complicity between speaker and audience, as well as advancing the plot and preparing the audience for what is to follow. Like his son, the future Richard III, he is a Machiavel, unscrupulous, with a strong will, a confidence in his own abilities, and a scorn for those who 'surfeit in the joys of love' or display other signs of weakness. In this speech, York shows political astuteness and an ability to plan ahead, making temporary alliances 'till time do serve', while never losing sight of his ultimate goal, the 'golden mark' of the crown he eventually plans to claim (1.1.242, 247–50). At the moment, he will 'make a show of love' to those he secretly despises and then, 'when I spy advantage, claim the crown' (1.1.240–1). Like his son Richard of Gloucester, who plays an increasingly prominent role in Parts 2 and 3, he understands the lessons of Machiavelli's *The Prince*, and is equally willing to embrace force and fraud in pursuit of his ends, playing the lion or the fox.

Here and elsewhere in the play, York is contemptuous of King Henry VI, considering him weak, unwarlike, 'bookish', unfit to rule. Like Margaret, later his bitter enemy, York sees King Henry as insufficiently manly and insufficiently regal, and therefore unqualified to

> ... hold the sceptre in his childish fist,
> Nor wear the diadem upon his head
> Whose church-like humours fits not for a crown.
>   (1.1.244–6, 258)

Later in the play, he openly defies the King, insulting him to his face, and in effect declares war on him, asserting his own claim to the throne not on the grounds of ancestral right, but on the grounds of being more fit to rule, more kinglike, more comfortable with the trappings of power.

Both the Yorkist claim and the rival Lancastrian claim are backed up with troops, brought on the stage. York's enemies try to arrest him, charging him with 'capital treason' for his remarks, but these words are empty, when each of the two rival kings, each with his own army and allies among the nobility, can call the adherents of the other traitors.

> YORK
> 'King' did I call thee? No, thou art not king,
> Nor fit to govern and rule multitudes
> ...
> That head of thine doth not become a crown;

> Thy hand is made to grasp a palmer's staff,
> And not to grace an aweful princely sceptre
> . . .
> Here is a hand to hold a sceptre up,
> And with the same to act controlling laws.
> Give place! By heaven, thou shalt rule no more
> O'er him whom heaven created for thy ruler.
>
> (5.1.93–107)

Despite the mention of 'heaven' in the last two lines, there is no appeal here or elsewhere in the *Henry VI* plays to divine right. The world of *2 Henry VI* is one where power rules, where justice is silenced, where claims of conscience are transparent excuses for breaking a solemn oath. In Act 4, Lord Saye, a loyal servant of the commonwealth, defends his conduct in terms of 'justice', probity, the public good:

> Justice with favour have I always done,
> Prayers and tears have moved me, gifts could never.
> When have I aught exacted at your hands,
> But to maintain the King, the realm, and you?
>
> (4.7.63–6)

His reward for 'pleading so well for his life' (4.7.100) is to be slaughtered by an angry mob and have his head chopped off.

York, as man of action and as adroit, unprincipled politician, is contrasted with Henry VI and with Duke Humphrey, concerned to 'labour for the realm' rather than for his 'own preferment' (1.1.180–1). Like Lord Saye, Duke Humphrey has remained constant to an ideal of public service, 'studying good for England' with 'heart unspotted' (3.1.100, 111). York is fully aware that 'the good Duke Humphrey' is 'the shepherd of the flock', a 'virtuous prince' (2.2.73–4), but nevertheless deliberately plots his downfall. If the first half of the play has as its central action the tragedy of the martyred Duke Humphrey, the second half of the play presents the unleashing of chaos in the naked struggle for power after his restraining hand is removed.

In his characterization of King Henry VI and Queen Margaret, Shakespeare follows the general outlines of Hall's account. Where Queen Margaret, according to Hall, was 'of stomack and corage, more like to a man, then a woman', her husband also displays characteristics ordinarily associated with the opposite gender. In comparing him unfavourably to her lover Suffolk, she sees him as less than a man, sexually neuter, one whose failings as a king are 'failings of masculinity':[30] Hall, like Shakespeare, in summarizing King Henry's character, emphasizes his piety and unworldliness, though giving a more balanced and nuanced view than the hostile remarks of York and Queen Margaret:

> For kyng Henry, whiche reigned at this tyme was a man of a meke spirite, and of a simple witte, preferryng peace before warre, reste before businesse, honestie before profite, and quietnesse before laboure . . . There could be none, more chaste, more meke, more holy, nor a better creature: In him reigned shamefastnesse, modestie, integritie, and pacience to be marveiled at, takyng and sufferyng all losses, chaunces, displeasures, and such worldely tormentes, in good parte, and with a pacient manner.
>
> (Bullough, *Narrative and Dramatic Sources*, III.105)

Even the terms of praise here present King Henry as a man ill-equipped for the responsibilities of monarchy and disinclined to assume them. The virtues of 'shamefastnesse', modesty, meekness, and chastity are not those normally associated with kingship, but with the Christian saint ready to embrace martyrdom or with the ideal of womanhood perpetrated in conduct books. Productions of the play have brought out these characteristics in Henry, with David Warner in *The Wars of the Roses* particularly emphasizing his saint-like passivity in 'takyng and sufferyng all losses' and Alan Howard his withdrawal from the world of action, his 'preferryng peace before warre'. Yet if Shakespeare, developing hints in Hall's chronicle, makes King Henry a tragic figure, he is not presented as a blameless victim but, in the standard tragic pattern, as to some degree responsible for his own downfall. His lack of political skills causes him to be 'negligent', 'governed of them whom he should have ruled', making errors of judgement with serious consequences.[31]

Where King Henry is concerned for the health of his soul and Duke Humphrey the health of the state, Queen Margaret, an amoral, destructive force throughout Parts 2 and 3, seeks only power. In Hall as in Shakespeare, her primary motivation is a burning desire 'to take upon her the rule and regiment, bothe of the kyng and his kyngdome'.[32] In all respects, she is the opposite of her husband, a 'coragious quene' with 'giftes and talentes of nature' that might in other circumstances be seen as virtues, but are inappropriate for her position, defying convention.

> But on the other parte, the Quene his wife, was a woman of a greate witte, and . . . of haute stomacke, desirous of glory, and covetous of honor, and of reason, pollicye, counsaill, and other giftes and talentes of nature belongyng to a man, full and flowying: of witte and wilinesse she lacked nothyng, nor of diligence, studie, and businesse.
>
> (Bullough, *Narrative and Dramatic Sources*, III.105–6)

In their excellent commentary on the *Henry VI* plays, Howard and Rackin, though recognizing that Margaret is 'a powerful stage presence' and the only woman in Shakespeare's histories able to 'dominate' a play as a central figure, nevertheless primarily see her as a Bad Example. She illustrates 'the danger which ambitious and sexual women pose to English manhood and to English monarchy', warning husbands and fathers to keep a close watch over their wives and daughters. But actresses who have played the part, from Peggy Ashcroft to Penny Downie and Fiona Bell, do not see Margaret as a monster but as 'one of the greatest parts ever written', a complex figure reacting to changing circumstances: 'She is amoral, in the strict sense of the word. She is not immoral, she simply has no morality, but responds to the world she has to operate in, reacting in a sense simply as an animal to stimuli, but then politicizing her responses.'[33] It is possible to see her actions in Parts 2 and 3 as instinctively moving to fill a power vacuum, exerting her will to do what her husband has declined to do, following the practical advice of Machiavelli. Yet even in Part 2, where she is not yet the 'tiger's heart wrapped in a woman's hide' (*3 Henry VI*, 1.4.137), capable of savage cruelty to the helpless, wounded York, she not only takes an active part in the conspiracy to bring about the downfall of Duke Humphrey, but urges her fellow conspirators to have him murdered. The King, she says, is 'too full of foolish pity' and may act to save Humphrey's life: 'This Gloucester should be quickly rid the world / To rid us from the fear we have of him' (3.1.225, 231–4).

On the discovery of Humphrey's sudden death, King Henry acts decisively for the only time in the play, banishing Suffolk, whom he suspects of being responsible for the murder and of plotting 'mischance unto my state' (3.2.288). After the King pronounces Suffolk's banishment, Margaret and Suffolk, alone on stage, have an extended love scene (with some details resembling the balcony scene in *Romeo and Juliet*), mourning their forthcoming separation. In Suffolk's death scene, Shakespeare, following hints in Hall, brings out popular resentment of Suffolk's malign political influence, as 'the most swallower up and consumer of the kynges treasure' and enemy of 'all good and verteous counsailors'.[34] The scene is particularly interesting as the eruption of the common people on the stage, contrasting, with considerable dramatic economy, Suffolk's arrogant contempt for his social inferiors with the colloquial vigour and decisiveness of the 'base men' who have captured him. These common soldiers show more concern for the commonweal than the haughty aristocrat who treats them as an inferior species, 'paltry, servile, abject drudges':

> SUFFOLK
> Obscure and lousy swain, King Henry's blood,
> The honourable blood of Lancaster,
> Must not be shed by such a jady groom.

> Hast thou not kissed thy hand and held my stirrup,
> Bare-headed plodded by my foot-cloth mule
> And thought thee happy when I shook my head?
>
> (4.1.51–6, 105)

The leader of the troops pronounces the judgement of the people's court on Suffolk, and in the dramatic context the verdict is a just one.

LIEUTENANT
Ay, kennel, puddle, sink, whose filth and dirt
Troubles the silver spring where England drinks,
Now will I dam up this thy yawning mouth
For swallowing up the treasure of the realm.
Thy lips that kissed the Queen shall sweep the ground.[35]

Act 4, which unlike the rest of the play is largely in prose, is devoted to Jack Cade's rebellion, a popular uprising eventually brought under control when Cade's supporters desert him. Prose in Shakespeare's plays is often the language of clowns – comic actors and the common people, urban or rural. In the confrontation between the erudite public servant Lord Saye and Cade, Lord Saye speaks in dignified blank verse, while Cade and his followers (Dick the Butcher, Smith the Weaver) speak colloquial prose. The original Cade may have been Will Kemp, the leading comic actor in Shakespeare's company.[36] Later productions have differed in the extent to which they bring out the comic aspects of Cade and his followers, or present them as terrifying symbols of mob violence and blood lust. As several critics point out, Cade in the chronicles is far from a buffoon: Hall, though he emphasizes his 'base byrthe' and his cruelty, presents Cade as a 'subtil capitayn', of 'goodley stature, and pregnaunt wit', 'sober in communication, wyse in disputing', while also 'arrogant in hart' and 'presumptuous'.[37] Cade and his followers in the chronicles have genuine grievances, where in Shakespeare they seem to be animated by a spirit of destruction, a deep-seated resentment against all they consider their social superiors.

In depicting Cade's rebellion, Shakespeare draws on a number of accounts of the Peasants' Revolt of 1381, including Holinshed and an anonymous play, *The Life and Death of Jack Straw*. In making the resentment of the labouring poor against the rich and privileged the motivation of the rebels, Shakespeare departs from Hall, taking hints from accounts of Wat Tyler, Jack Straw, and John Ball in the Peasants' Revolt. Cade's talk of 'liberty' in stirring up his troops is patently hypocritical, especially since he has just described himself as 'rightful heir' to the throne and shortly afterwards declares it to be 'treason for any that calls me other than Lord Mortimer' (4.2.122, 173; 4.6.5–6). Though the term 'class' is anachronistic in the Elizabethan period, there is at least an incipient class-consciousness in Cade's appeal to his followers, with its assumption that every 'gentleman' is his enemy and all those wearing 'clouted shoon' or 'leather aprons' his natural allies, even if some of them are too timid to recognize their class interests (4.2.12–13, 174–7).[38] Cade gives his followers 'a license to kill', burning down ancient buildings and wantonly destroying everything in their path. Anarchy, Shakespeare suggests here and elsewhere, is tyranny under another name in the unbridled rule of will, the sleep of reason: 'Away, burn all the records of the realm. My mouth shall be the Parliament of England.' In turning the land into a 'slaughterhouse', Cade's rebellion anticipates the action of Part 3, though in darkly comic rather than tragic mode, projecting a nightmare vision of blind, self-destructive carnage.[39]

Though Cade is an opportunist, ultimately believing in nothing but his own advancement, the prose scenes in Act 4, like the confrontation of Suffolk and the soldiers and the false miracle of Saunder Simcox in Act 2, introduce an element which will become more prominent in Shakespeare's later histories. In the disruptive, aggressive words of Cade, as in the tavern scenes of *1* and *2 Henry IV* and the truculence of the soldiers Bates and Williams in *Henry V*, we hear the voice of the common people, and an indication of conflicts within the society that cannot easily be resolved. When the eloquent humanist Lord Saye, spokesman for civilized values and the rule of law, confronts an armed mob, the dramatic context creates a degree of sympathy for a virtuous man victimized. But Cade's words, equating education and the processes of law with unjustified privilege, complicate the situation: as often in Shakespeare, it is not a confrontation of right against wrong, but a juxtaposition of two incompatible perspectives.

> CADE
> I am the besom that must sweep the court clean of such filth as thou art.
> Thou hast most traitorously corrupted the youth of the realm in creating
> a grammar school; and whereas before, our forefathers had no other
> books but the score and the tally, thou hast caused printing to be
> used . . . It will be proved to thy face that thou hast men about thee that
> usually talk of a noun and a verb and such abominable words as no
> Christian ear can endure to hear. Thou hast appointed justices of peace
> to call poor men before them about matters they were not able to
> answer. Moreover, thou hast put them in prison, and because they could
> not read, thou hast hanged them.   (4.7.28–41)[40]

A speech which starts out as a defence of blind ignorance against learning turns into a critique of a legal system which perpetuates privilege and injustice. If we laugh at the comic exaggerations of the Shakespearean clown, with its parody of the language of the law courts, we may also feel uncomfortable.

3 Henry VI: Tiger's heart

Civil war in Part 3 is presented as the breakdown of natural and social ties, the erosion of feudal loyalties, feelings of patriotism or community. There is no equivalent here of Talbot or Duke Humphrey: the only spokesman for traditional values in this play is King Henry VI, neither warrior nor statesman, but shoved to the margins of the action as an impotent looker-on. Kingship in *3 Henry VI* is entirely desacralized, stripped of mystery or dignity, as it is treated throughout as transferable property, to be passed from hand to hand. The word 'crown' occurs sixty times in the text, more than in any other Shakespeare play, but almost always as token of possession or object of desire – as for example, it is for Richard of Gloucester, in lines echoing Marlowe's *Tamburlaine:*

> RICHARD
> And, father, do but think
> How sweet a thing it is to wear a crown,
> Within whose circuit is Elysium
> And all that poets feign of bliss and joy.
> (1.2.28–31)[41]

To have two kings asserting 'I am thy sovereign' and 'I am thine' (1.1.76) is the equivalent of having no king. When, in one of a series of uncrownings, Warwick removes the crown from Edward's head, saying 'Henry now shall wear the English crown / And be true king indeed' (4.3.49–50), the irony is clear enough.

Oaths are broken freely again and again. Richard advises his father early in the play that 'for a kingdom any oath may be broken', claiming sophistically that the authority before whom he swore the oath was not 'true and lawful' (1.2.16, 23). When the park keepers, seizing the king to whom they were 'sworn true subjects', disclaim that oath because they are now 'true subjects to the king: King Edward', they follow the example of the great men of the realm, who assiduously watch the way the wind blows (3.1.78–95). Clarence, brother to Richard and Edward, flits back and forth from side to side, following the lure of self-interest at the expense, first, of loyalty to his brother and then, breaking yet another 'holy oath' (5.1.92), of fidelity to his father-in-law, Warwick. At each turn, he finds an excuse to justify his conduct.

Hall's account of the battle of Towton accurately describes the world depicted throughout *3 Henry VI*, a world in which conventional ideas of 'nature' and the bonds of nature are routinely violated.

> This conflict was in maner unnaturall, for in it the sonne fought against the father, the brother against the brother, the nephew against the uncle, and the tenaunt against his lord, which slaughter did . . . sore debilitate and much weken the puyssance of this realm.
>
> (Bullough, *Narrative and Dramatic Sources*, III.183)

In the opening scene, King Henry, faced with a superior force and the defection of some of his supposed allies, agrees to entail the crown to the Duke of York and his heirs, in order to avoid bloodshed. Queen Margaret upbraids him ('I shame to hear thee speak') in terms which anticipate Lady Macbeth:

> MARGARET
> Had I been there, which am a silly woman,
> The soldiers should have tossed me on their pikes
> Before I would have granted to that act.
> But thou preferr'st thy life before thine honour.
>
> (1.1.233, 245–8)

Margaret takes on the role of leader of the Lancastrian army because, in her view, Henry has failed to perform his duties as king and father: she is more of a man than he is. Lady Macbeth similarly accuses her husband of being irresolute, insufficiently manly ('When you durst do it, then you were a man'), presenting her own iron resolution as overriding any bonds of nature, any traditional notions of femininity (*Macbeth*, 1.7.49, 54–9).

In the powerful scene where Margaret torments the captured Duke of York, gloating at his anguish, York, with no weapons left other than his tongue, attacks her as unnatural, embodying 'the opposite' of all those virtues normally associated with women:

> YORK
> Women are soft, mild, pitiful and flexible:
> Thou stern, obdurate, flinty, rough, remorseless.
>
> (1.4.134, 141–2)

In the play's most celebrated line, he calls her a 'tiger's heart wrapped in a woman's hide' (1.4.137): women don't do such things. Weeping at the death of his young son and at his own humiliation, York is presented as a piteous spectacle, whose sufferings should provoke tears in any observer, and not the 'inhuman' response of his 'inexorable' enemy (1.4.154). Indeed, Northumberland,

an ally of Margaret, responds in exactly that way ('His passion moves me so /
That hardly can I check my eyes from tears' (150–1)), heightening the contrast between 'natural' compassion and the stifling of remorse, and indicating
a likely audience response to the scene as staged.

Kinship bonds among the Yorkist and Lancastrian factions are used to autho-
rize cruelty. Margaret's ostensible justification for her behaviour throughout
Part 3 is that she is defending her son's rights as heir to the throne. The word
'father' occurs sixty-eight times in the play, even more often than the word
'crown'.[42] In mocking York, Margaret lays particular stress on the failure of his
dynastic hopes and the failure of his sons to rescue him. When, in an earlier
scene, Clifford slaughters the innocent, defenceless child Rutland, the desire
for revenge dehumanizes him. Kinship ties, the duty of revenge, Clifford tells
Rutland, cancel out all other human feelings.

> CLIFFORD
> In vain thou speak'st, poor boy: my father's blood
> Hath stopped the passage where thy words should enter.
> (1.3.21–2)

Again, the passage anticipates *Macbeth* – in this case, Lady Macbeth's terrifying 'unsex me here' soliloquy, wilfully embracing the unnatural, the
inhuman.

> LADY MACBETH
> Make thick my blood,
> Stop up th'access and passage to remorse;
> That no compunctious visitings of Nature
> Shake my fell purpose,   (1.5.39–44)

Clifford characterizes his desire for revenge as insatiable, tormenting him and
causing him to 'live in hell'. His own suffering has turned him into a monster,
a killing machine, resisting any impulses of 'pity'.

> CLIFFORD
> Had I thy brethren here, their lives and thine
> Were not revenge sufficient for me;
> No, if I digged up thy forefather's graves
> And hung their rotten coffins up in chains,
> It could not slake mine ire nor ease my heart.
> (1.3.25–9, 33, 36–7)

Margaret, unlike her ally Clifford, expresses pleasure in the pain of her enemy. The monosyllabic directness of her language contrasts with the formal dignity of York's response.

> MARGARET
> Why, art thou patient, man? Thou should'st be mad;
> And I, to make thee mad, do mock thee thus.
> Stamp, rave, and fret, that I may sing and dance.
> Thou wouldst be feed, I see, to make me sport:
> York cannot speak unless he wear a crown. –
> A crown for York! And, lords, bow low to him.
> Hold you his hands whilst I do set it on.
>   [*Putting a paper crown on his head.*]
> Ay, marry, sir, now looks he like a king!
>
> (1.4.89–96)

The paper crown mocks York's aspirations and, by an implication of which the speaker is unaware, all human dignity, the presumed sacredness of monarchy and the belief that kings are set apart from ordinary men. In its bleak dismissal of 'tradition, form and ceremonious duty', the scene prefigures Richard II's realization that a king is 'subjected' to the same sorrows and vicissitudes as anyone else (*Richard II*, 3.2.173, 176). Here and elsewhere in the play, right is equated with the naked exercise of power, and power is equated with the ability to inflict pain without restraint. The obscene ritual crowning is also a re-enactment of the crucifixion, affording York no release from suffering.

If Margaret and Clifford can invoke the ties of blood as overriding all other considerations, in a second tragic episode the violence of civil war is shown to be destructive of natural kinship bonds. The scene begins with an extended soliloquy by King Henry, and its formal patterning is characteristic of the scene as a whole. King Henry presents himself as a neutral, passive observer, watching as from a great distance the tide of battle 'sways . . . this way' and that. In the midst of carnage, he longs for a peace and tranquillity he has never been able to attain, imagining an idealized pastoral existence void of care, moving at a slow pace in accordance with the rhythms of nature:

> O God, methinks it were a happy life
> To be no better than a homely swain;
> To sit upon a hill, as I do now,
> To carve out dials quaintly, point by point,
> Thereby to see the minutes how they run:
> How many makes the hour full complete,
> How many hours bring about the day,

How many days will finish up the year,
How many years a mortal man may live.
(2.5.5, 21–9)

This moment of contemplation and repose, with its contrast of the world of public affairs, where kings and other great men are afflicted by 'care, mistrust, and treason' (2.5.54), and the peaceful life of the simple shepherd, is interrupted by the sudden appearance of some actual peasants, simple men caught up in the war.

The scene that follows is staged as a tableau, a play within the play, with the king as onstage observer and chorus, voicing the expected response of the theatrical audience to the 'piteous spectacle' before their eyes.

> *Alarum. Enter a* SON *that has killed his father, at one door.*
>
> SON
> Ill blows the wind that profits nobody:
> This man whom hand in hand I slew in fight
> May be possessed with a store of crowns . . .
>
> *Enter a* FATHER *that has killed his son, at another door.*
>
> FATHER
> Thou that so stoutly hast resisted me,
> Give me thy gold – if thou hast any gold –
> For I have bought it with an hundred blows.
> (2.5.55–7, 73, 79–81)

Shakespeare clearly points out the element of self-interest and self-preservation in these men, seeking to profit materially from a war in which they have been forced to fight. Yet those who have done the killing are no less victims than those they have killed: all have been pressed into service unwillingly, as the common soldiers who do the fighting in their masters' quarrels. The son explains that feudal obligations, with his father 'the Earl of Warwick's man' and himself 'pressed forth' by the King, have led father and son to fight on different sides (2.5.64–6). Unlike Queen Margaret and Clifford, they do not seek to justify their acts, but pronounce moral judgement on them as 'butcherly, / Erroneous, mutinous, and unnatural' (2.5.89–90), responding with a flow of tears indicating heartfelt remorse. The ritual incantation of son, father, and king links the pain of the individual family, ripped apart by war, with the maimed commonwealth:

> FATHER
> I'll bear thee hence; and let them fight that will,
> For I have murdered where I should not kill.
> (2.5.121–2)

In the second half of the play, family bonds among the victorious Yorkists rapidly unravel. Edward, the oldest brother, now claiming the title of king, commits a series of rash acts, abuses of power, which antagonize his closest supporters. Led by lust and wilfulness, he impulsively offers marriage to the widow Lady Grey, even though he is fully aware that his powerful ally Warwick is at that moment negotiating a politically advantageous marriage for him in France. When his brothers Clarence and Richard criticize the 'hasty marriage' as foolish and impolitic, his answer is to assert his arbitrary will as monarch:

> KING EDWARD
>   I am Edward,
> Your king and Warwick's, and must have my will.

And, when he grants preferment to Lady Grey's relatives in preference to his own brothers, he again asserts, tyrannically, 'my will shall stand for law' (4.1.15–18, 50).

Predictably, the reaction of Warwick and of Clarence, both directly insulted by Edward's behaviour, is anger at what they consider betrayal: if Edward is false to them, they will reciprocate in kind. Machiavelli had pointed out that princes with an insecure grasp on power should take care not to antagonize those who had helped them gain power, remaining wary of them as potential enemies, and that men have a strong desire to protect their own property.[43] Clarence's reaction to his brother's ill-judged behaviour is to assert the priority of self-interest, finding his own advantage in breaking off any alliance with his brother. Warwick's reaction invokes honour rather than naked self-interest, though the repeated first-person pronouns suggest that for him honour is identified with the demands of self to be recognized and fed. Edward has rewarded him with 'shame' instead of the expected material benefits, and therefore Edward is 'no more my king': in revenge, he will put Henry back on the throne (3.3.184, 190–1).

Richard of Gloucester, unlike his brother Clarence, hides his feelings in public and does not openly oppose King Edward. Instead, in the first of two great soliloquies, he reveals to the audience his overwhelming desire 'to catch the English crown' (3.2.179) and his determination to allow nothing to stand in his way. Here, emerging from his chrysalis, is the Richard of legend, the Machiavel, consummate actor, free from all moral restraints, embodiment of the will to power in its most concentrated form.

> RICHARD
> Why, I can smile, and murder whiles I smile,
> And cry 'Content' to that which grieves my heart
> . . .

> I'll play the orator as well as Nestor,
> Deceive more slily than Ulysses could.
> . . .
> I can add colours to the chameleon,
> Change shapes with Proteus for advantages,
> And set the murderous Machiavel to school.
> (3.2.182–95)

This is the first time in the play we hear in any detail about Richard's bodily deformity: previously 'valiant Richard' (2.1.198) has appeared mostly as a warrior. In this speech, as in the soliloquy that begins *Richard III*, he descants on his unfitness for, and contempt of, the softnesses of love. Richard's awareness of the 'disproportion' within himself can be seen as motivating his behaviour, leading him to disavow all human ties, or as symptomatic, a logical consequence of the world he inhabits, and illustrative of the recurrent imagery of nature and the 'unnatural' that, in *3 Henry VI* as in *Macbeth*, runs through the play.

> Why, Love forswore me in my mother's womb
> And, for I should not dwell in her soft laws,
> She did corrupt frail Nature with some bribe
> To shrink mine arm up like a withered shrub;
> To make an envious mountain on my back
> Where sits Deformity to mock my body;
> To shape my legs of an unequal size;
> To disproportion me in every part.
> (3.2.153–60)

Richard's second soliloquy occurs after he has killed Henry VI in the play's penultimate scene. Henry's last words, as well as cursing Richard as 'an indigested and deformed lump' from the time of his birth and associating him with ill omens and emblems of darkness, are a prophecy of disasters to follow. What Henry prophesies is not retribution on Richard, a restoration of order and justice, but 'slaughter', continued civil war – indeed, he summarizes what we have already seen in the play, the destruction of families, with maimed survivors left to mourn fruitlessly:

> KING HENRY
> And many an old man's sigh, and many a widow's,
> And many an orphan's water-standing eye –
> Men for their sons', wives for their husbands',
> Orphans for their parents' timeless death.
> (5.6.39–42, 51, 59)

Richard's defiant proclamation of the sovereignty of self and the abandonment of all human ties contains the germs of the first half of *Richard III*, in which, acting on this principle, he rises to power on a heap of corpses: 'Henry and his son are gone; thou, Clarence, next, / And one by one I will dispatch the rest' (5.6.90–1). But, beyond this, it serves as the culmination of a process apparent throughout *3 Henry VI*, the erosion of the traditional bonds of nature and society, to be replaced first by adherence to a clan, with all outside the closed circle defined as enemies, and then by pure self-interest, knowing no restraint. In this final phase, embodied by Richard of Gloucester, all outside the ravenous self are lawful prey, and the will to power is identified with the urge to destroy.

> RICHARD
> I had no father, I am like no father;
> I have no brother, I am like no brother;
> And this word 'love', which greybeards call divine,
> Be resident in men like one another
> And not in me: I am myself alone.
>
> (5.6.80–4)

Chapter 4

Determined to prove a villain: *Richard III*

Stage and screen

Richard III is both an independent play and the conclusion of a tetralogy. Richard of Gloucester, a prominent figure in *3 Henry VI*, is basically the same person in this play and in the first half of *Richard III*, a man who has 'neither pity, love, nor fear', ruthless in his single-minded pursuit of power. Much of the action of the first two acts of *Richard III* is summarized proleptically in Richard's soliloquy near the end of *3 Henry VI*:

> For I will buzz abroad such prophecies
> That Edward shall be fearful of his life
> And then, to purge his fear, I'll be thy death.
> Henry and his son are gone; thou, Clarence, next,
> And one by one I will dispatch the rest.
> (3 Henry VI, 5.6.68, 87–91)

Productions of the play on its own, more common than those in which it forms part of a cycle, face the problem of what to do about antecedent action and links to the *Henry VI* plays. Both Olivier and McKellen in their film versions splice bits of Richard's soliloquies from *3 Henry VI* into the first scene of *Richard III*. McKellen inserts three lines from the earlier play into the soliloquy that begins *Richard III*, as he scrutinizes his face in a mirror:

> Why, I can smile, and murder whiles I smile
> . . .
> And wet my cheeks with artificial tears,
> And frame my face to all occasions.[1]

McKellen (or his director, Richard Loncraine) also adds, as prologue to the 'winter of our discontent' soliloquy, nearly five minutes of virtually wordless action depicting the deaths, at Richard's hands, of Henry VI and his son Prince Edward, followed by the celebrations of the victorious Yorkists at a grand ball, with Richard prowling malevolently on the sidelines.[2]

Both McKellen and Olivier cut Shakespeare's text freely, eliminating Queen Margaret, the only character who appears in all four plays of the tetralogy. Her presence in the film as 'a symbol of the past', McKellen comments, might confuse cinema audiences, unless passages were added 'explaining clearly who she is and has been'. In its truncated version of Clarence's dream in the scene in which he is murdered at Richard's orders (1.4.1–68), the McKellen film omits all mention of Clarence's guilty conscience, his awareness of his 'false, fleeting, perjured' behaviour in the earlier play:

> O Brakenbury, I have done these things,
> That now bear evidence against my soul.[3]

Richard III was first performed by Shakespeare's company, the Chamberlain's Men, in 1594, with Richard Burbage as Richard – probably two years or so after *2* and *3 Henry VI* were performed, also with Burbage as Richard, by a short-lived earlier company, Pembroke's Men. Critics have often commented on the greater complexity and more assured 'control over dramatic materials' in *Richard III* as compared with the earlier plays in the tetralogy. This may suggest a gap of some time in the writing of *3 Henry VI* and *Richard III*.[4] Richard III was the role which made Burbage's reputation as a leading actor, and since Burbage's time this demanding role, dominating the play and longer than any Shakespearean part other than Hamlet, has always attracted bravura performances by star actors. The version which held the stage for nearly two centuries was Colley Cibber's adaptation, *The Tragical History of King Richard III* (1700), performed by David Garrick in the eighteenth century and by John Philip Kemble and Edmund Kean, among others, in the nineteenth century. Cibber's version omits Clarence and Hastings as well as Queen Margaret, and adds a new Act 1, partly drawn from *3 Henry VI*, depicting the imprisonment of Henry VI in the Tower of London and his murder by Richard. In later scenes, Cibber adds at least seven soliloquies for Richard, not only fattening his own star role, but materially altering Shakespeare's characterization, making Richard an 'aspiring Soul' motivated by ambition, both more transparently villainous and more heroic in stature than Shakespeare's Richard:

> Why were Laws made, but that we're Rogues by Nature?
> . . .
> There's not a Slave but has his share of Villain;
> Why then shall after Ages think my deeds
> Inhumane? Since my worst are but Ambition:
>
>> Ev'n all Mankind to some lov'd Ills incline,
>> Great Men chuse Greater Sins – Ambition's mine.[5]

1. Antony Sher as Richard III, Penny Downie as Lady Anne, *Richard III*,
Royal Shakespeare Company, 1984, directed by Bill Alexander.

At the end of Cibber's play, the victorious Richmond pays tribute to his adversary (after borrowing some passages from *1 Henry IV* and *Henry V*, to enhance
the dignity of their final encounter):

> Had thy aspiring Soul but stir'd in Vertue
> With half the Spirit it has dar'd in Evil,
> How might thy Fame have grac'd our *English* Annals:
> But as thou art, how fair a Page thou'st blotted.[6]

As Olivier's and McKellen's performances in stage productions and on screen illustrate, Richard of Gloucester is a particularly juicy role for star performers, dwarfing the other characters in the play. Other notable Richards in recent years include Antony Sher's mesmerizing, sexy Richard in Bill Alexander's 1984 RSC production, who whizzed around the stage on crutches which turned him into a cyborg, half-human and half-mechanical, both illustrating and compensating for his bodily deformity. Unlike Olivier and McKellen, Sher's production retained Queen Margaret and, though dominated by a charismatic Richard, gave full recognition to the forces surrounding and opposing Richard and ultimately bringing about his downfall.[7] McKellen, in the stage and screen versions, and Sher both included a visually impressive and symbolically potent coronation scene, not in Shakespeare. McKellen's coronation, in the film and in the 1990 National Theatre production directed by Richard Eyre, is a fascist rally, with cheering crowds and a ring of black-shirted uniformed police (in the film, vast numbers of extras multiplied by trick photography). In the Sher/Alexander production, the impressive, quasi-religious coronation, with the entire cast singing a Gloria, is the moment when Richard throws away his crutches, prefiguring his decline.[8]

Productions of the play as the conclusion of a cycle, like the Hall–Barton *Wars of the Roses* (1963) and Michael Boyd's 2000 production, rarely have a barnstorming, bravura Richard. Reviewers commented on the low-key approach of Ian Holm in *The Wars of the Roses*, which had a powerful Queen Margaret in Peggy Ashcroft to provide a counterbalance. The same general pattern – a greater emphasis on the other characters, sense of ensemble, awareness of the larger historical patterns underlying the play – characterized other productions of *Richard III* as the culmination of a series of interconnected plays, rather than as a vehicle for heroic acting. As Anton Lesser, Richard of Gloucester in Adrian Noble's *Henry VI* and *Richard III* (1988), says in an interview:

> The virtue of doing the play in sequence . . . was that, by the time you got to *Richard III*, you knew exactly who everybody was; you knew why Margaret was mad and why she is still around the court . . . The great virtue of this new situation was that I didn't have to make up for these shortcomings by doing some sort of extraordinary one-man show . . . Instead, I had to build a real person, not a two-dimensional figure of evil, but a person whose seeds I found in the play we called *Henry VI* (our version of Shakespeare's *1 Henry VI* and the first half of *2 Henry VI*), in which Richard does not even appear.[9]

Shakespeare and More

In this play, as in his other history plays, Shakespeare follows a source closely, selecting and arranging his material in the interest of dramatic effectiveness. The source of *Richard III*, providing Shakespeare with the basic outlines of his characterization of Richard and, in considerable detail, the action of the first three acts of the play, up to Richard's coronation, is Thomas More's *History of King Richard III*. In all probability, Shakespeare did not consult the separate edition of More's *History* published in 1557, but used Hall's Chronicle of 1548, which prints More's unfinished History up to the point where it breaks off, supplementing it with an account of the last part of Richard's brief reign.[10] More's Richard is, in all essential qualities, Shakespeare's Richard. His physical appearance, his bitterness at being 'Cheated of feature by dissembling nature, / Deformed, unfinished', his plotting and dissimulation, his scorn for conventional morality and indifference to family ties, are as vividly present in the character sketch near the beginning of More's history as in Shakespeare:

> Richarde the third sonne . . . was in witte and courage egall with either of them, in bodye and prowess farre under them both, little of stature, ill fetured of limmes, croke backed, his left shoulder much higher then his right, hard favoured of visage . . . He was malicious, wrathfull, envious . . . He was close and secrete, a deepe dissimuler, lowlye of counteynaunce, arrogant of heart, outwardly familier where he inwardely hated, not letting to kisse whom hee thought to kill: dispitious and cruell, not for evill will alway, but often for ambicion, and either for the suretie or encrease of his estate. Frende and foo was muche what indifferent, where his advauntage grew, he spared no mans death, whose life withstoode his purpose.[11]

More's *History* provided Shakespeare with more than the details of characterization and plot. More's Richard is not simply a villain, but a wit, a consummate actor, skilled in deceiving and manipulating others by assuming one or another mask and concealing his 'close and secrete' intent. In the darkly comic scene where Richard and his ally Buckingham put on a performance before the Mayor and other prominent citizens, with Richard, entering 'between two bishops, aloft', pretending piety and reluctance to take the crown, Shakespeare closely follows More – not least, in the consciousness of the two principal actors and the audience that it was all a charade. In this instance, More, like Shakespeare, finds a degree of complicity between the deceivers and the deceived:

> There was no man so dul that heard them, but he perceived well inough,
> yᵗ all the matter was made betwene them . . . And menne must
> sommetime for the manner sake not be a knowen what they know.
>
> (*History*, p. 80)

In More and in Shakespeare, the entire episode is marked by the frank admission of theatricality by the performers, confident in their ability to 'counterfeit the deep tragedian' in pursuit of their 'stratagems' (*Richard III*, 3.5.6–12). Shakespeare adds a further level of irony in having the deceivers openly confess their tricks to the theatrical audience, while leaving it uncertain to what extent the onstage audience are fooled by the performance.

> BUCKINGHAM
> When he had spoke, some followers of mine own,
> At the lower end of the Hall, hurled up their caps,
> And some ten voices cried 'God save King Richard!'
> 'Thanks, loving citizens and friends', quoth I,
> 'This general applause and loving shout
> Argues your wisdom and your love to Richard'
> – And so brake off and came away.
>
> RICHARD
> What, tongueless blocks were they? Would they not speak?
>
> BUCKINGHAM
> No, by my troth, my lord.   (3.7.30–38)[12]

Where Olivier brings out the comic aspects of the scene, the McKellen film, with explicitly twentieth-century analogies, focuses on the ability of those in power to manipulate public opinion.

In his version of this episode, More develops the theatrical metaphor in several directions, suggesting that 'Kynges games' resemble 'stage playes', with 'pore men' as passive spectators.[13] Here More not only satirizes the hypocrisy of politicians, but suggests the instability of power, the rapidity with which the royal stage can turn into the executioner's scaffold. The advice he gives to lookers-on, like that argued by Raphael Hythloday in Book I of *Utopia*, is that 'wise men' will 'refrain to meddle in the commonwealth', knowing that any advice they give will be ignored and may well put them in danger: 'If I should propose to any king wholesome decrees . . . think you not that I should forthwith either be driven away or else made a laughing-stock?'[14] An anonymous 'Third Citizen', fearing the disruption in 'a troublous world', makes a similar comment in *Richard III*: 'When clouds appear, wise men put on their cloaks' (2.3.9, 32).

The pattern of history, as More presents it in *The History of King Richard III* and Shakespeare in *Richard III*, is ironic. Richard knows more than those he is deceiving – Clarence, Hastings, the Mayor and citizens, eventually his ally Buckingham – and we know more than Richard. As Richard Sylvester suggests, the model underlying More's *History* is Tacitus' account of the reign of Tiberius, a quintessential tyrant.[15] Shakespeare's play is an anatomy of tyranny, dramatizing the tyrant's rise and fall. As McKellen notes, 'audiences across the world' took the touring version of the National Theatre production as a warning against tyranny, applying it to their individual circumstances:

> The more specific a production, the more general its relevance. Although our story was obviously an English one, audiences took the message personally wherever we toured. In Hamburg, Richard's blackshirt troops seemed like a commentary on the Third Reich. In Bucharest, when Richard was slain, the Romanians stopped the show with heartfelt cheers, in memory of their recent freedom from Ceaucescu's regime.[16]

Tyrant, seducer, and clown

Besides the scene with the Mayor and citizens, other major episodes in Acts 1–3, depicting Richard's rise to power, are closely indebted to More's *History*. As in More, Richard uses his skills in dissimulation to bring about the downfall of possible rivals, playing off the Queen and her faction against Clarence and Hastings, and ruthlessly dispatching both Clarence and Hastings while pretending friendship to them. Virtually all the details in the mini-drama of the fall of Hastings come from More: the dying King's attempt to patch up the quarrel between Hastings and the Queen's relations (2.1); the attempt, through an intermediary, to sound out Hastings about Richard's becoming king (3.1 and 2); the omen of a dream ignored by Hastings (3.2); even the strawberries Richard sends for, before springing the trap on Hastings (3.4). In More, 'the protectour and the Duke of Buckingham made very good semblaunce unto the Lord Hastinges, and kept him much in company',[17] and in Shakespeare, Hastings is blind to Richard's true nature:

HASTINGS
His grace looks cheerfully and smooth today
. . .
I think there's never a man in Christendom
Can lesser hide his love or hate than he;
For by his face straight shall you know his heart.

(3.4.53–8)

In both accounts, Hastings is 'too fond', 'trusting too much', and one lesson to be learned from his fall is homiletic:

> HASTINGS
> O momentary state of worldly men,
> Which we more hunt for than the grace of heaven!
> Who builds his hopes in air of your fair looks
> Lives like a drunken sailor on a mast,
> Ready with every nod to tumble down
> Into the fatal bowels of the deep.
>
> (3.4.86, 101–6)[18]

Both More and Shakespeare use the episode to illustrate the arbitrary nature of tyrannical power, but Shakespeare, to a greater extent than More, shows Hastings deserted by his fellow courtiers, concerned to save their own skins.

> RICHARD
> Off with his head! Now by Saint Paul,
> I will not dine today, I swear,
> Until I see the same. Some see it done.
> The rest that love me, come and follow me.
>   *Exeunt; Cateby [and soldiers] remain with Hastings.*
>
> (3.4. 81–4)

The Olivier film at this point has all the courtiers at the council table, including Hastings's friend Lord Stanley, move away from Hastings, as if in fear of contamination; McKellen comments that 'Stanley and the Archbishop are prepared to swear black is white if only they can get out of the room alive' (p. 178). Richard's unexpected brandishing of his withered arm as he accuses Hastings is a stunning theatrical moment:

> RICHARD
> Then be your eyes the witness of this ill.
> See how I am bewitched. Behold, mine arm
> Is like a blasted sapling withered up.
>
> (3.4. 72–4)

More's comments make it clear that the assembled courtiers are fully aware that the accusation of witchcraft is fraudulent and that Richard is putting on a performance.

> And thereupon every mannes mind sore misgave them, well perceiving that this matter was but a quarel. For wel they wist, that ye quene was to wise to go aboute any such folye . . . And also no man was there present, but wel knew that his harme was ever such since his birth.
>
> (More, *History*, p. 48)

Here as elsewhere in More as in Shakespeare, Richard uses his skill as an actor – his ability to 'frame my face to all occasions . . . Change shapes with Proteus for advantages', aware at having 'nothing to back my suit at all / But the plain devil and dissembling looks' – to aid him in his shameless pursuit of power.[19]

In dramatizing Richard's machinations against his brother Clarence, Shakespeare relies on a mere hint in More, who with a historian's caution remarks that there is 'no certaintie' in the rumours that Richard 'was gladde of his brothers death yᵉ Duke of Clarence, whose life must nedes have hindered hym' in his ambition 'to be kyng himself':

> Somme wise menne also weene, that his drift covertly convayde, lacked not in helping forth his brother of Clarence to his death: which hee resisted openly, howbeit somewhat (as menne demed) more faintly than he yᵗ were hartely minded.[20]

Shakespeare's Clarence, like Hastings, is fooled by Richard's skilful dissimulation, his pretence that 'this deep disgrace in brotherhood / Touches me deeper than you can imagine' and that he will do his utmost in interceding with the King on Clarence's behalf. In an aside, after Clarence's exit under guard, Richard reveals his true intentions, taking the audience into his confidence:

> RICHARD
> Go tread the path that thou shalt ne'er return.
> Simple plain Clarence, I do love thee so
> That I will shortly send thy soul to heaven,
> If heaven will take the present at our hands.
>   (1.1.111–12, 117–20)

Both Olivier and McKellen address these lines, like all of Richard's soliloquies and asides, directly to the cinema audience, turning the viewers into accomplices.

> I never doubted that in the film he would have to break through the fourth wall of the screen and talk directly to the camera, as to a confidant. If this unsettled the audience, so much the better . . . They would also better appreciate his ability to fool, deceive and seduce his hapless victims.   (McKellen, *Richard III, a Screenplay*, p. 23)

Richard's cosy, intimate relationship with the theatrical audience complicates any moral judgement and keeps us from siding entirely with his victims (other than the two young princes): he is too clever, prompting laughter and grudging admiration at the way he 'offers the false as more attractive than the true'. A consummate actor, he takes an 'artist's delight in his craft'.[21]

One of Richard's roles is that of the clown, generating 'roars of laughter at wickednesses (whether of deed or word) which the audience would immediately condemn in real life'.[22] As such, he is the direct descendant of the Vice in the medieval morality play, an affinity which he himself acknowledges, inviting the audience to admire his skill at equivocation:

> RICHARD [*aside*].
> Thus like the formal Vice Iniquity,
> I moralize two meanings in one word.
>   (3.1.82–3)

It has been argued that the traditional Vice, like Richard himself, exulting in his role as demonic jester, is ultimately the servant of conventional morality, rather than its subverter: the comic displays of the Vice 'delighted the popular audience and reconciled them to . . . the homiletic theme'. But, as recent productions of *Richard III* bring out, the performative dimension of the Vice and of his descendant Richard is 'highly transgressive', suggesting an unlimited potential for destruction, hypnotic in its appeal.[23]

In the scene, not in More, in which Clarence awakes from a dream 'full of dismal terror' (1.4.7) to confront his murderers, there are suggestions of a system of values other than Richard's corrosive nihilism. Except for the two young princes, murdered in the Tower, none of Richard's victims is entirely innocent: all are active participants in a world of multiple betrayals, subject to the appeal of self-interest. Clarence's dream foreshadows his death (drowned in a butt of malmsey) and, in equivocating terms, warns against Richard as a false friend – one of many passages where the audience can read the signs a character is unable to interpret:

> As we paced along,
> Upon the giddy footing of the hatches,
> Methought that Gloucester stumbled, and in stumbling
> Struck me, that sought to stay him, overboard
> Into the tumbling billows of the main.   (1.4. 15–19)

Clarence is vulnerable not simply because he, like Hastings, is too trusting, but because he is guilty, has failed to heed the promptings of conscience. Though he considers himself 'a Christian-faithful man', he has given in to temptation, and now suffers pangs of remorse for his past acts:

> CLARENCE
> Then came wand'ring by
> A shadow like an angel with bright hair,
> Dabbled in blood, and he shrieked out aloud,

'Clarence is come, false, fleeting, perjured Clarence,
That stabbed me in the field by Tewkesbury'.
(1.4.4, 49–53)[24]

The stings of conscience, the conflict between self-interest and traditional
ethical principles, are central concerns in the comic dialogue between the two
murderers, in a prose scene which, like the Jack Cade episode in *2 Henry VI*,
introduces ordinary men into a world of contending dukes and princes. Like
Macbeth, the second murderer worries about the possibility of 'judgement
here' and in 'the life to come'.

2 MUR.
The urging of that word 'judgement' hath bred a kind of remorse in me.

1 MUR.
What, art thou afraid?

2 MUR.
Not to kill him, having a warrant for it, but to be damned for killing him,
from which no warrant can defend us.

1 MUR.
Back to the Duke of Gloucester, tell him so.[25]

The two murderers, like Tyrrell later in the play, find 'warrant' for their
behaviour in obedience to those in power and in the promise of financial
gain or preferment. They can resist the 'dregs of conscience' within them when
they remind themselves of practical material considerations.

1 MUR.
Remember our reward when the deed is done.

2 MUR.
Zounds, he dies. I had forgot the reward.

1 MUR.
Where is thy conscience now?

2 MUR.
In the Duke of Gloucester's purse.
(1.4.110, 112–17)

Tyrants throughout history have relied on finding followers with flexible consciences, the Catesbys, Tyrrells, and Buckinghams of the world, intent on their
own advancement. The Second Murderer's brief aria on the inconveniences
of conscience anticipates Falstaff's disquisition on honour, though here the

passage, with its biblical echoes, invokes the moral standards by which the speaker can be judged, implying its own refutation:

> 2 MUR.
> I'll not meddle with it, it is a dangerous thing, it makes a man a coward.
> A man cannot steal, but it accuseth him; he cannot swear, but it checks
> him; he cannot lie with his neighbour's wife, but it detects him . . . It
> beggars any man that keeps it. It is turned out of all towns and cities for
> a dangerous thing, and every man that means to live well endeavours to
> trust to himself and live without it.   (1.4.123–32)

When Clarence wakes, facing imminent death, he appeals to earthly justice, the 'course of law', and to the prospect of heavenly judgement, the hope of 'redemption / By Christ's dear blood'.

> CLARENCE
> Are you called forth from out a world of men
> To slay the innocent? What is my offence?
> Where are the evidence that do accuse me?
>   (1.4.162–4, 168, 170–1)

In this confrontation, each of the speakers challenges his opponent's assumptions: no one's hands are clean. As in the earlier prose dialogue of the two murderers, the grounds of moral judgement are made explicit. All by their past and present deeds are at risk of 'God's dreadful law', and the excuses by which they justify their conduct are shown to be hollow.

> CLARENCE
> The deed you undertake is damnable.
>
> 1 MUR.
> What we will do, we do upon command.
>
> 2 MUR.
> And he that hath commanded is the King.
>
> CLARENCE
> Erroneous vassal, the great King of kings
> Hath in the tables of his law commanded
> That thou shalt do no murder, and wilt thou then
> Spurn at his edict, and fulfil a man's?
> Take heed, for he holds vengeance in his hands
> To hurl upon their heads that break his law.
>
> 2 MUR.
> And that same vengeance doth he throw on thee,
> For false forswearing, and for murder too . . .

1 MUR.
How can thou urge God's dreadful law to us,
When thou hast broke it in so dear degree?

(1.4.173–83, 190–1)

In his audacious courtship of Lady Anne, in the open presence of the 'bleeding witness' reminding her (and the audience) that he has 'killed her husband and his father' (1.3.216–19), Richard shows his open scorn for traditional morality. The episode, invented by Shakespeare, with no precedent in the chronicles, displays Richard's powers of seduction, as, against all odds, he bends Anne to his will. As McKellen remarks: 'On the page, it seems incredible that Lady Anne would ever succumb to her husband's killer. In performance, the scene . . . is invariably convincing.'[26] In seducing Anne, Richard seduces the theatrical or cinematic audience by the skill and conviction of his performance, the charismatic force by which he dominates Anne, overriding her objections and keeping moral judgement at bay. The performance is both rhetorically astute and emotionally charged, a display of quick wit and sexual energy. Olivier and Sher, in interpretations of the role different in other ways, bring out Richard's sexual appeal: Claire Bloom in the Olivier film keeps swaying into Richard's arms, drawn by sexual magnetism. In their exchange, Richard is initially content to parry Anne's blows.

ANNE
Out of my sight, thou dost infect mine eyes.

RICHARD
Thine eyes, sweet lady, have infected mine.

(1.2.146–7)

Throughout the scene, Richard has full command of the conventional rhetoric of the Petrarchan lover, using it to wear down her defences.

RICHARD
Teach not thy lips such scorn, for they were made
For kissing, lady, not for such contempt.

(1.2.157–8)

In unsheathing the phallic sword and handing it to her, pointing it at his breast, he challenges her to assert or surrender mastery, in terms overtly sexual: 'Take up the sword again, or take up me' (1.2.169). From this point on, he knows he has won, and can dictate the terms of the Petrarchan love exchange that follows, as her resistance crumbles.

ANNE
I would I knew thy heart.

RICHARD
'Tis figured in my tongue.

ANNE
I fear me both are false.

RICHARD
Then never was man true.
(1.2.178–81)

In the exultant soliloquy that follows, Richard crows over his triumph, show-ing contempt for his female victim, who has succumbed so readily, forgetting 'that brave prince', her husband, whom 'some three months since' he has slaugh-tered.

Was ever woman in this humour wooed?
Was ever woman in this humour won?
I'll have her, but I will not keep her long.
(1.2.213–15, 224–6)

His delight in the brilliance of his performance is shared with the audience, treated as his allies, as fellow connoisseurs of the art of acting.[27] The McKellen film provides a superb visual counterpoint to the soliloquy, bringing out his callousness and amorality by setting it in a hospital ward, as McKellen's Richard chortles with glee, dancing a demonic jig at the end, to the accompaniment of a jaunty tune.

Shine out, fair sun – till I have bought a glass –
That I may see my shadow as I pass.
(1.2.247–8)

Olivier and McKellen treat the final lines of the speech differently: for McKellen, the emphasis lies on the 'looking-glass' by which the deformed actor can trans-form himself, as if by magic, into 'a marv'lous proper man' (1.2.239–40), where for Olivier, the emphasis is on the sinister shadow Richard casts on the wall, blighting the lives of all who cross his path. The ambivalence of Richard, and the power of theatrical illusion, are nowhere more striking than in this episode: he is both a moral leper and irresistibly attractive.

Deformity

The one thing that everyone knows about Richard III is that he is deformed, 'misshapen' (*3 Henry VI*, 1.3.170), a hunchback with a withered arm. Richard calls attention to his bodily deformity as motivating his behaviour in soliloquies in *3 Henry VI* and *Richard III*, using much the same terms as his enemies when they taunt him as 'an indigested and deformed lump'. Nature has 'cheated' him, making him 'unfinished', incomplete, with arms and legs 'of an unequal size'.

> To disproportion me in every part,
> Like to a chaos or an unlicked bear-whelp
> That carries no impression like the dam.[28]

His outward appearance, in its blatant violation of 'fair proportion' (*Richard III*, 1.1.18), reflects – or, as Richard suggests, has shaped, has helped determine – his inward nature:

> Then, since the heavens have shaped my body so,
> Let hell make crook'd my mind to answer it.
>   (*3 Henry VI*, 5.6.78–9)

Richard is 'determined to prove a villain' in more ways than one: he has chosen to be a villain by a conscious exercise of his will, like Milton's Satan in proclaiming 'Evil be thou my good', or, alternatively, he has been acted on, propelled in a particular direction, by determining forces not under his control.[29]

Richard's visible deformity, breaking through his many disguises, can appear to other characters as a legible sign of the monstrous and unnatural. In the tetralogy as a whole, Richard's deformed body is emblematic of a disordered world, torn apart by civil war and the unleashing of the will to destruction. To Richard himself, an awareness of deformity provides a spur to action, an impetus for revenge on the 'dissembling nature' which has mocked and cheated him. In the terms of Francis Bacon's essay 'Of Deformity', deformity is not so much 'a sign' as it is 'a cause, which seldom faileth of the effect':

> Deformed persons are commonly even with nature: for as nature hath done ill by them, so do they by nature . . . Whosoever hath anything fixed in his person that doth induce contempt, hath also a perpetual spur in himself to rescue and deliver himself from scorn . . . Also, it stirreth in them industry . . . to watch and observe the weaknesses of others, that they may have somewhat to repay . . . In a great wit, deformity is an advantage to rising.[30]

2. Ian McKellen as Richard III, Bill Paterson as Ratcliffe, *Richard III*,
directed by Richard Loncraine, produced by Lisa Katselas and
Stephen Bayly, screenplay adapted by Ian McKellen and Richard
Loncraine, 1995.

In his soliloquy at the beginning of the play, Richard presents himself in precisely
this way, as motivated by a burning desire to overcome his bodily disadvantages,
thus arming himself against any possible scorn and contempt in the pitiless gaze
of others:

> I that am curtailed of this fair proportion,
> Cheated of feature by dissembling nature,
> Deformed, unfinished, sent before my time
> Into this breathing world scarce half made up,
> And that so lamely and unfashionable
> That dogs bark at me as I halt by them.

(1.1.18–23)

Here and elsewhere, by dramatizing, even parodying his deformity, Richard
acts out his will to conquer it.

Both McKellen and Sher in their performances present a Richard of Gloucester, badly damaged physically, who compensates for his disability by his strong
will and commanding physical presence. Sher's Richard, on crutches, has lost

the use of his legs and has a grotesque hump, painful to behold (and, according to his memoir, *The Year of the King*, painful to wear). But in Sher's performance, an 'astonishingly mobile' Richard moves so fast, changes emotional direction so swiftly and convincingly, that his audience, on stage and in the auditorium, is 'half mesmerized': 'The speed with which Antony Sher rises on crutches and reaches the front of the stage, apparently on six legs . . . has the audience drawing back in alarm.'[31] McKellen's Richard is a soldier, whose disabilities look more like war wounds than genetic defects. He has the use of only one arm, with the damaged arm strapped inside his uniform shirt, and he walks with a pronounced limp. His powerful will is exercised in the overcoming of his disability and in a hypnotic control over others: both are shown in the extraordinary moment when, with the words 'Vouchsafe to wear this ring'(1.2.187), he removes a ring from his one good arm with his teeth and places it, wet with saliva, on Anne's finger. McKellen's fascist dictator enacts the moral of Auden's 'September 1, 1939': 'Those to whom evil is done / Do evil in return.' Freud, describing Richard III as 'an enormously magnified representation of something we can all discover in ourselves', finds the source of Richard's power over beholders in a guilty recognition of affinity, a 'possible inner fellowship' with him:

> Nature has done me a grievous wrong in denying me that beauty of form which wins human love . . . I have a right to be an exception, to overstep those bounds by which others let themselves be circumscribed. I may do wrong myself, since wrong has been done to me.[32]

Nemesis

Not all the characters in the play are susceptible to Richard's charismatic appeal. As early as Act 1, Shakespeare is careful to establish countervailing forces opposed to Richard, suggesting that Richard's ascendancy may be only temporary. In an interview, McKellen characterizes the play's structure (and the challenge faced in any production) as 'putting into the rise to power the seeds for the fall and the collapse afterwards'. In the course of the play, Richard is increasingly unable to exercise control over events.[33]

In the first part of the play, the principal force in opposition to Richard is old Queen Margaret. One of her functions is to serve as a reminder of past events, calling the attention of the theatrical audience to the earlier plays in the tetralogy and upbraiding the other characters with their past deeds and her past injuries. In bringing her onstage, a ghost from the past, Shakespeare rewrites history and his sources in the chronicles, since the historical Margaret had died in exile some years earlier.

Margaret refuses to accept the victory of her enemies in the civil war, considering herself still the rightful Queen and the Yorkists usurpers, interlopers. The baleful Queen Margaret is a figure in the Senecan tradition, who could as easily have been given the allegorical name Revenge, framing the action of the play (as in Kyd's *Spanish Tragedy*) by foreshadowing future reversals of fortune and calling down curses on the heads of her enemies.[34] Again and again, her prophecies come true, as in these lines addressed to Queen Elizabeth:

> Thyself a queen, for me that was a queen,
> Outlive thy glory like my wretched self;
> Long may thou live, to wail thy children's loss
> And see another, as I see thee now,
> Decked in thy rights, as thou art stalled in mine.
> Long die thy happy days before thy death,
> And after many lengthened hours of grief
> Die neither mother, wife, nor England's queen.
>
> (1.3.199–206)

Productions which emphasize the role of Margaret as Richard's principal antagonist present her as an 'ageless figure of moral nemesis', whose ritual incantations give her an unearthly, supernatural quality: Penny Downie, in Adrian Noble's 1988 production, played her as '200 years old'. The bleak future she prophesies for most of the other characters is in part motivated by hatred, a desire to make others suffer as she has suffered, but her speeches have a visionary quality. As one reviewer commented on the Margaret in the Alexander/Sher production, at each of her appearances she 'conjured up a world of sin and retribution'.[35] Some of Margaret's prophecies, like that addressed to Buckingham, who is smugly confident that 'curses never pass / The lips of those that breathe them in the air', are warnings:

> O Buckingham, beware of yonder dog.
> Look when he fawns, he bites; and when he bites,
> His venom tooth will rankle thee to death.
> Have not to do with him, beware of him.
>
> (1.3.285–6, 289–92)

Her curse on Richard does not reach fruition immediately, and in his inexorable rise to power it may at first glance seem a mere desire to wish the most 'grievous plague' possible on her enemy, calling him 'bitter names'. But, in fact, all these predictions come true in Acts 4 and 5.

On thee, the troubler of the poor world's peace[,]
The worm of conscience still begnaw thy soul.
Thy friends suspect for traitors while thou livest,
And take deep traitors for thy dearest friends.
No sleep close up that deadly eye of thine,
Unless it be whilst some tormenting dream
Affrights thee with a hell of ugly devils.

(1.3.214, 218–24, 236)

The fate prophesied for Richard here is the appropriate fate for a tyrant, whose misdeeds have made him hated, distrusted, and able to trust no one, like Macbeth afforded only 'curses, not loud but deep, mouth-honour'. By the end of the play, Richard like Macbeth suffers sleeplessness and terrifying dream visions. But it is open to question whether the fulfilment, one by one, of Margaret's dire prophecies reflects a dramatic universe in which, as Tillyard and others have argued, all sins are punished by a just God in 'a tit-for-tat scheme of crime and punishment', demonstrating 'the working out of God's will in English history'. Margaret's curses are more bloodthirsty than such a reading suggests, and are far removed from a Christian pattern of 'penitence . . . forgiveness and regeneration'.[36] Though she may try to identify herself with 'an upright, just, and true-disposing God', she is in some ways Richard's mirror image, no less a 'hell-hound' than he is, a ravenous beast 'hungry for revenge', made monstrous by her suffering.

> MARGARET
> From forth the kennel of thy womb hath crept
> A hell-hound that doth hunt us all to death
> . . .
> O upright, just, and true-disposing God,
> How do I thank thee that this charnel-cur
> Preys on the issue of his mother's body,
> And makes her pew-fellow with others' moan.
>
> DUCHESS OF YORK
> O Harry's wife, triumph not in my woes.
> God witness with me, I have wept for thine.

(4.4.44–5, 50–56)

The relentless parallelism in the ritual mourning by the assembled female victims (Penny Downie compares them to 'refugees . . . women in black wandering round Europe', displaced by war) has a choric dimension which includes an element of fellow feeling, shared woe. But there is no sense of divine justice in this endless cycle of revenge, in which even the names of the dead lose their individuality.[37]

> MARGARET
> If sorrow can admit society,
> Tell over your woes again by viewing mine.
> I had an Edward, till a Richard killed him.
>
> [*To the Queen*]
> Thou hadst an Edward, till a Richard killed him.
> Thou hadst a Richard, till a Richard killed him.
>
> DUCHESS OF YORK
> I had a Richard too, and thou didst kill him.
> I had a Rutland too, thou holp'st to kill him.
>   (4.4.35–42)

Margaret may gloat over the sufferings of her enemies, but the powerful incremental rhetoric of her catalogue of disasters and humiliation is tragic in effect. Rather than 'the course of justice', it invokes the wheel of fortune, reminding the audience of the transiency of earthly power and earthly happiness. The only certainties are pain and loss.

> Where is thy husband now? Where be thy brothers?
> Where are thy children? Wherein dost thou joy?
> Who sues to thee, and cries 'God save the Queen'?
> Where be the bending peers that flattered thee?
> Where be the thronging troops that followed thee?
> Decline all this, and see what now thou art:
> For happy wife, a most distressèd widow,
> For joyful mother, one that wails the name,
> For queen, a very caitiff crowned with care,
> For being sued to, one that humbly sues,
> For one commanding all, obeyed of none,
> For one that scorned at me, now scorned of me.
>   (4.4.87–99)

From this point in the play, power and confidence seep away from Richard, whose domination over events, undermined in prophecies such as this, is defied successively by the defection of his principal ally Buckingham, the resistance (somewhat equivocally presented) of Queen Elizabeth, the divided loyalties of Stanley, and the arrival on English soil of Richmond, with troops armed with the conviction that their adversary 'hath no friends but who are friends from fear, / Which in this greatest need will shrink from him' (5.2.20–1). The scene with the mourning women is followed immediately by Richard's entry, 'with drums and trumpets', to be confronted by his mother, who tells him that he has come 'on earth to make the earth my hell'.

> DUCHESS OF YORK
> A grievous burden was thy birth to me;
> Tetchy and wayward was thy infancy;
> Thy schooldays frightful, desp'rate, wild, and furious;
> Thy prime of manhood daring, bold and venturous;
> Thy age confirmed proud, subtle, bloody, treacherous.
> What comfortable hour canst thou name
> That ever graced me in thy company?   (4.4.159–66)

This confrontation of mother and son comes across powerfully in the McKellen film (which, shortly afterwards, gives the Duchess some of the best lines from Margaret's 'Where is thy husband now' speech), and other recent productions make much of the mother's 'loathing of her own son' and its effect on Richard.[38] Bidding farewell to her son ('I shall never see thee more'), she leaves him with her parting curse, yet another prophecy the audience can expect to see fulfilled:

> Therefore take with thee my most heavy curse,
> Which in the day of battle tire thee more
> Than all the complete armour that thou wear'st.
> My prayers on the adverse party fight
> . . .
> And promise them success and victory.
> Bloody thou art, bloody will be thy end.
>   (4.4.171, 177–84)

Richard continues to meet resistance in a second wooing scene, in which Queen Elizabeth, unlike Anne, has the upper hand in their exchanges, seemingly immune to his seductive powers as, having slain her two sons, he seeks an advantageous marriage with her young daughter.

> KING RICHARD
> Now by the world –
>
> QUEEN
>   'Tis full of thy foul wrongs.
>
> KING RICHARD
> My father's death –

QUEEN
                    Thy life hath that dishonoured.

KING RICHARD
Then by myself –

QUEEN
                    Thyself thyself misusest.

KING RICHARD
Why then, by God –

QUEEN
                    God's wrong is most of all.
                              (4.4.295–8)

The scene ends on a note of uncertainty, as Elizabeth wavers in her determination, allowing Richard to think he has made another conquest. Hall,
Shakespeare's source, leaves no doubt that Elizabeth, 'seduced by flatterynge
wordes' and 'fayre & large promises', is guilty of 'inconstancie' and gives in to
Richard.

QUEEN
Shall I go win my daughter to his will?

KING RICHARD
And be a happy mother by the deed.

QUEEN
I go. Write to me very shortly.

KING RICHARD
Bear her my true love's kiss. *[Kissing her.]* Farewell. *Exit Queen.*
Relenting fool, and shallow, changing woman.   (4.4.346–50)[39]

The McKellen film removes any ambiguity by having Elizabeth, trembling with
horror from the encounter with Richard, immediately bring about her daughter's marriage to Richmond – and for good measure, adds a nude wedding-night
scene for the newlyweds on the eve of the battle.

In Act 5, Richard meets his most formidable adversary in Richmond, the
future Henry VII. Dramatically, the two characters are given equal weight,
with parallel scenes devoted to each. Richmond, surrounded by his 'fellows in
arms', is presented marching against 'the yoke of tyranny' in 5.2, and Richard,
with his weary followers, pitches his tent in Bosworth Field in 5.3. Each delivers
an oration to his soldiers before the battle, and the two men, on opposite sides

of the stage, see a procession of ghosts pass before them, addressing each of
them in turn.

> GHOST [*to Richard*]
> Let me sit heavy on thy soul tomorrow.
> Think how thou stabb'st me in my prime of youth
> At Tewkesbury. Despair, therefore, and die.
>
> [*to Richmond*]
> Be cheerful, Richmond, for the wrongèd souls
> Of butchered princes fight in thy behalf.
>   (5.2.1–2; 5.4.97–101)

Where Richmond awakens from 'the sweetest sleep' confident of victory,
encouraged by 'so fair a dream', Richard, shaken by his terrible dream, tells
Ratcliffe 'I fear, I fear' (5.4.193, 206–12). Productions which, like Olivier's film,
have the ghosts appear only to Richard, cutting Richmond's part while fattening
that of the star actor, distort the play, ignoring Shakespeare's careful patterning.
The Olivier and McKellen films have impressively choreographed battle scenes,
but underplay the sense of prophecies fulfilled, an important element in the
play's tightly unified structure, in which 'all the lines of action converge on
Bosworth' and on Richard's inevitable, precipitous decline.[40]

  The two battlefield orations are carefully contrasted. Richard's, effective in its
way, denigrates the opposing army as 'vagabonds, rascals and runaways . . . base
lackey peasants' and appeals to the self-interest of his followers, urging them to
defend their property against the 'famished beggars' who would seize it from
them:

> Shall these enjoy our lands, lie with our wives,
> Ravish our daughters?
>   (5.5.45–6, 50, 58, 65–6)

Richmond's speech appeals more to principle than to self-interest, characterizing Richard as 'God's enemy', a tyrant, a usurper 'falsely set' upon the throne of
England (5.5.231–2). Far from being 'the Lord's anointed' (4.4.144), Richard
is excoriated as 'a bloody tyrant and a homicide', whom it is the patriotic and
moral duty of the citizen-soldiers of Richmond's army to resist.

> RICHMOND
> Yet remember this,
> God and our good cause fight upon our side;
> The prayers of holy saints and wrongèd souls,
> Like high-reared bulwarks, stand before our forces.
> . . .

> Thus if you fight against God's enemy,
> God will, in justice, ward you as his soldiers.
> If you do sweat to put a tyrant down,
> You sleep in peace, the tyrant being slain.
> If you do fight against your country's foes,
> Your country's fat shall pay your pains the hire.
>
> (5.4.218–21, 232–7)

The effect of these lines, addressed as much to the audience as to the assembled troops, is not, as Tillyard suggests, to establish Richmond as literally God's soldier, fulfilling a divine plan – 'the new and fruitful unity that God is to construct out of Richard's impartial wickedness'.[41] Rather, it is to direct the sympathies of the audience and prepare it for Richmond's eventual victory over a Richard who, earlier in the scene, has admitted, 'I have not the alacrity of spirit / Nor cheer of mind that I was wont to have' (5.4.52–3).

The dramatic structure of the play, critics have argued, depends on 'the conception of a supernatural order that surrounds and contains the main action and from which judgement will eventually come'. As Phyllis Rackin puts it, 'Richard thinks he is living in a world governed by Machiavellian *Realpolitik*', where he can assert unchallenged mastery, and is proved wrong. But if there is a providence at work in *Richard III*, it is to be identified more with the shaping hand of the playwright than with any ideology of retributive justice, a God who strikes down his enemies and showers rewards on his obedient servants.[42]

Richard tells his troops that nothing exists beyond the individual will: no moral restraints should hamper those who are resolute in the pursuit of their desired ends.

> Conscience is but a word that cowards use,
> Devised at first to keep the strong in awe.
> Our strong arms be our conscience, swords our law.
>
> (5.5.38–40)

Yet, when he awakens from the terrifying dream in which the ghosts of his murdered victims parade before him, his outward assurance is shaken and he shows, for the first time in the play, an inner turmoil, with the self divided against itself, anticipating such later tragic heroes as Macbeth.[43] Richard, the consummate actor, has no stable self, and now that he has no audience to dazzle with his tricks, faces an inner void.

> Is there a murderer here? No. – Yes, I am.
> Then fly. – What, from myself? Great reason why:
> Lest I revenge. – What, myself upon myself?

Alack, I love myself. – Wherefore? – For any good
That I myself have done unto myself. –
O no, alas, I rather hate myself
For hateful deeds committed by myself.

                    (5.4.163–9)

The stuttering, incoherent language, with each phrase cancelling out the one before, reflects his shattered confidence. In his terror, the claims of morality, which Richard has consistently denied, are brought home to him through the dream and given expression in the powerful soliloquy. In this scene, the McKellen film uses the resources of cinema in a close-up of his sweating face and agonized writhing, and, after the soliloquy, in showing Richard weeping like a child in the arms of his attendant Ratcliffe. As with Clarence before him, the 'forcible impression' of the dream, leaving him 'trembling', forces him to acknowledge his own guilt, rendering a severe judgement on his earlier actions:

My conscience has a thousand several tongues
And every tongue brings in a several tale,
And every tale condemns me for a villain. –
Perjury, perjury, in the high'st degree! –
Murder, stern murder, in the dir'st degree,
And several sins, all used in each degree,
Throng to the bar, crying all, 'Guilty, guilty!'

                    (1.4.58, 60; 5.4.172–80)

This soliloquy gives Richard a tragic dimension somewhat at odds with the homiletic framework of Richmond's final speech, looking forward to 'smiling plenty, and fair, prosperous days' after the death of 'the bloody dog', murderer, and tyrant (5.7.2, 34). What Richard comes to realize in this moment of tragic insight is the inevitable consequence of his embracing a defiant isolation, rejecting all human ties: 'I have no brother . . . I am myself alone' (*3 Henry VI*, 5.6.80, 83). Richard recovers from the bleak despair of this soliloquy, seeking on the battlefield to convince his soldiers and himself that 'a thousand hearts are great within my breast' (5.5.76). Olivier, in presenting a dauntless Richard, ready to fight to the very last, excises the soliloquy altogether. But the awakening of conscience in Richard is the moment of the play closest to tragedy, when the play's protagonist, stripped of all his customary defences, realizes that he has created around himself a universe devoid of love:

I shall despair. There is no creature loves me,
And if I die, no soul shall pity me.

                    (5.4.179–80)

Chapter 5

Gain, be my lord: *King John*

The uncertainties of *King John*

If *Richard III* is one of Shakespeare's most popular plays, *King John* is one of the least popular. Though it was a staple of the repertoire in the eighteenth and nineteenth centuries, in elaborate productions full of pageantry, with countless spear-carriers crowding the stage, there have been few productions in recent years. In an opening scene in which there are three speaking parts, King John, his mother Queen Eleanor, and the French ambassador, Macready in 1823 brought fifty-nine actors on stage, and eighty-eight for the confrontation of the English and French forces before Angers in Act 2.

> When the curtain rose, and discovered King John dressed as his effigy appears in Worcester Cathedral, surrounded by his barons sheathed in mail, with cylindrical helmets and correct armorial shields, and his courtiers in the long tunics and mantles of the thirteenth century, there was a roar of approbation, accompanied by four distinct rounds of applause.[1]

Beerbohm Tree in 1899 outdid Macready by staging a wordless tableau of the Signing of Magna Carta (an event unmentioned in Shakespeare's play). Modern productions have tended to be minimalist in staging and resolutely anti-heroic, treating the play as black comedy. RSC productions in 1970 and 1974 cut and rewrote Shakespeare's text severely, and small-scale RSC productions in 1988–9 and 2001, though more faithful to the text, were heavily slanted towards satire. The 2006 RSC production used medieval pageantry ironically, in sharp contrast to the undignified, self-seeking behaviour of the characters.

Critical accounts of *King John* have generally been dismissive, calling attention to its formal incoherence and 'apparent lack of unity'. Emrys Jones sees it as 'a strangely faltering, uncertain work', episodic and uneven in quality, with 'a tendency to start and stop'.[2] King John is the least prepossessing of Shakespeare's monarchs, creating problems for any actor undertaking the role because of the puzzling inconsistency of his behaviour. John stoutly defies the

French in Act 1; patches up an uneasy alliance with them in Act 2; confronts the Pope's emissary, Cardinal Pandulph, as a 'meddling priest', in Act 3; basely submits to him, surrendering his crown to the authority of the Pope, in Act 5; orders the murder of a rival claimant to the throne, young Arthur, in Act 3; tries to rescind that order in Act 4; and dies abjectly, 'a clod / And module of confounded royalty', in Act 5 (3.1.163; 5.7.57–8). In the 1988–9 RSC production, the actor playing King John was the smallest man in the company, dwarfed in a huge tin helmet and a sword three times his size, while in 2001, an ungainly King John was 'a kingly klutz', twitchy and petulant. In 2006, Richard McCabe's feeble, posturing despot was patently unequal to the burdens of kingship.[3]

Of all Shakespeare's history plays, *King John* is the one which fits least well into the Tillyardian moral pattern of order disrupted and restored, demonstrating the workings of divine providence. Though the play ends with a rousing patriotic speech, the lines seem tacked on, inconsistent with what has gone before, possibly even inappropriate for the character speaking the words.

> BASTARD
> This England never did, nor never shall,
> Lie at the proud foot of a conqueror
> But when it first did help to wound itself.
> Now these her princes are come home again,
> Come the three corners of the world in arms
> And we shall shock them! Naught shall make us rue,
> If England to itself do rest but true.   (5.7.112–18)

Similar words conclude *The Troublesome Raigne of King John*, an anonymous play of 1588–91 which is Shakespeare's principal source, and they fit that play much better than *King John*.

> *They crowne yong Henry.*
> BAST.
> Thus *Englands* peace begins in *Henryes* Raigne,
> And bloody warres are closde with happie league.
> Let *England* live but true within it selfe,
> And all the world can never wrong her State
> . . .
> If Englands Peeres and people joyne in one,
> Not Pope, nor *Fraunce*, nor *Spaine* can do them wrong.[4]

The Troublesome Raigne is a play of 'simple affirmations', ending with the surrender of the Dauphin ('I am contented to depart the Realme'), a vow by the rebellious English lords 'to fight for *England* and her King', and the crowning of Prince Henry as 'lawfull king' (lines 1118, 1175, 1184, Bullough,

Narrative and Dramatic Sources, IV.149–51). *King John*, in contrast, ends in anticlimax and uncertainty. After John dies with a whimper, we are told that the Bastard's army has been destroyed by an 'unexpected flood' (5.7.64) and then learn that the Dauphin has dismissed his troops and is willing, through the devious Pandulph, to negotiate peace. The inconclusive final moments of *King John* are characteristic of a play in which 'the relationship between power and legitimacy is endlessly contested' and in which 'there is no unblemished cause and no unquestioned authority'.[5]

Though Tillyard tries hard to find evidence of 'the great and godlike principle of order' and warnings against 'the sin of sedition' in *King John*, capricious Fortune, or the spirit of muddle, appears to rule in the action of the play, rather than the hand of providence.[6] In rapid succession in Act 4, Hubert, sent by John to murder Arthur, agrees to spare the young prince's life; John is confronted by the rebellious lords, accusing him of 'apparent foul play' in bringing about the death of 'this poor child'; Hubert returns and tells John, who now feels the stings of conscience, that Arthur is alive after all; and Arthur, trying to escape, is killed accidentally as he jumps from the castle walls. The Bastard's comment after discovering Arthur's dead body applies not only to this incident but to the play generally:

> I am amazed, methinks, and lose my way
> Among the thorns and dangers of this world.
>   (4.2.93, 97; 4.3.140–1)

King John is a play in which the audience as well as the characters can easily lose their way, with their expectations confounded. Rackin has suggested that the episodic structure of the play accurately reflects 'a world without faith and ceremony, where failure and success ride on the shifting wings of chance'.[7]

One possible explanation for the formal incoherence of *King John* is its dependence, virtually scene by scene, on an earlier play, *The Troublesome Raigne*. Rather than selecting and shaping material from Hall or Holinshed, as in his other history plays, Shakespeare leaves this task to the author of *The Troublesome Raigne*. The resemblance of the two plays is one of plot and not of style: there are few verbal echoes, and where *King John*, like *Richard II*, is entirely in verse, *Troublesome Raigne* is in a 'medley' style, a mixture of rhymed couplets, blank verse, fourteeners, and comic scenes in prose.[8] The two plays dramatize the same events, largely derived from Holinshed, in the same order. Neither mentions Magna Carta, and neither presents King John as in John Bale's *King Johan* (1539), John Foxe's *Acts and Monuments* (1563), and the Protestant tradition, as a stalwart opponent of and eventual martyr to Papist tyranny. *Troublesome Raigne* includes scenes of knockabout comedy with corrupt monks and friars absent from *King John*, along with battle scenes involving the Bastard Faulcon-bridge, avenging his father's death at the hands of the Duke of Austria and proving himself a worthy knight (treated much more briefly in *King John*, where the Bastard enters 'with Austria's head' and exits ten lines later). The characterization of the Bastard differs greatly in the two plays. In *Troublesome Raigne*, he is a figure out of heroic romance, rising from rustic obscurity to demonstrate by his actions –'honour is my desire' – that he is the true, 'wor-thie' son of 'so great a sire', Richard I (lines 291–2, Bullough, IV.80). In *King John*, the Bastard is a far more complex and interesting figure, who frequently stands apart from the action of the play as a satiric commentator and is given three soliloquies, the only ones in the play. In his irreverence, his comic energy, and the colloquial vitality of his language, Shakespeare's Bastard resembles Richard III, Mercutio, and Falstaff, and, like them, he can be seen as a lineal descendant of the Vice of the Morality plays.[9]

Mad world, mad kings

In Act 2 of *King John* (and in *Troublesome Raigne* as well), two rival kings, at the head of two rival armies, confront one another before the besieged town of Angers. Each, supported by his followers, calls the other usurper in an exchange of insults. John and his mother, earlier in the play, had admitted privately that his title to the throne, after the death of his brother Richard I, rested more upon 'possession' than on 'right' (1.1.40), and that Arthur's claim, as the son of John's older brother, was as good or better.

Each of the two opposing kings addresses the citizens of Angers with the same formulae of loyalty and obedience: the repetition shows how empty the words are. Recent productions of the play have brought out the comic potential of this scene, treating the pretensions of puny, blustering monarchs as patently ludicrous.

> KING JOHN
> You men of Angers, and my loving subjects –
>
> KING PHILIP
> You loving men of Angers, Arthur's subjects,
> Our trumpets called you to this gentle parle –
>
> KING JOHN
> For our advantage; therefore hear us first.
>
> (2.1.203–6)

The spokesman for the citizens of Angers, speaking from the upper stage, uses cautious words which demystify the claims of the two kings to sovereignty, obedience, and divine right.

> KING JOHN
> Acknowledge then the King, and let me in.
>
> CITIZEN
> That we can not. But he that proves the King,
> To him will we prove loyal; till that time
> Have we rammed up our gates against the world.
>
> KING JOHN
> Doth not the crown of England prove the King?
> And if not that, I bring you witnesses,
> Twice fifteen thousand hearts of England's breed
> . . .
>
> KING PHILIP
> As many and as well-born bloods as those –
>
> BASTARD [ASIDE]
>   Some bastards too.
>
> KING PHILIP
> Stand in his face to contradict his claim.
>
> CITIZEN
> Till you compound whose right is worthiest,
> We for the worthiest hold the right from both.
>   (2.1.269–82)[10]

With two contesting claims, 'right' and worthiness remain uncertain, held in suspension, unknowable.

When the citizens of Angers continue obdurate, refusing to surrender to either of the rival armies, then the Bastard offers the cynical advice that the two enemies should band together, 'be friends a while', and jointly turn their 'battering cannon' on the walls of Angers (2.1.379, 382). According to Guy Henry, King John in the 2001 production, John's reply to the suggestion always drew a laugh.

> KING JOHN
> Now, by the sky that hangs above our heads,
> I like it well. France, shall we knit our powers
> And lay this Angers even with the ground,
> Then after fight who shall be king of it?
>   (2.1.397–400)[11]

At this point, the spokesman for the citizens of Angers proposes a way of keeping the peace and reconciling the enemies: Blanche, John's niece, should be married to the French Dauphin, thus uniting the two warring nations in 'amity' by a 'friendly treaty', with a substantial dowry to be paid by England to France (2.1.482, 538). Blanche – treated as a blank sheet of white paper, as her name implies – obediently accepts her role in a patriarchal society of power-brokers, recognizing that in these matters she has no will of her own. She will do what she is told to do.

> BLANCHE *[to Louis]*
> My uncle's will in this respect is mine.
> If he see aught in you that makes him like,
> That anything he sees which moves his liking,
> I can with ease translate it to my will.
> (2.1.511–14)[12]

The Dauphin Louis, prompted by John's promise to make the bride 'rich / In titles, honours, and promotions', duly finds 'a wondrous miracle' in the eyes of a young woman he hadn't noticed before:

> I do protest I never loved my self
> Till now infixèd I beheld myself,
> Drawn in the flattering table of her eye.
> (2.1.492–3, 498, 502–4)

To the Bastard, whose robust colloquial language deflates the pretences of the other characters onstage, the language of diplomacy and the conventional diction of courtly love are equally fraudulent, masking the true motives of the characters.

Greg Doran's 2001 production brought out the comic and satiric elements in the play. Nearly all reviewers commented on how the production emphasized 'Shakespeare's corrosively ironic view of power politics', in which 'among the movers and shakers, the only principle seems to be self-interest'. According to Guy Henry, audiences consistently found 'Shakespeare's savage satire on political spin (a key element in the play)' to be 'relevant and accessible to us today'.

> We know so much more now, more even than just a few years ago, mainly through the probing of the various media, about those who rule over us, that we can be certain that the great and good are usually neither of those things. To see this demonstrated so wittily by Shakespeare was a huge pleasure.[13]

'Commodity' is the term the Bastard uses, in his soliloquy that ends Act 2, scene 1, for the calculating self-interest, 'the bias of the world', which leads the French and English kings to patch up their differences, abandoning their former vows and loyalties.

> Mad world, mad kings, mad composition!
> John, to stop Arthur's title in the whole,
> Hath willingly departed with a part,
> And France, whose armour conscience buckled on,
> Whom zeal and charity brought to the field
> As God's own soldier, rounded in the ear
> With that same purpose-changer, that sly devil
> . . .
> This bawd, this broker, this all-changing word,
> Clapped on the outward eye of fickle France,
> Hath drawn him from his own determined aid,
> From a resolved and honourable war,
> To a most base and vile-concluded peace.
>
> (2.1.562–8, 575, 583–7)

The Bastard is rapidly becoming educated in the ways of the world, but until the closing lines of this speech he retains a satirist's detachment, addressing the audience directly as a commentator on a world that is 'morally askew'. In his diction and in his stance, the Bastard positions himself in this soliloquy as speaking the truth where all around him are liars. In the 2006 production, this aspect of the Bastard came across particularly well in the performance of Joseph Millson, taking the audience into his confidence in his soliloquies.

Like Hotspur, the Bastard sees war as 'honourable' and the 'half-faced fellowship' and intrigues of a 'vile politician' as base and unworthy (*1 Henry IV*, 1.3.207, 239). In the next scene, Constance, horrified by the betrayal of her hopes for her son Arthur, inveighs against the broken promises of her former allies, who treat 'a king's oath' as meaningless (3.1.10). Like the Bastard, she sees war as an honourable calling and 'painted peace' as false and shameful.

> CONSTANCE
> War! War! No peace! Peace is to me a war.
> O Limoges, O Austria, thou dost shame
> That bloody spoil.
> . . .
> Hast thou not spoke like thunder on my side,
> Been sworn my soldier, bidding me depend
> Upon thy stars, thy fortune, and thy strength,
> And dost thou now fall over to my foes?
>
> (3.1.105, 113–15, 124–7)

The difference between Constance and the Bastard is that her reaction to 'this day of shame, oppression, perjury' (3.1.88) is overwhelming grief, mingled with anger at her own helplessness, where the Bastard is more ambivalent, more detached. He is able to laugh, not weep at the all-embracing power of 'that smooth-faced gentleman, tickling Commodity', and he ends his soliloquy, somewhat unexpectedly, with the resolve that if he wishes to thrive in the world, he must serve Commodity like everyone else.

> And why rail I on this Commodity?
> But for because he has not wooed me yet.
> Not that I have the power to clutch my hand
> When his fair angels would salute my palm,
> But for my hand, as unattempted yet,
> Like a poor beggar raileth on the rich.
>   (2.1.574, 588–93)

In this speech, the Bastard retains a degree of satiric distance in commenting on the follies and hypocrisy of others, while pointing out that, if presented with the opportunity, he would act the same way.

> Well, whiles I am a beggar, I will rail
> And say there is no sin but to be rich;
> And being rich, my virtue then shall be
> To say there is no vice but beggary.
> Since kings break faith upon commodity,
> Gain, be my lord, for I will worship thee!
>   (2.1.594–9)

The cynical amorality of the closing lines of the soliloquy has occasioned a good deal of critical commentary. Jones, pointing out that the Bastard does not behave like a Machiavel later in the play, ignoring his own advice, sees the Bastard as basically a virtuous, attractive figure capable of 'irony directed against himself' as well as others.

> In performance it is unambiguously clear from his first appearance what the Bastard's moral standing is – a sympathetic man who eventually becomes a good one, whose many jocular remarks never violate the simple outlines of his character . . . An audience will respond with a complex amusement, quite clear about its moral bearings.

Weimann and other critics see the Bastard as a 'hybrid', ambivalent figure, akin in some respects to self-aware Machiavels like Richard III and Edmund in *Lear*, who is partly complicit in the 'commodification of politics' he satirizes, and who serves to destabilize conventional ideas of morality and authority.[14] Not only in this speech, but in his later actions in the play, the Bastard's words and behaviour seem problematical in a number of ways.

Machiavels and victims

One character who is unquestionably a Machiavel, unprincipled and ruthless in the pursuit of power, is Cardinal Pandulph, described by reviewers of the 2001 production as 'sadistically manipulative', 'an ecclesiastical spin-master'.[15] The initial exchange between King John and Pandulph is full of fine, ringing phrases on both sides. Pandulph speaks of his 'holy errand' and his 'lawful power', sprinkling his utterances wth terms like 'religious' and 'blessed' (3.1.137, 140, 172, 174), while John, in one of the few references in the play to divine right monarchy, is at the outset forthright in his defiance of the 'usurped authority' of the Pope.

> KING JOHN
> What earthy name to interrogatories
> Can test the free breath of a sacred king?
> . . .
>   From the mouth of England
> Add thus much more: that no Italian priest
> Shall tithe or toil in our dominions.
> But . . . we, under God, are supreme head.
>   (3.1.147–8, 152–5, 160)

To an Elizabethan audience, aware that a few years earlier, Pope Gregory XIII had excommunicated Queen Elizabeth, decreeing that she was not a lawful monarch and authorizing armed rebellion against her, the confrontation between John and Pandulph would have had particular topical relevance.[16] Pandulph, in a brutal assertion of naked power, not only pronounces anathema on John but threatens Philip of France with a similar decree unless he renounces his newly sworn alliance with England.

> PANDULPH
> Thus, by the lawful power that I have,
> Thou shalt stand cursed and excommunicate,
> And blessèd shall he be that doth revolt
> From his allegiance to an heretic,
> And meritorious shall that hand be called,
> Canonizèd and worshipped as a saint,
> That takes away by any secret course
> Thy hateful life.   (3.1.172–8)

The two monarchs, for all their claims of 'supremacy' in their 'dominions' (3.1.154–6), are reduced to impotence by the implacable Cardinal, who has no compunctions about the exercise of power, and makes no distinction between spiritual and worldly weapons.

King Philip of France, like the besieged city of Angers in the earlier scene, is faced with 'two irreconcilable claims', the power of Rome, threatening him with eternal damnation if he disobeys, and the 'sacred vows' of marriage, the 'deep-sworn faith' of the treaty between the two previously warring nations (3.1.229–31). Blanche, confronted with the prospect of being widowed on the day of her marriage, is even more distraught at the perceived conflict of loyalties, seeing herself as literally torn asunder.

> BLANCHE
>   Upon thy wedding day?
> Against the blood that thou hast married?
> What, shall our feast be kept with slaughtered men?
>   . . .
> Which is the side that I must go withal?
> I am with both; each army hath a hand.
> And in their rage, I having hold of both,
> They whirl asunder and dismember me.
>   (3.1.300–2, 327–30)[17]

Cardinal Pandulph is immune to the claims of human feeling, and coolly denies the efficacy of moral absolutes: truth is what we want it to be, what suits us at a particular moment. One falsehood, he argues in a display of Jesuitical equivocation, cancels out or 'cures' another (3.1.277).

The wily Pandulph, experienced in the ways of the world, tells the Dauphin, scornfully, 'Your mind is all as youthful as your blood . . . How green you are' (3.4.125, 145). After the French forces have been defeated in battle, Pandulph predicts that John, momentarily victorious, will bring about his own downfall by actions which will 'cool the hearts / Of all his people' and lead them to 'revolt from him' (3.4.149–50, 165). Now that Arthur is in John's power, Pandulph says, it is inevitable that John, like any tyrant, will find a way to eliminate his feared rival.

> John has seized Arthur, and it cannot be
> That whiles warm life plays in that infant's veins,
> The misplaced John should entertain an hour,
> One minute, nay, one quiet breath, of rest.
> A sceptre snatched with an unruly hand
> Must be as boisterously maintained as gained.
>   (3.4.131–6)

The first part of this prediction has already started to come true, in a scene where John promises unspecified rewards to his retainer Hubert in return for killing the young prince. John begins his courtship of Hubert with vague phrases, saying that eventually there will be a 'cause . . . for me to do thee good':

> KING JOHN
>   O my gentle Hubert,
> We owe thee much. Within this wall of flesh
> There is a soul counts thee her creditor,
> And with advantage means to pay thy love.
> . . .
> Give me thy hand. I had a thing to say,
> But I will fit it with some better time.
>   (3.3.19–26, 30–2)

John's language is circuitous and euphemistic, as though he is unwilling to express his thoughts directly, exposing them to the light of day. He hopes that Hubert will understand the hints he drops, and that Hubert is willing to act as a tyrant's willing emissary, like Tyrrell and the two Murderers in *Richard III*, without any need to have the terms of the bargain stated explicitly. As Milton says, tyrants have a ready supply of 'bad men' who 'have been always readiest with the falsified names of loyalty and obedience to colour over their base compliances'.[18] In a later scene, when John has begun to feel the consequences of 'the foul corruption of a sweet child's death', in the disaffection of nobles and the mutterings of the common people 'in the streets', he blames Hubert for prompting him to commit an act 'which both our tongues held vile to name' (4.2.81, 185, 241). A similar pattern can be found in *Richard II*, where Exton, seeking reward, takes a hint from the newly crowned King to murder the deposed Richard II, only to be rejected afterwards by the King, who would like to deny his own complicity.

> EXTON
> From your own mouth, my lord, did I this deed.
>
> BULLINGBROOK
> They love not poison that do poison need.
> Nor do I thee. Though I did wish him dead,
> I hate the murderer, love him murderèd.
> The guilt of conscience take thee for thy labour,
> But neither my good word nor princely favour.
>   (*Richard II*, 5.6.37–42)

In the temptation scene in *King John*, Hubert chooses to answer John's dark hints in terms of feudal service, honour, and loyalty, responding to the King's 'I think thou lov'st me well'.

> HUBERT
> So well that what you bid me undertake,
> Though that my death were adjunct to my act,
> By heaven I would do it.   (3.3.56–8)

For John, these formulaic words are enough, and he speaks more plainly, though Hubert's response remains ambiguous: either that he will fulfil his trust as 'keeper' to the imprisoned Arthur, or that he will do whatever is necessary to secure the King against the threat that Arthur represents.

> KING JOHN
>   Hubert, Hubert, throw thine eye
> On yon young boy. I'll tell thee what, my friend,
> He is a very serpent in my way,
> And wheresoe'er this foot of mine does tread,
> He lies before me. Dost thou understand me?
> Thou art his keeper.
>
> HUBERT
>   And I'll keep him so
> That he shall not offend your majesty.
>   (3.3.59–65)

The bareness of the lines that follow, free from euphemism, resembles Richard III's 'Shall I be plain? I wish the bastards dead', except that as a dialogue (presumably spoken on stage with pregnant pauses before each of Hubert's responses), the words generate a subtext, with Hubert accepting the role of murderer and the implied rewards that go along with it.[19]

> KING JOHN
> Death.
>
> HUBERT
>   My lord.
>
> KING JOHN
>   A grave.
>
> HUBERT
> He shall not live.
>   (3.3.66–7)

This is the most chilling moment in the play, and serves to withdraw any sympathy from John, as well as motivating his precipitous decline in Acts 4 and 5. John here has failed to heed Machiavelli's advice that a prudent prince must avoid actions 'which will make him hated or despised': 'when the people are hostile and regard him with hatred he must go in fear of everything and everyone'.[20] The collapse of John's authority is shown by his surrender to Pandulph at the beginning of Act 5, and by the imagery of disease, fever, and poison that accompanies him throughout the last part of the play. It is as though 'civil tumult' and foreign invasion are outward manifestations of his guilty conscience, as the body politic succumbs to a raging disease.

> My nobles leave me, and my state is braved,
> Even at my gate, with ranks of foreign powers;
> Nay, in the body of this fleshy land,
> This kingdom, this confine of blood and breath,
> Hostility and civil tumult reigns
> Between my conscience and my cousin's death.
>   (4.2.243–8)

When Hubert attempts to carry out his commission from the King, he indicates in a number of asides ('I must be brief, lest resolution drop / Out at my eyes in tender womanish tears' (4.1.35–6)) that he has conscientious scruples. The contrast between Hubert's brusque manner, threatening physical violence, and the innocent prattle of the young victim is calculated to build suspense and create sympathy for Arthur. Braunmuller's Oxford edition includes a photograph of a Victorian painting, showing an anguished Hubert, hand to his brow, turning aside from a kneeling, beseeching Arthur.

> ARTHUR
> Have you the heart? When your head did but ache,
> I knit my handkerchief about your brows –
> The best I had, a princess wrought it me –
> And I did never ask it you again.   (4.1.41–4)

As several critics have pointed out, the equivalent scene in *The Troublesome Raigne* is very different. In that play, Hubert and Arthur engage in an extended political debate in rhymed couplets, weighing the duty of obedience owed to a king against the sovereign commands of conscience. When Hubert relents, it is because he has been convinced by Arthur's arguments, which awaken his dormant moral sense.

HUBERT
My Lord, a subject dwelling in the land
Is tyed to execute the Kings command.

ARTHUR
Yet God commands, whose power reacheth further,
That no command should stand in force to murther.[21]

None of this enters into the scene in *King John*, where it is the human emotion of pity (in Hubert as in the audience) rather than the prospect of divine judgement on the sinner that leads the would-be murderer to relent. The innocent child Arthur invokes 'mercy', saying that even inanimate objects, 'fierce fire and iron', rebel against the deed. Though he mentions in passing 'the breath of heaven', the terms of his appeal to the natural instinct of 'compassion' are almost entirely secular (4.1.88, 109, 118–20).

In deciding to spare Arthur's life, Hubert explicitly rejects the claims of self-interest, 'all the treasure that thine uncle owns . . . the wealth of all the world', and Arthur praises the emergence of a better self, previously obscured: 'O, now you look like Hubert. All this while / You were disguised' (4.1.122, 125–6, 130). But Hubert's good deed is unavailing, as, in one of the many instances in this play of 'accidental judgements, casual slaughters . . . purposes mistook' (*Hamlet*, 5.2.335–7), Arthur dies shortly afterwards in a fall. On the page, the scene of Arthur's death seems undramatic, rushed, though in Greg Doran's 2001 production the fall 'seemed a genuine accident' and was theatrically effective: 'a heart-stoppingly convincing crash to the floor'.[22] In the performance I saw of the 2006 production, there was an audible gasp from the audience when Arthur fell. Later in this scene, when the disaffected lords discover Arthur's body, they immediately conclude that Hubert has murdered him on the orders of the King, and take a solemn oath absolving them from obedience to John and vowing to avenge Arthur's death. Hubert, whose puzzled 'I left him well' (4.3.139) is accurate, protests his innocence, but no one believes him. From this point on, the realm is engulfed in war, with a bewildering series of shifting allegiances and changes in fortune (Guy Henry comments on the 'switchback quality' of the action).[23] Cardinal Pandulph, who shortly before had urged war, now, having secured John's submission to Rome, tries unsuccessfully to broker a peace, and the rebellious nobles, when they discover that the Dauphin plans to 'recompense the pains you take / By cutting off your heads' once he has won the battle (5.4.15–16), suddenly discover they are loyal Englishmen after all. Salisbury's convenient conversion to 'old right' and 'obedience . . . to our great King John', like most of the political language in the play, rings hollow (5.4.56–7, 61).

The Bastard's progress

The Bastard, unlike the other major characters in *King John*, is not a historical figure, but is invented by the author of *The Troublesome Raigne* and developed further by Shakespeare. He takes his origins from a single sentence in Holinshed: 'Philip, bastard sonne to king Richard, to whome his father had given the castell and honor of Coinacke, killed the vicount of Limoges, in revenge of his fathers death.'[24] In *Troublesome Raigne*, he is generally referred to as 'Philip', but in *King John*, he abandons this name after the first scene, when the King renames him as 'Sir Richard and Plantagenet' and makes him a knight (1.1.160–2). In both plays, he erupts upon the scene in a dispute with his brother Robert Faulconbridge. Robert, the younger brother, claims that he should be the heir to an estate worth 500 pounds a year, on the grounds that his brother is illegitimate, the product of an adulterous liaison between his mother and the deceased King Richard. In *Troublesome Raigne*, Philip Faulconbridge takes a high moral stand, initially refusing to 'open my mouth to unrippe the shamefull slaunder of my parents, the wicked dealing of my brother', and later goes into a trance ('Fond man, ah whether art thou carried?') on hearing 'Birds, bubbles, leaves, and mountaines, Eccho, all / Ring in mine Eares, that I am *Richards* Sonne'.[25] *King John* turns this into a comic scene, making the Bastard 'a good blunt fellow', 'a madcap', with a devil-may-care attitude and a witty, colloquial turn of phrase, strongly contrasted with his materialistic, conventional brother. He has no hesitation in renouncing the security of 'land' for the prospect of adventure.

> BASTARD
> Brother, take you my land; I'll take my chance.
> Your face hath got five hundred pound a year;
> Yet sell your face for five pence and 'tis dear.
> Madam, I'll follow you unto the death.
>   (1.1.71, 84, 151–54)

Where Philip Faulconbridge in *Troublesome Raigne* chooses the path of 'honour' (the term recurs six times in this scene), the Bastard in *King John* subjects both honour and his own elevation to satiric scrutiny in his first soliloquy.

BASTARD

A foot of honour better than I was,
But many a foot of land the worse.
Well, now I can make any Joan a lady;
'Good den, Sir Richard', 'God-a-mercy, fellow' –
And if his name be George, I'll call him 'Peter'.
For new-made honour doth forget men's names.

(1.1.182–7)

The actor who played the Bastard in Greg Doran's 2001 production described this soliloquy as 'undercutting the establishment he has just joined'. This soliloquy is a 'crowd-pleasing' comic performance, appealing to the audience (and providing opportunities for the actor) in its mimicry of different voices, its improvisatory quality.[26] In his irreverence and the pleasure he takes in putting on 'a play extempore' (*1 Henry IV*, 2.4.271), the Bastard resembles Falstaff, as well as such Shakespearean clowns as Touchstone and Feste.

And when my knightly stomach is sufficed,
Why then I suck my teeth and catechize
My pickèd man of countries: 'My dear sir' –
Thus leaning on mine elbow I begin –
'I shall beseech you'
. . .
'O sir', says Answer, 'at your best command,
At your employment, at your service, sir'.
'No sir', says Question, 'I, sweet sir, at yours'.

(1.1.191–9)

In the later part of this soliloquy, the tone changes, bringing out resemblances between the Bastard and a later Shakespearean bastard, Edmund, as well as Richard III and Iago. As Weimann points out, there is more than a touch of the Machiavel in the Bastard, with his 'aggressive mobility' and sardonic running commentary on the 'worshipful society' in which he is at all times an outsider.[27] A 'mounting spirit', the Bastard announces his intention to rise still further, using 'deceit' if that is necessary for his own advancement: 'observation' from the sidelines will allow him to 'learn' how to rise in the world.

For he is but a bastard to the time
That doth not smack of observation,
And so am I whether I smack or no;
And not alone in habit and device,
Exterior form, outward accoutrement,

But from the inward motion to deliver
Sweet, sweet, sweet poison for the age's tooth,
Which though I will not practise to deceive,
Yet to avoid deceit I mean to learn,
For it shall strew the footsteps of my rising.

(1.1.207–16)

Though like Iago and Richard III he contrasts 'exterior form' and clothing with a hidden 'inward' core, even sees himself as potentially a venter of 'poison', it is significant that he says not that he will deceive, but that he could. Aware that he is surrounded by hypocrites and schemers, he will be able to fortify himself against the deceit of others. The lines can be seen as illustrative of the Bastard's ambivalence, his capacity, at this early point in the play, to pursue more than one path, towards 'covetous self-interest' or towards service of an ideal beyond the self.[28]

As we have seen, the Bastard's soliloquy on commodity raises similar problems. The motto 'Gain, be my lord' would appear to fit nearly all the characters in the play: only Arthur and Blanche, innocents buffeted by fortune and subjected to the intrigues of those surrounding them, are immune from the temptations of self-interest. Arthur is onstage throughout 3.1, and the only line he speaks is 'I do beseech you, madam, be content' (3.1.42). When he is captured, his one line is 'O, this will make my mother die with grief!' (3.3.5). Constance is victim and outcast, conscious of being 'oppressed with wrongs' (3.1.13), but she is also an eager participant in the struggle for power, who mourns for the failure of her dynastic ambitions as well as for the imprisonment and death of her son. Hubert is tempted to commit murder in order to gain preferment, but finally overcomes the temptation. In each of his soliloquies in the first half of the play, the Bastard starts out as a detached, ironic commentator and ends by stating his intent to participate, sharing in the spoils. When King John assigns him the responsibility of raiding the monasteries in search of booty, to 'shake the bags / Of hoarding abbots' – an episode presented in detail in *Troublesome Raigne* – the Bastard comments, 'gold and silver becks me to come on' (3.3.7–8, 13). It is possible then to see the Bastard, halfway through the play, as, like Hubert, susceptible to the appeal of 'gain', but also capable of resisting: in Miltonic terms, 'sufficient to have stood, though free to fall' (*Paradise Lost*, III.99).

The next time the Bastard appears, he brings the King news of disaffection among the populace, 'possessed with rumours . . . full of fear', and then agrees to act as the King's emissary to the discontented nobles (4.2.145–6). When the body of Arthur is discovered, he, like Salisbury and Pembroke, condemns the apparent murder as 'a damnèd and bloody work', but unlike them withholds judgement as to whether Hubert is guilty of 'this most cruel act'. He tells Hubert

'I do suspect thee very grievously', but leaves open the possibility that Hubert is sincere in his protestations of innocence (4.3.57, 126, 134).

His third soliloquy, as Hubert carries off Arthur's body, like the first two begins one way and ends another. The uncertainty, gravity, and tragic dimensions in the Bastard's language here are absent from his previous utterances, and appear to reflect a new level of understanding, prompted by the death of Arthur.[29] The first part of the speech is a lament for the death of Arthur, presented (more or less as in John of Gaunt's famous 'sceptred isle' speech in *Richard II*) as the death of England, the death of the traditional commonwealth and traditional ideals.

> I am amazed, methinks, and lose my way
> Among the thorns and dangers of this world.
> How easy dost thou take all England up!
> From forth this morsel of dead royalty,
> The life, the right, the truth of all this realm
> Is fled to heaven, and England now is left
> To tug and scramble, and to part by th' teeth
> The unowed interest of proud-swelling state.
>
> (4.3.140–7)

Here the Bastard is closer to Kent or Gloucester than to Edmund: rather than joining in the 'tug and scramble', picking over the bare bones of the state like a bird of prey, the Bastard grieves for the wounded commonwealth. 'Vast confusion' in a state of 'doggèd war' does not provide an opportunity, but a cause for deep sorrow. The advice he gives is similar to what the Fool and Kent urge on Lear: in a tempest, it's best to seek any shelter and stay dry.

> Now for the bare-picked bone of majesty
> Doth doggèd war bristle his angry crest
> And snarleth in the gentle eyes of peace.
> Now powers from home and discontents at home
> Meet in one line; and vast confusion waits,
> As doth a raven on a sick-fall'n beast,
> The imminent decay of wrested pomp.
> Now happy he whose cloak and ceinture can
> Hold out this tempest.   (4.3.148–56)

What is most surprising about this speech is its conclusion: 'I'll to the King'. Faced with a state of chaos and 'imminent decay' for which King John is partly responsible, the Bastard chooses without hesitation to offer his services to the King. From this point on, he abandons his stance of satiric observer and becomes an active participant.

> Bear away that child
> And follow me with speed. I'll to the King.
> A thousand businesses are brief in hand,
> And heaven itself does frown upon the land.
>
> (4.3.156–9)

In Act 5, the Bastard is the King's general and chief political adviser. He counsels the King to 'put on / The dauntless spirit of resolution', not to sink into lassitude and depression ('But wherefore do you droop? Why look you sad?'), but to be 'great in act, as you have been in thought'. In response, King John tells him, 'Have thou the ordering of this present time' – in effect, to become the King's deputy, as the King himself retreats more and more into impotent passivity (5.1.44–5, 52–3, 77).

Tillyard praises the Bastard's 'masterful strength' in this part of the play, saying that 'only a man of the firmest character could have made up his mind so quickly when beset with such terrible perplexities' (p. 227). Other critics have found the last part of the play unconvincing, full of hollow, conventional oratory, once the Bastard assumes his new role as spokesman for the King.

> BASTARD
> No! Know the gallant monarch is in arms
> And like an eagle o'er his eyrie towers
> To souse annoyance that comes near his nest
> . . .
> Do but start
> An echo with the clamour of thy drum,
> And even at hand a drum is ready braced
> That shall reverberate all as loud as thine.
>
> (5.2.148–50, 167–70)

Burckhardt comments that 'with the Bastard turned serious, Shakespeare no longer had a language adequate to his real purpose'. 'In the first three acts his task had been to expose an order and a language that had become false . . . When he accepts the king's responsibilities . . . he also takes over the king's language.'[30]

The actor who played the Bastard in the 2001 production found the 'large speeches' in Act 5 problematical – a 'torrent of words', 'verbal fireworks' with little substance: the Bastard's 'defiant salvo of image upon image of "warlike John"' is 'all the more vehement because of his awareness of how altogether unwarlike John had appeared at their last meeting'.[31] In the 2006 production, the irony is pointed up by bringing a feeble, corpse-like John onstage, behind the main action. What the Bastard is doing in this act is to attempt to prop up a faltering monarchy. John is in all respects a bad king, both weak and tyrannous – a usurper, a murderer, yet irresolute, ready to cave in at the slightest provocation. But the Bastard chooses to take responsibility for 'the ordering of this present time' in the absence of any viable alternative, making the best of an unattractive and unpromising situation – thus providing one possible answer to the problem the play sets forth, 'how to live in a world dangerously stripped of absolutes'.[32]

In the play's final scene, the Bastard sounds very much like Kent in *Lear*, expressing an uncomplicated ideal of service to his feudal lord and indicating that he is willing to follow his master's example and die:

> BASTARD
> Art thou gone so? I do but stay behind
> To do the office for thee of revenge,
> And then my soul shall wait on thee to heaven,
> As it on earth hath been thy servant still.
>
> (5.7.70–3)

In Shakespeare's text, once John has died, the Bastard immediately offers his allegiance to John's son, the child Prince Henry (a character appearing for the first time in this scene), followed by the once rebellious nobles, all kneeling:

> On my knee
> I do bequeath my faithful services
> And true subjection everlastingly.
>
> (5.7.103–5)

In the 2006 production, the Bastard's closing lines were not addressed to the audience but to the young prince, as counsel and encouragement. In 2001, in contrast, there was a destabilizing moment of uncertainty, making the play end 'as cynically as it had begun':

> The assembled barons and the Bastard eyed each other suspiciously to see who would make the first move, and what it would be. Then, as if at some invisible signal, and in unison, they scurried across to Prince Henry, now King Henry III, scrambling to be the first to kneel at his feet.[33]

In Deborah Warner's 1988 production, the Bastard's transformation from 'bruisingly sardonic outsider to patriotic spokesman and moral centre of the play' was simply omitted, so that lines like 'This England never did, nor never shall, / Lie at the proud feet of a conqueror' (5.7.112–13) were treated with heavy irony. In this production, the Bastard was turned into a thoroughly unsympathetic figure, a thug and bully, ruled throughout by self-interest and a love of violence, 'an appallingly literal and consistent embodiment of the nationalist triumphalism inscribed in his final words'.[34] Such a radical reinterpretation of the character, making the Bastard morally indistinguishable from the other characters and robbing him of his quality of ironic detachment in the first half of the play, is one way of resolving the play's contradictions and anomalies. But the problematical aspects of *King John* remain, and not the least of these is that its closing lines express conventional sentiments that seem at variance with the previous action and with the character speaking them.

Chapter 6

The death of kings: *Richard II*

'I am Richard II. Know ye not that?'

Ideologically, *Richard II* is complex and problematical. As the first play in a tetralogy, it is central to the 'Tudor myth' of 'sacramental kingship' and divinely ordained order in the state and the universe. To Tillyard and his followers, the play is profoundly conservative in its doctrine, arguing, like the *Homily against Disobedience and Wilfull Rebellion* (1571), for 'the 'sanctity of monarchy' and 'the enormity of rebellion'.[1] In contrast with Marlowe's *Edward II*, a play on a similar theme which strongly influenced Shakespeare, *Richard II* is full of allusions to sacred kingship. Though there are marked structural similarities (in the counterpoint of the rise of Bullingbrook and the fall of Richard, the rise of Mortimer and the fall of Edward), *Edward II* has none of the 'ceremonial stateliness' in language and visual pageantry of Shakespeare's play, and not a single reference to the doctrine of Divine Right.[2] The word 'sacred' occurs more times in *Richard II* than in any other Shakespeare play, and the honorific terms of feudal loyalties and traditions – 'sovereign', 'liege', 'duty', 'knighthood', 'crown' – reverberate throughout the play.[3] King Richard's opening lines, formulaic words spoken from the throne, set the tone:

> Old John of Gaunt, time-honoured Lancaster,
> Hast thou according to thy oath and bond
> Brought hither Harry Herford, thy bold son.
>
> (1.1.1–3)

This is a world steeped in tradition, where oaths and bonds are honoured, and where family ties matter: the father presents the son, testifying to his status as a 'good subject' (1.1.10) and proper deference to his father and his monarch. *Edward II* begins with the Machiavel Gaveston, a hated upstart and parasite, describing in soliloquy the advantages he can gain from being 'the favourite of a king'.[4] In Marlowe's play, no one, including the King himself, has much respect for monarchy and its institutions.

John of Gaunt's famous lines on the endangered 'demi-paradise', the 'sceptred isle' of England, encapsulate the difference between the two plays, associating the privileged, protected state of the island kingdom with the 'earth' of English soil, breeding successive generations of kings and chivalrous noblemen:

> This blessèd plot, this earth, this realm, this England,
> This nurse, this teeming womb of royal kings
> Feared by their breed and famous by their birth,
> Renownèd for their deeds as far from home
> For Christian service and true chivalry
>
> (2.1.40–2, 50–4)

The related terms 'earth' (occurring 29 times), 'land' (28 times), and 'ground'(12 times), along with the related theme of England as garden, make up a recurrent symbolic pattern, frequently noted by critics. In Steven Pimlott's 2000 RSC production, a pile of earth (the soil of England, the grave) was present onstage from the beginning of the play.[5]

John of Gaunt is not the only spokesman for order and tradition prominent in *Richard II*. No more comprehensive and unequivocal statement of the ideology of Divine Right and the sanctity of tradition can be found than the Bishop of Carlisle's speech in 4.1, reacting with horror to Bullingbrook's blunt 'In God's name I'll ascend the regal throne'.

> CARLISLE
> What subject can give sentence on his king,
> And who sits here that is not Richard's subject?
> . . .
> And shall the figure of God's majesty,
> His captain, steward, deputy, elect,
> Anointed, crownèd, planted many years,
> Be judged by subject and inferior breath
> And he himself not present?
>
> (4.1.113, 121–2, 125–9)

This is precisely the position argued in *An Homily against Disobedience*, in James VI and I's *Trew Law of Free Monarchies* (1598), and, some years later, by Charles I in challenging the jurisdiction of his judges in 1649: for subjects to sit in judgement on their rulers is 'as though the foot must judge of the head', and no actions by a king, however reprehensible, can justify his forcible removal:

Shall it lie in the hands of the headless multitude, when they please to weary of subjection, to cast off the yoke of government that God has laid on them, to judge and punish him, whom-by they should be judged and punished?[6]

And yet, however unimpeachable the sentiments in Carlisle's eloquent speech, and however prescient his predictions of destructive civil war as a legacy to 'future ages' from 'this foul act' (4.1.138), the response by Northumberland and Bullingbrook, curt and efficient, shows that they are motivated by an entirely different set of values.

> NORTHUMBERLAND
> Well have you argued, sir, and for your pains
> Of capital treason we arrest you here.
> My Lord of Westminster, be it your charge
> To keep him safely till his day of trial.
> . . .
>
> BULLINGBROOK
> Fetch hither Richard, that in common view
> He may surrender. So we shall proceed
> Without suspicion.   (4.1.150–7)

The practical politicians immediately clap him into jail, and get down to the business of consolidating their power. Richard, no longer given an honorific title, is summoned to put on a public show, stage-managed by Bullingbrook, in an attempt to allay 'suspicion' and minimize possible opposition to the *coup d'état.*

This confrontation is a characteristic instance of Shakespearean 'negative capability' in its juxtaposition of opposites: both positions are true, according to their separate perspectives. *Richard II*, like Marvell's 'Horatian Ode', anatomizes political power, subjecting kingship and its associated institutions to searching analysis, as it examines conflicting loyalties and the problems of allegiance in unsettled times.

> Though Justice against Fate complain
> And plead the ancient rights in vain;
>> But these do hold or break
>> As men are strong or weak.

As Phyllis Rackin has pointed out, Shakespeare's histories can be read as supporting a providentialist or a Machiavellian view of historical causation: either the claim, argued here by Carlisle, that 'the ancient rights' and traditional values of service and loyalty retain their validity throughout changing circumstances, or the more cynical belief that strong men seeking power make their own rules.[7]

Richard II, like *Macbeth* and *King Lear*, is a play about the killing or forcible supplanting of a king, about the ways in which kings both are and aren't like ordinary men, and about the temptations and responsibilities of power. As with Macbeth's murder of Duncan, much of the effect of the play is predicated upon the assumption that the killing of a king is a particularly monstrous and unnatural act and is thus likely to have unpleasant consequences. The medieval and Renaissance *topos* of the dual nature of kingship, examined by E. H. Kantorowicz in *The King's Two Bodies*, can be used to invest a monarch with a particular sanctity. Any individual king is mortal and fallible, 'subject to Passions and Death as other Men are', but, as a legal fiction, 'what the King does in his Body politic, cannot be invalidated or frustrated by any Disability in his natural Body'. At his death 'there is a Separation of the two Bodies' by which 'the Body politic is transferred and conveyed . . . from one Body natural to another': the King is dead, long live the King.[8] The legal fiction of the king's two bodies can be applied not only to exalt the institution of monarchy and protect the king from criticism, but to justify opposition to a king, even, in the 1640s, to raise an army against the king in the king's name. Parliament in 1642 declared its actions to have 'the stamp of Royal Authority, although His Majesty . . . do in his own Person oppose or interrupt the same'.[9]

In Shakespeare, the monarch's dual nature – 'twin-born with greatness', yet 'subject to the breath / Of every fool', as Henry V puts it, rather testily (*Henry V*, 4.1.231–2) – is often given tragic dimensions. Sometimes the emphasis is on the discrepancy between the king as embodiment of tradition and as mere man, sometimes in an ironic awareness of the flimsiness of the trappings of power: the king as actor, assuming a role as he dons his costume. John Barton's celebrated 1973 production, with two actors alternating in the roles of Richard and Bullingbrook, began each night with one of the two, onstage, dressing himself in the robes denoting majesty. In both *Richard II* and *King Lear*, the monarch moves from an exaggerated sense of his own power and dignity to a recognition of kinship with ordinary mortals.

> RICHARD
> I live with bread like you, feel want,
> Taste grief, need friends. Subjected thus,
> How can you say to me I am a king?
>
> (3.2.175–7)

The simplicity of the largely monosyllabic language here suggests that Richard is not simply wallowing in abjection, playing yet another role, but has reached some degree of understanding not available to him earlier. As with Lear on the heath, there is at least a hint that his new-found awareness of 'poor naked wretches' entails a sense of his own failure in exercising the responsibilities that accompany power.

> LEAR
>
>   O, I have ta'en
> Too little care of this. Take physic, pomp,
> Expose thyself to feel what wretches feel,
> That thou mayst shake the superflux to them
> And show the heavens more just.
>
>   (*King Lear*, 3.4.28, 32–6)

To an Elizabethan audience, the most disconcerting aspect of *Richard II* is that it uses the notion of the king's two bodies to show onstage the uncrowning of a king, in an 'inverted rite . . . in which the order of coronation is reversed'.[10] By asserting his own agency in stripping himself of the visible symbols of monarchical power, Richard retains the upper hand psychologically, denying Bullingbrook centre stage, but the effect, as he fully realizes, is to reduce himself to 'nothing' once he stops talking, with little to look forward to but death.

> RICHARD
> With mine own tears I wash away my balm;
> With mine own hands I give away my crown;
> With mine own tongue deny my sacred state;
> With mine own breath release all duteous oaths.
> All pomp and majesty I do forswear;
> My manors, rents, revenues I forgo;
> My acts, decrees, and statutes I deny.
>
>   (4.1.200, 206–12)

If Queen Elizabeth, commenting 'I am Richard II. Know ye not that?', expressed her disapproval of public performances of a play depicting Richard's deposition and death, it is because any play on such a topic was, in potential at least, politically explosive. Parallels between the reign of Richard II and the latter years of Queen Elizabeth, with the succession in doubt and an ambitious favourite, the Earl of Essex, at times openly challenging the Queen, were widely recognized by contemporaries. As early as 1578, Sir Francis Knollys complained in a letter:

> For who woll persiste in gyvinge of safe counsayle, if her Majestie woll persiste in myslyking of safe counsayle? Nay who woll not rather . . . play

> the partes of King Richard the Second's men, then to enter into the
> odious office of crossing of her Majesties' wille?[11]

The historian Sir John Hayward was imprisoned for three years in 1600 for
publishing *The First Part of the Life and Raigne of King Henrie the IIII* in the
previous year, and the book was suppressed by the Privy Council. At his trial,
Hayward was accused of 'making this time seem like that of Richard II', with
seditious intent, both in the historical account itself and in the preface addressed
to Essex.

> What moved him to set down . . . that the nobility were then had in
> contempt, or that they were but base that were called about that King? . . .
> What moved him to maintain, with arguments never mentioned in the
> history, that it might be lawful for the subject to depose the King?[12]

The deposition scene does not appear in the three Quarto editions of
Richard II (1597–8) published during the Queen's lifetime. It first appeared,
in different political circumstances, in the Quarto of 1608, when the issue of
succession was no longer topical. What made the deposition scene particularly problematical, and might well, as with Hayward's book, have attracted
the notice of the censors, was the implicit support it might provide for the
dangerous assumption 'that it might be lawful for the subject to depose the
King'. In 1596 the Jesuit Robert Parsons had published a book, *a conference
about the next succession*, seized and banned by the censors, which made precisely that argument, justifying the deposition of Richard II on the grounds
that the King openly admitted 'his unworthy goverment, and [was] brought to
confesse that he was worthily deprived, and that he willingly and freely resigned
the same'.[13] The version of 4.1 in the 1597–8 Quartos, omitting lines 161–317,
is much more orthodox politically, including Carlisle's spirited defence of the
King, but leaving out the actual 'resignation' of Richard's 'state and crown / To
Henry Bullingbrook' (4.1.179–80), the ceremony of unkinging and the transfer
of power to a new monarch.

The 1608 Quarto advertises on its title page 'new additions of the Parliament
Scene, and the deposing of King Richard. As it hath been lately acted by the
Kinges Majesties servants, at the Globe.' Scholars disagree as to the extent to
which the deposition scene fell foul of the censor and whether the deposition
scene was ever acted during the reign of Queen Elizabeth. My view is that
the words 'new additions . . . lately acted' suggest that the scene in question
had appeared neither on stage nor in print previously. Presumably what was
perceived as dangerous in print would be equally so onstage.[14]

Rival monarchs

The central paradox at the heart of *Richard II* is that, of the two claimants to the throne, one possesses legitimacy but shows himself to be unfit to rule, while the other, lacking legitimacy, demonstrates the political skills and self-control his opponent lacks. Shakespeare's dramatic technique in this play encourages a suspension of judgement, a balance of sympathies towards the two main figures.

Two extended metaphors present closely matched antagonists contending for power, suggesting a momentary equipoise, followed by a decisive victory for one of them. In the deposition scene, the opening lines of Richard's speech addressed to Bullingbrook indicates the staging, with the two men, stage centre, and the crown poised between them:

> RICHARD
> Give me the crown. Here, cousin, seize the crown,
> On this side my hand and on that side thine.
> Now is this golden crown like a deep well
> That owes two buckets, filling one another,
> The emptier ever dancing in the air,
> The other down, unseen and full of water.
> That bucket, down and full of tears, am I,
> Drinking my griefs whilst you mount up on high.
>
> (4.1.181–8)

Richard's metaphor of the two buckets implies reciprocity, mutual dependency, while at the same time denying agency to either man. He sees himself here as passive victim of Fortune, weighed down by 'care' (l. 195) and his own sorrow at his overthrow, while his adversary is the happy recipient of Fortune's gifts. In effect, he is absolving himself of responsibility for what has happened to him. A second passage, in the gardeners' scene, uses a similar metaphor of weight and balance (this time, scales rather than two buckets) to very different effect.

> GARDENER
> Their fortunes both are weighed.
> In your lord's scale is nothing but himself
> And some few vanities that make him light,
> But in the balance of great Bullingbrook
> Besides himself are all the English peers,
> And with that odds he weighs King Richard down.
>
> (3.4.84–9)

Men make their own fortunes. Here, as throughout this scene, responsibility for Richard's downfall is placed squarely on his own shoulders. Despite the stately allegorical language, the Gardener makes a practical political point. Richard has failed because of his faults of character and his alienation of the powerful nobles who might have supported him; Bullingbrook has won because he has more troops and other material resources to back him up. Richard is characterized as 'light' because of his vanity and frivolity, where in the other passage Bullingbrook is lighter because unburdened as yet with the cares of office.

A problem in productions of the play is that Richard's part is much larger than that of Bullingbrook, and that he is a more attractive and interesting character, giving more opportunities to the actor. Yeats, in an amusing passage, is contemptuous towards Bullingbrook, waxing lyrical about Richard's grace and eloquence:

> To suppose that Shakespeare preferred the men who deposed his king is to suppose that Shakespeare judged men with the eyes of a Municipal Councillor weighing the merits of a Town Clerk . . . He saw indeed, as I think, in Richard II the defeat that awaits all, whether they be artist or saint, who find themselves where men ask of them a rough energy and have nothing to give but some contemplative virtue.[15]

Modern productions, reacting against the Gielgud tradition of mellifluous Richards, the King as Poet in a world of philistines, have attempted to redress the balance, both by fattening the part of Bullingbrook and by refusing to play for sympathy in the portrayal of Richard. John Barton's 1973 production tried to give Bullingbrook a tragic dimension (and a soliloquy, which he lacks in Shakespeare's original) by splicing into the text a version of his lines on sleeplessness from *2 Henry IV*.

> How many thousand of my poorest subjects
> Are at this hour asleep! O sleep, O gentle sleep,
> Nature's soft nurse, how have I frighted thee
> That thou no more will weigh my eyelids down
> And steep my senses in forgetfulness?[16]

In Steven Pimlott's 2000 production, Bullingbrook, aware of the hollowness of power, 'the realization that being a king is nothing', ends the play by repeating Richard's lines from the prison scene: 'I have been studying how I may compare / This prison where I live unto the world' (5.5.1–2).[17]

The deposition scene brings out the contrast between the two rivals and the interplay between them particularly strongly. In 4.1.181–308, Richard speaks

3. Richard Pasco as Richard II, Ian Richardson as Bullingbrook,
Richard II, Royal Shakespeare Company, 1973, directed by John Barton.

214 lines, most of them in long lyrical cadenzas (one speech of 22 lines, one of
19, one of 15, one of 14), where Bullingbrook has only five laconic utterances
of a single line and one of a line and a half. The contrast between words and
deeds, the expression of emotion and the control of emotion, could hardly
be more marked. Each line that Bullingbrook speaks suggests self-discipline,
practicality, a desire to maintain control over the situation, focusing on the
immediate moment: no metaphors, no lyrical flights.

> I thought you had been willing to resign.
> . . .
> Part of your cares you give me with your crown.
> . . .
> Are you contented to resign the crown?
> . . .
> Urge it no more, my Lord Northumberland.
> . . .
> The shadow of your sorrow hath destroyed
> The shadow of your face.
>   (4.1.189, 193, 199, 267, 270, 291–2)

Yet as recent productions make clear, Bullingbrook's apparent victory is a defeat. If earlier in the play Richard had shown himself to be an unworthy occupant of his exalted position, in his downfall he acquires tragic dimensions, with insights made possible by the loss of the comfortable illusions of power.

> O flattering glass,
> Like to my followers in prosperity
> Thou dost beguile me . . .
> (4.1.277–9)

The wasteful king

In the opening scenes of the play, Richard demonstrates his unworthiness by blatant abuses of power. He shows himself at his worst in seizing Bullingbrook's inheritance after the death of John of Gaunt. Here as elsewhere in the play, the aged Duke of York, a wise counsellor, acts as moral spokesman, pointing up the folly and immorality of the King's irresponsible, tyrannous act. Kent in the opening scenes of *King Lear* serves a similar dramatic function, warning Lear against banishing Cordelia.

> YORK
> Is not Gaunt dead? And doth not Herford live?
> Was not Gaunt just? And is not Harry true?
> Did not the one deserve to have an heir?
> Is not his heir a well-deserving son?
> Take Herford's rights away and take from time
> His charters and his customary rights.
> Let not tomorrow then ensue today.
> Be not thyself. For how art thou a king
> But by fair sequence and succession?
> (2.1.191–8)

Arrogantly, the King snaps in reply:

> RICHARD
> Think what you will, we seize unto our hands
> His plate, his goods, his money and his lands.
> (2.1.209–10)

Richard's behaviour here is not only morally unjustifiable, it is self-destructive, since as York warns him, by such conduct 'You pluck a thousand dangers on your head, / You lose a thousand well-disposed hearts' (ll. 205–6).

Machiavelli in *The Prince* warned rulers against seizing the property of their subjects and thus unnecessarily making enemies of those who felt themselves aggrieved.[18]

In earlier scenes, John of Gaunt, another representative of the traditional values of an older generation, had, in the play's most famous lines, presented Richard as a destructive force, endangering the traditions and the very life of 'this royal throne of kings', the 'dear, dear land' of England (2.1.40, 57). The abuses Gaunt warns against in his 'wholesome counsel' (2.1.2) are stated in rather general terms, but phrases like 'leased out', 'like to a tenement', 'rotten parchment bonds', and, in a later speech, 'landlord of England' suggest that he is referring to practices of tax-farming, devices of dubious legality by which Richard, encouraged by parasitic courtiers, is attempting to raise money (2.1.59–60, 64, 113). Similar charges against Richard are spelled out in more detail in the earlier play, *Woodstock.*[19] The essence of the charge is that Richard has brought 'shame' on the kingdom and has been an unworthy custodian of his legacy:

> That England that was wont to conquer others
> Has made a shameful conquest of itself.
>
> (2.1.63–6)

Later in this scene, Gaunt makes similar accusations directly to the King himself, and, predictably, enrages Richard. As well as being unheeded counsel, Gaunt's impolitic speech to Richard is one of several prophecies of impending disaster – in this case warning Richard of the possibility that he may eventually be deposed.

> Oh, had thy grandsire with a prophet's eye
> Seen how his son's son should destroy his sons,
> From forth thy reach he would have laid thy shame,
> Deposing thee before thou wert possessed,
> Which art possessed now to depose thyself.
>
> (2.1.104–8)

In Act 2 of the play, then, Richard is presented as an incipient tyrant, surrounded by flatterers. The parasitic courtiers themselves, Bushy, Bagot, and Green, are rather shadowy figures, not nearly as vividly portrayed as the equivalent figures in *Woodstock* or in Marlowe's *Edward II*. Thomas of Woodstock, the principal character in the earlier, anonymous play, is a possible model for Shakespeare's John of Gaunt: a patriot, a spokesman for traditional values, an honest counsellor critical of the misgovernment of his nephew Richard. In *Woodstock* and in *Richard II*, Woodstock and Gaunt are portrayed in consistently favourable terms, providing a moral touchstone, where in the chronicles and in accounts by modern historians, Gaunt is 'a contentious and ambitious baron' and Woodstock is 'hasty, wilful . . . ever repining against the king in all things'.[20] Politically, *Woodstock* is more daring than *Richard II*, since Richard there, a thoroughly unsympathetic figure, is unequivocally portrayed as tyrant and voluptuary, whose response to the criticisms of Woodstock is to order his uncle's murder. There is no evidence that *Woodstock* was ever performed, and the manuscript shows clear evidence of censorship, deletion of lines that might be considered especially provocative. One such instance is Woodstock's lines addressed to Richard:

> See here King Richard: whilst thou liv'st at ease
> Lulling thyself in nice security,
> Thy wronged kingdom's in a mutiny.[21]

More clearly than either *Richard II* or *Edward II, Woodstock* presents a version of contract theory, justifying resistance against a tyrant: the proposition 'that a king must protect his realm', with a care to the public interest, 'or lose his right to govern'.[22]

In Act 1 of *Richard II*, the King's actions are opaque, and these scenes have been interpreted in a number of ways in different productions. The death of Woodstock is mentioned in the early scenes, but Richard's responsibility for that death is never stated explicitly, as it is in *Woodstock*.[23] In the highly formal, ceremonial opening scene, Bullingbrook accuses Thomas Mowbray, Duke of Norfolk, of treason in plotting the murder of Woodstock and of misappropriating funds; Mowbray denies the charges and asks for the dispute to be settled by 'chivalrous design of knightly trial' (1.1.81). The two characters use essentially the same vocabulary ('honour's pawn', 'the rites of knighthood') in their lengthy speeches (1.1.74–5), and for a theatrical audience unlikely to know the details of the story beforehand, there is no clear way of judging between them. In 1.3, with its marshal, heralds, trumpets, and armed warriors facing one another, Shakespeare sets up the dramatic expectation that the knightly combat will take place on stage, so that when Richard suddenly orders them to stop, it comes as a shock. As Samuel West says, 'it must *look* for all the world as if we're going through with the duel'. Critics may speculate about Richard's motives, but in this scene of ritual and formal utterance, the audience is given no access to the King's thoughts. According to West, 'there's a choice here: the cancellation can be a spur-of-the-moment decision, but I felt premeditated action was more in keeping' with an interpretation of Richard in the opening scenes as politically astute, aware of the danger to him of letting either contestant win. In Deborah Warner's 1995 production, Fiona Shaw, in contrast, portrayed Richard as 'desperately unsure what to do . . . in complete panic. He threw his warder down as a last-second reaction, surprising himself as much as anyone else by his action.'[24]

In the early scenes, West played Richard as ice-cold and supercilious, with 'a smug sense of his own primacy'. One reviewer commented that in this modern-dress production, 'Richard is convincingly shown as a tin-pot dictator, with the courtiers his apparatchiks'. Shaw played Richard in these scenes as 'an impish and irresponsible boy-king', a Peter Pan unwilling to grow up, constantly 'trying to make jokes' and uncomfortable in the exercise of power.[25] Other Richards – Ralph Fiennes in 2000, Derek Jacobi in a BBC production in 1978 – played Richard in these scenes as self-indulgent, arrogant, encouraged in his abuses by compliant courtiers who, as in *Edward II*, evidently also served as his catamites. In all of these productions, and in Shakespeare's text, the Richard of the opening scenes is a relatively unsympathetic character, either indifferent to his responsibilities or consciously abusing his power.

The name of king

The political issues central to *Richard II* are expressed clearly and explicitly in several speeches by York in 2.2 and 3. Richard is absent from the kingdom, and Bullingbrook, returning from exile, is at the head of a group of rebellious nobles, with a large army. York's position, as the King's representative and as a counsellor whose prudent advice the King has constantly rejected, is ambivalent. His role in the play, like that of Enobarbus in *Antony and Cleopatra*, is partly to direct the sympathies of the audience, serving as a kind of moral touchstone.[26] Here he can see merit in both sides of the dispute between Bullingbrook and the King, recognizing that the King has 'wronged' Bullingbrook, but also aware that his 'oath and duty' require obedience to his sovereign (2.2.111–15).

At this point in the play, Bullingbrook claims to have returned to England, backed up by an army, only to claim his inheritance.

> BULLINGBROOK
> Will you permit that I shall stand condemned
> A wandering vagabond, my rights and royalties
> Plucked from my arms perforce and given away
> To upstart unthrifts? Wherefore was I born?
> If that my cousin king be king in England
> It must be granted I am Duke of Lancaster.
>
> (2.3.118–23)

York had given fruitless counsel to Richard, and now gives fruitless advice to Bullingbrook, warning him against 'gross rebellion' in 'braving arms against thy sovereign' (2.3.108–11). York's language of Divine Right, invoking the magic of a monarch's sacred name, sanctified by tradition and authority derived from God, is the kind of language King Richard uses in the scenes that follow and that the Bishop of Carlisle uses in protesting against Richard's deposition:

> YORK
> Comest thou because the anointed king is hence?
> Why, foolish boy, the king is left behind
> And in my loyal bosom lies his power.
>
> (2.3.95–7)

Yet though symbolically York exercises the King's power, acting as the monarch's designated deputy, he is aware, as is the audience, that his 'power is weak and all ill-left' (2.3.153), as an old man presiding over a bankrupt kingdom, with no reliable troops at his disposal, facing a formidable, well-armed force of determined men. As Richard says, with some bitterness, at the end of the Flint Castle scene, where he yields the initiative to Bullingbrook, 'do we must what force will have us do' (3.3.206).

Richard's long and eloquent speeches in 3.2 and 3.3, great favourites with actors, are full of the characteristic language and imagery of Divine Right. In an extended conceit, Richard imagines his enemy quailing at the very appearance of the royal sun, darkness overcome by the glorious effulgence of light. Once 'the cloak of night' is removed at sunrise, then Bullingbrook, obedient to the terms of Richard's metaphor:

> Shall see us rising in our throne the east
> His treasons will set blushing in his face,
> Not able to endure the sight of day,
> But self-affrighted tremble at his sin.
>
> (3.2.45, 50–3)

In stirring lines, Richard expresses his faith in his sacred role: once a king, always a king. God has appointed him, and God will protect him.

> Not all the water in the rough rude sea
> Can wash the balm off from an anointed king.
> The breath of worldly men cannot depose
> The deputy elected by the Lord.   (3.2.54–7)

The lines gain poignancy from their ironic context, since the audience, knowing the story in advance, are aware that 'worldly men', indifferent to arguments such as these, will depose Richard. Richard's assertion that the king cannot be deposed carries within it the possibility that he *can*: indeed, Richard mentions this possibility long before Bullingbrook does.

The fragility of Richard's confidence at this point in the play is indicated in the extravagance of his claim that God will send angels to fight on his behalf. Here as elsewhere he is taking metaphor for reality, rejecting as 'discomfortable' the hard facts of dwindling support and the large number of troops under Bullingbrook's command.

> For every man that Bullingbrook hath pressed
> To lift shrewd steel against our golden crown
> God for his Richard hath in heavenly pay
> A glorious angel.   (3.2.36, 58–61)

When he hears 'the tidings of calamity' from successive messengers, Richard's reaction is to sink into despair.

> Have I not reason to look pale and dead?
> All souls that will be safe fly from my side,
> For time hath set a blot upon my pride.
>   (3.2.70, 79–81, 105, 119)

Actors relish Richard's rapid oscillations of emotion in this scene, from the heights to the depths in an instant, embracing abjection and then castigating himself for admitting unworthy thoughts. By calling up 'the name of king' to strengthen his resolve, investing that name with magical, charismatic power, he is of course admitting that all he has at his disposal in this crisis is a mere name, empty of significance.

> Awake, thou coward! Majesty, thou sleepest.
> Is not the king's name twenty thousand names?
> Arm, arm, my name! A puny subject
> Strikes at thy great glory.   (3.2.84–7)

In the next scene, at Flint Castle, Richard for the first time admits a disjunction between name and reality. By the incantational repetition of the terms 'king', 'name', and 'must', he is in a sense asserting a form of agency through words, while stripping these words of their magical associations, divesting himself of the robes of kingship. The lines enact the transfer of sovereignty to the triumphant 'King Bullingbrook'.

What must the king do now? Must he submit?
The king shall do it. Must he be deposed?
The king shall be contented. Must he lose
The name of king? A God's name let it go.

(3.3.143–6)

Richard's great lyrical speech on 'the death of kings' abandons all ideas that kings are privileged beings, to be treated with 'solemn reverence' and ceremony. The tragic aspects of the play, brought out in the Quarto title, *The Tragedie of King Richard the Second*, are particularly notable in this speech, in which Richard generalizes from his own example, to anatomize the folly of all those who, with 'vain conceit', pretend to 'monarchise' over others, unaware of their own vulnerability.

For God's sake let us sit upon the ground
And tell sad stories of the death of kings.
How some have been deposed, some slain in war,
Some haunted by the ghosts they have deposed,
Some poisoned by their wives, some sleeping killed,
All murdered. For within the hollow crown
That rounds the mortal temples of a king
Keeps Death his court . . .   (3.2.155–62, 165–6)

As with Lear in the prison scene ('So we'll live / And pray, and sing, and tell old tales, and laugh / At gilded butterflies' (*King Lear*, 5.3.11–13)), the simplicity of the utterance is an index of the insight achieved once the outward trappings of power are stripped away. It is an artful simplicity, with marked rhetorical patterning (some . . . some . . . some): Richard is telling sad stories to his audience, an actor taking advantage of the moment.

The metaphor of the king as actor, playing a role chosen for him by another, is implicit in the lines that follow (brought out in the terms 'antic' and 'little scene'). Earthly monarchs occupy their thrones on a temporary basis, on sufferance: the only true monarch is death. Syntactically, these lines differ from the earlier part of the passage, with long suspended clauses, enjambement, strings of participles (scoffing . . . grinning . . . allowing), doublets (a breath, a little scene; be feared and kill; self and vain). In terms of the play's overall structure, one function of the lines is to project a Richard who is capable of development, recognizing a kinship with others ('our life'), and thus can gain the audience's sympathies.

Keeps Death his court, and there the antic sits
Scoffing his state and grinning at his pomp,
Allowing him a breath, a little scene
To monarchise, be feared and kill with looks,
Infusing him with self and vain conceit
As if this flesh which walls about our life
Were brass impregnable, and humoured thus
Comes at the last and with a little pin
Bores through his castle wall and farewell king!

(3.2.162–70)

'Down, down, I come like glistering Phaëton'

In the next scene, a direct confrontation between the two rival claimants, Richard attempts for a moment to summon up the old trumpet tones. The staging is clearly indicated: Richard on the upper stage, flanked by his handful of followers, Bullingbrook and his supporters on the main acting area below. Throughout the scene there is much play with kneeling and other conventional signs of deference: early in the scene York scolds Northumberland for speaking of 'Richard' without the honorific title. Richard's opening lines, clothed in regal dignity, address Northumberland's refusal to kneel.

RICHARD
We are amazed, and thus long have we stood
To watch the fearful bending of thy knee
Because we thought ourselves thy lawful king.
And if we be, how dare thy joints forget
To pay their awful duty to our presence?

(3.3.72–6)

As in the earlier scene, he employs the standard Divine Right tropes to bolster his position: the King is God's deputy, wielding a 'sacred' sceptre, and the mere presence of Bullingbrook on 'my land' without permission, is 'dangerous treason'.

If we be not, show us the hand of God
That hath dismissed us from our stewardship.
For well we know no hand of blood and bone
Can gripe the sacred handle of our sceptre,
Unless he do profane, steal or usurp.

(3.3.77–81, 92–3)

As before, he summons up imaginary legions of heavenly troops to compensate for his lack of actual troops, papering over his awareness that, in hard fact, he is 'barren and bereft of friends' to defend him. This time, the supernatural 'armies' he imagines acting on his 'behalf' will not keep him on his throne, but punish Bullingbrook and his allies afterwards. Like Carlisle in the deposition scene, Richard prophesies a legacy of disaster in 'future ages', a deluge of 'blood' overwhelming English fields.

> Yet know: my master, God omnipotent,
> Is mustering in his clouds on our behalf
> Armies of pestilence, and they shall strike
> Your children yet unborn and unbegot
> That lift your vassal hands against my head
> And threat the glory of my precious crown.
>   (3.3.84–90, 100; 4.1.137–8)

Richard's aside to his follower Aumerle openly recognizes that both he and Northumberland are putting on a performance, engaging in a ritual in which the words they use do not convey an inner reality but seek to disguise it. When he speaks of the 'fair demands' of his 'noble cousin' and praises the 'gracious utterance' of Northumberland, or when Northumberland swears that Bullingbrook, in 'faithful service to the King', has raised an army 'with no further scope / Than for his lineal royalties', both are uttering diplomatic untruths, using words they know to be false.

> *[to Aumerle]*
> We do debase ourselves, cousin, do we not,
> To look so poorly and to speak so fair?
> Shall we call back Northumberland and send
> Defiance to the traitor and so die?
>   (3.3.112–13, 118, 122–5, 127–30)

The aside can be read both as an admission that the formulae of politeness are transparently insincere and an expression of anguished self-recrimination at having to resort to such paltry stratagems. Indeed, the claim that he might unsay what he has just said and breathe defiance to Northumberland embodies a tacit recognition that he is no longer in a position to do any such thing.

> Oh that I were as great
> As is my grief, or lesser than my name,
> Or that I could forget what I have been,
> Or not remember what I must be now.
>   (3.3.136–9)

Richard, who had previously claimed that 'the king's name' was more powerful than an army of twenty thousand, is now coming to see the name of king
as a burden, bringing only 'grief'. Later, in the deposition scene, he characterizes himself as nameless, losing all identity once he has been stripped of his
hereditary title, and calls for a mirror, to find out what shreds of identity are
left him, now 'bankrupt of his majesty'.

> I have no name, no title,
> No, not that name was given me at the font,
> But 'tis usurped. Alack the heavy day
> That I have worn so many winters out
> And know not now what name to call myself.
> (4.1.254–8, 266)

Still later, in prison, he concludes that the desire to be reduced to 'nothing',
facing the oblivion of death, is the ultimate end of vain human hopes and
ambition.

> But what'er I be
> Nor I nor any man that but man is
> With nothing shall be pleased till he be eased
> With being nothing. (5.5.38–41)

In the Flint Castle scene, Richard's farewell to earthly pomp has a self-
consciously theatrical quality. Nearly all commentators see Richard's lines in
praise of the simple life of religious meditation as 'outbursts of self-pity', yet
another role for him to assume, as he takes pleasure in his flights of fancy,
seeking to 'play the wantons with our woes' (3.3.164).[27] When, in comparable lines in *3 Henry VI*, the saintly and ineffective King Henry commends
the ordered, quiet life of 'a homely swain', his soliloquy suggests a genuine
alternative to bloodshed, a shadow life in which, under other circumstances,
King Henry might have been happy, free from 'care, mistrust and treason'
(*3 Henry VI*, 2.5.21–54). In *Richard II* there is no suggestion that Richard
seriously contemplates taking up a religious vocation, or that, in an access of
piety, he renounces the life of luxury. Indeed, the account of Richard's 'misgovernance' in Holinshed, Shakespeare's principal source, places much greater
emphasis on the 'prodigall' extravagance of Richard's court than Shakespeare's
play.

> He kept the greatest port, and maintained the most plentifull house that
> ever any king in England did either before his time or since. For there
> resorted dailie to his court above ten thousand persons that had meat
> and drinke there allowed them . . . And in gorgious and costlie apparell

> they exceeded all measure, not one of them that kept within the bounds
> of his degree. Yeomen and groomes were clothed in silkes.[28]

Richard's lines, in neat patterns, express his awareness of the pain of loss, the
contrast between 'what I have been' and 'what I must be now', and seek to evoke
tears from sympathetic onlookers: 'Aumerle, thou weep'st, my tender-hearted
cousin' (3.3.138–9, 160). Walter Pater, in a felicitous phrase, speaks of Richard's
'appreciation of the poetry of his own hapless lot, an eloquent self-pity, infecting
others in spite of themselves'.[29]

> I'll give my jewels for a set of beads,
> My gorgeous palace for a hermitage,
> My gay apparel for an almsman's gown,
> My figured goblet for a dish of wood,
> My sceptre for a palmer's walking staff,
> My subjects for a pair of carved saints,
> And my large kingdom for a little grave,
> A little, little grave, an obscure grave.
> Or I'll be buried in the king's highway,
> Some way of common trade, where subjects' feet
> May hourly trample on their sovereign's head.
>
> (3.3.147–57)

By the end of the passage, the pleasure that Richard takes in self-abasement,
courting oblivion, becomes overt, in the loving repetition of 'little, little, little'
and the vision of himself as trodden underfoot. No gilded monument for
him, but a nameless grave, an infinite prolongation of humiliation and pain
extending beyond death.

    The scene ends with a literal descent from on high, as Richard relinquishes
the elevation of the upper stage for the common acting surface below. His language brings out his awareness of the symbolic role of this agreement to 'come
down' from above, presenting it as a form of abdication, a formal acknowl-
edgement of his loss of power and prestige. His scornful repetition of 'base' and
the imperative 'down' represent the physical descent as a violation of natural
hierarchy: 'kings grow base' when they surrender to the demands of their social
inferiors.

NORTHUMBERLAND
My lord, in the base court he doth attend
To speak with you. May it please you to come down?

RICHARD
Down, down, I come, like glistering Phaëton,

Wanting the manage of unruly jades.
In the base court? Base court where kings grow base
To come at traitors' calls and do them grace!
In the base court come down. Down court, down king,
For night owls shriek where mounting larks should sing.

(3.3.176–83)

Here as elsewhere in this scene, Richard projects himself as victim, giving vent to his 'sorrow and grief of heart' (l. 184) while attempting to hold on to the tattered shreds of his dignity. But the implications of the myth of Phaëton, who brought destruction on himself by his inability to control the chariot of the sun, a classic instance of unwarranted pride and nemesis, suggest an alternative reading. By an irony of which Richard is not yet fully aware, the myth fits his own situation precisely: he is, by his rash actions, responsible for his own downfall.

The lamentable tale of me

The gardeners' scene, which follows immediately, presents a variant of the Phaëton myth. In many ways, this scene is an oddity: where other scenes in Shakespeare's histories involving ordinary people rather than princes and baron – the Jack Cade episode in *2 Henry VI*, the Boar's Head Tavern in *1 Henry IV* – are in colloquial prose, often with a pronounced comic element, the gardeners' scene is in highly formal, elevated verse. John Barton's 1973 production tried to introduce a degree of verisimilitude by turning the gardeners into monks, who might be expected to speak this way.

GARDENER
Go thou, and like an executioner
Cut off the heads of too-fast-growing sprays
That look too lofty in our commonwealth.
All must be even in our government.

(3.4.33–6)

The terms the Gardener and his assistant use are implicitly political at first (the garden needs to be maintained like a commonwealth) and then explicitly directed at the 'disordered' state, 'full of weeds . . . unpruned . . . swarming with caterpillars' (the state needs to be managed with care, like a garden). The Gardener applies the terms of the allegory to 'the wasteful king', who has suffered a disaster, a 'fall', as a direct consequence of his lack of foresight, his failure to act responsibly.

> Oh what pity is it
> That he had not so trimmed and dressed his land
> As we this garden!   (3.4.44–7, 49, 55–7)

In its overall dramatic function, the allegory of the unweeded and disease-ridden 'sea-wallèd garden' is associated with John of Gaunt's lament for the 'demi-paradise' of England, threatened with destruction. As in earlier scenes with Gaunt and York, Richard is accused of irresponsibility in the exercise of his office and of excessive reliance on 'too lofty', parasitic courtiers (3.4.35).

The gardeners' scene begins and ends with weeping, the Queen's copious tears at her husband's fate. As Altick says, 'the idea of tears and weeping' is more 'insistently presented' in *Richard II* than in any other of Shakespeare's histories: 'grief', 'sorrow', 'weeping', 'the heavy thought of care' echo throughout the scene.[30] In the Queen's next appearance, meeting her husband on his way to prison, the function of the scene, quite overtly, is to extort sympathetic tears from the audience.

> QUEEN
>   Yet look up, behold,
> That you in pity may dissolve in dew
> And wash him fresh again with true love tears.
>
>   (5.1.8–10)

This scene is Shakespeare's invention, with no basis in Holinshed: the historical Queen Isabel, Richard's second wife, was eleven years old at the time, and apparently had no contact with her husband after his return from Ireland.[31] Husband and wife weep together at his sad fate, kiss one another goodbye, mourning their separation as well as his downfall. Richard tells his wife to abandon all thought of earthly happiness and to think of him as dead: their parting must be a final one. The one task remaining for her, Richard says, is like Hamlet's dying request to Horatio, to tell his story – only here it is not to act as a living witness or as his advocate, but to make the listeners weep, to give the narrative of his life the form and emotional force of tragedy.

> Tell thou the lamentable tale of me
> And send the hearers weeping to their beds.
> . . .
> The senseless brands will sympathise
> The heavy accent of thy moving tongue
> And in compassion weep the fire out.
>
>   (5.1.43–7)

If Bullingbrook and his supporters see the last part of the action as confirmation of their success, giving the newly crowned king an opportunity to
rule more justly and efficiently than his predecessor, Richard sees it as the final
scene in his tragedy. Act 5 of *Richard II* includes foreshadowing and prophecy
of events to occur in later plays as yet unwritten. Bullingbrook complains 'Can
no man tell me of my unthrifty son?' and Richard warns Northumberland that
before long he and the new king will quarrel over the spoils of victory (5.1.55–
61; 5.3.1). Further evidence of dissension in the realm after the fall of Richard,
problems as yet unresolved, comes in the odd episode of Aumerle's conspiracy,
a moment of slapstick comedy out of keeping with the prevalent tone of the last
part of the play. These scenes, 5.2 and 3, are often cut in performance, though
they do show how skilfully Bullingbrook can deal with a political crisis.

But the overall mood of the last part of the play is tragic, and Richard is its
dominant figure. In the deposition scene, Richard compares himself to Jesus,
despised and rejected, betrayed by his former followers.

> RICHARD
>   Yet I well remember
> The favours of these men. Were they not mine?
> Did they not some time cry 'All hail' to me?
> So Judas did to Christ, but he in twelve
> Found truth in all but one, I in twelve thousand none.
>
>   (4.1.167–71)

Speeches like this one are not so much attempts by Richard, as earlier in the
play, to clothe himself in divinity, as they are a recognition of the transiency
of earthly power. The dramatic function of this passage, in an overall tragic
pattern, is to present the fallen King as an object of pity, in contrasting his
present and former state. As such, it is closely akin to the speech by the Duke
of York in 5.2 describing Richard's patient endurance, with 'gentle sorrow',
of the humiliation of having 'dust . . . thrown upon his sacred head' by the
fickle crowd, or the speech of the loyal Groom in 5.5, describing Bullingbrook's
triumphant coronation.

> Oh how it erned my heart when I beheld
> In London streets that coronation day
> When Bullingbrook rode on roan Barbary,
> That horse that thou so often hast bestrid,
> That horse that I so carefully have dressed.
>
>   (5.2.28–31; 5.5.76–80)

Both of these speeches evoke sympathetic tears from an audience, while suggesting the possibility of continued loyalty to the fallen King and to traditional values. York's speech makes explicit the analogy between the deposed monarch and the man of sorrows, acquainted with grief. But in Richard's own words, there is no suggestion of forgiveness of his enemies or of saintlike 'patience'.

Richard's comparison of himself to Jesus tried before Pilate presents his enemies as 'marked with a blot, damned in the book of heaven', and himself as an innocent victim. Elsewhere in the play the recurrent image of a blot staining a white surface is used to suggest a diseased commonwealth (with Gaunt associating the 'inky blots' of 'shame' with Richard's misrule, Mowbray with false accusations of treason, Richard himself with how 'time has set a blot upon my pride'). But here Richard suggests that he alone is sinless.[32]

> RICHARD
> Nay, all of you that stand and look on me
> Whilst that my wretchedness doth bait my self
> Though some of you with Pilate wash your hands,
> Showing an outward pity, yet you Pilates
> Have here delivered me to my sour cross
> And water cannot wash away your sin.
>
> (4.1.236–41)

Bullingbrook himself ends the play with a version of the comparison with Pilate, when, though disclaiming direct responsibility for the death of Richard, he makes a vow of pilgrimage to Jerusalem 'to wash his blood off from my guilty hand' (5.6.49–50). The legacy of guilt is a recurrent theme in the three later plays in the tetralogy.

When, in the deposition scene, Richard first addresses and then shatters the 'flattering glass' (4.1.278) he asks to be brought to him, the gesture can be seen as a step towards self-knowledge or as further confirmation of his narcissism and vanity. Modern productions have brought out visual mirror symbolism here: John Barton saw the broken mirror, placed over Richard's head as he was led off to prison, as both crown and noose, where Steven Pimlott, whose mirror was a large oblong box, saw it as doubling as coffin.[33] A looking glass is of course a familiar metaphor both for self-delusion and for confronting the truth, as in Hamlet's 'You go not till I set you up a glass / Where you may see the inmost part of you' (*Hamlet*, 3.4.18–19). As Richard develops the conceit, he moves from the apparent contrast between outward appearance and inner reality (grief has not yet carved 'deeper wrinkles' on his face) to a rejection of the trappings of monarchical power as flattering and deceptive.

> Was this face the face
> That every day under his household roof
> Did keep ten thousand men? Was this the face
> That like the sun did make beholders wink?
>
> (4.1.276, 280–3)

Shattering the glass is a gesture of impotence, an admission that he has been defeated, 'outfaced' by the 'silent king', Bullingbrook. But the 'moral' he draws is applicable to Bullingbrook, now bearing the burden of the crown, as well as to himself: all earthly glory is 'brittle', and outward prosperity cannot disguise the 'unseen grief' eating away within (4.1.285–6, 289, 296–7).

Richard's longest and most complex speech is his soliloquy in prison. This speech is unlike any other in the play, giving the impression of a man thinking, working out his arguments patiently, in a 'quietly meditative' tone.[34]

> I have been studying how I may compare
> This prison where I live unto the world,
> And for because the world is populous
> And here is not a creature but myself
> I cannot do it. Yet I'll hammer't out.
>
> (5.5.1–5)

The Richard of the earlier scenes would have been incapable of speaking these lines. Deprived of an audience to play to and comforting illusions to ward off pain, his only companions are 'a generation of still breeding thoughts', restlessly circulating, which populate his solitude (5.5.8–9).

In this soliloquy, Richard contrasts 'thoughts tending to ambition' with 'thoughts tending to content', and finds neither satisfying: both 'flatter themselves' (5.5.18–30). The stage metaphor prevalent throughout the play reaches its culmination here: Richard is an actor, with no choice over the roles he is asked to play.

> Thus play I in one person many people,
> And none contented. Sometimes I am a king,
> Then treasons make me wish myself a beggar,
> And so I am. Then crushing penury
> Persuades me I was better when a king,
> Then am I kinged again, and by and by
> Think that I am unkinged by Bullingbrook,
> And straight am nothing.   (5.5.31–8)

There is a dreamlike quality here, as everything seems to flash by, speeded up. All is illusion: no role in the stage of the world, high or low, is lasting, and none brings contentment. Here as in the earlier 'I live with bread like you, feel want, / Taste grief, need friends' (3.2.175–6), the bareness of the language suggests a truth learned through suffering. The conclusion is bleak: the only 'ease' obtainable is in the peace of oblivion, a final reduction to 'being nothing' (5.5.41).

At this point, Richard hears offstage music, and the terms of the metaphor shift. Music, depending on 'proportion', keeps time, so do clocks and watches, so do (or should do) 'men's lives'. In the solitude of prison, clock time ceases to have much meaning, but the imagination takes on the role of a 'numbering clock'.

> My thoughts are minutes, and with sighs they jar
> Their watches on unto mine eyes, the outward watch,
> Whereto my finger like a dial's point
> Is pointing still, in cleansing them from tears.
>
> (5.5.43–4, 50–4)

'Watch' here means wakefulness, sentries on parade, the faculty of sight, and the face of a clock, and the dial's point is the minute hand of the clock. To Richard, his time (the Arden edition glosses this as 'time on earth') is subordinated to Bullingbrook who has become the master of time, while he, humiliated, has been reduced to a mechanical 'Jack of the clock' (5.5.58–60). But the ultimate conclusion Richard reaches, remaining within the terms of the metaphor, suggests that he has gained an insight not available to him earlier.

> And here have I the daintiness of ear
> To check time broke in a disordered string,
> But for the concord of my state and time
> Had not an ear to hear my true time broke.
> I wasted time and now does time waste me.
>
> (5.5.45–9)

Able to recognize discord or false notes in music when he hears it, Richard admits for the first time in the play that he has been the cause of discord and disorder in the state. He does not see himself here as an innocent victim, an object to be pitied, but as the author of his own misfortunes, responsible by his previous actions for the predicament he now finds himself in.

Chapter 7

Lord of Misrule: *1* and *2 Henry IV*

Kings and clowns

Though the action of *1 Henry IV*, the second play in a tetralogy, follows directly from *Richard II*, it is an entirely different kind of play. Where *Richard II* is in highly formal, elevated verse throughout, *1 Henry IV* employs a mixed style, mingling kings and clowns. In 'The Defence of Poesy', Sir Philip Sidney argues that to 'thrust in the clown by head and shoulders to play a part in majestical matters' is indecorous, akin to mixing 'hornpipes and funerals'.[1] Rejecting such notions of decorum, *1 Henry IV*, like a number of Shakespeare's comedies – *Much Ado about Nothing, The Merchant of Venice, Twelfth Night* – has a double plot, ingeniously worked out, juxtaposing different worlds in its two distinct strands. Of the two plot lines in *1 Henry IV* and its sequel, *2 Henry IV*, one can be described as 'history', largely in verse, with its material drawn from the chronicles as in Shakespeare's earlier history plays, and the other, far less dependent on the chronicles and largely in prose, as comedy.

The comic world of the Boar's Head Tavern and the political world of the King's council chamber are presented from the beginning of the play as incompatible in their values. Falstaff's opening words are 'Now, Hal, what time of day is it, lad?' (1.2.1). You could never imagine King Henry IV (the astute, laconic Bullingbrook of *Richard II*) not knowing what time of day it was, or sleeping on a bench in the tavern until afternoon, or talking in such an informal, relaxed manner. Prince Hal's reply, like Falstaff's affectionate 'Hal' and 'lad', establishes a bond of friendship between the two men, with no insistence on hierarchy or deference, as well as vividly characterizing the kind of life Falstaff habitually leads:

> PRINCE HENRY
> Thou art so fat-witted with drinking of old sack, and unbuttoning thee
> after supper, and sleeping upon benches after noon, that thou hast
> forgotten that truly which thou wouldst truly know. What a devil hast
> thou to do with the time of day? (1.2.2–6)

King Henry's opening words, in contrast, are a public utterance, using the royal 'we', concerning matters of state, and with an emphasis on 'care', the weight of responsibility, the uncertain hope of escaping from the legacy of destructive civil war:

> KING HENRY
> So shaken as we are, so wan with care,
> Find we a time for frighted peace to pant,
> And breathe short-winded accents of new broils
> To be commenced in strands afar remote.
> No more the thirsty entrance of this soil
> Shall daub her lips with her own children's blood.
>   (1.1.1–6)

The scene that follows shows the moment of 'frighted peace' to be brief indeed, with the great barons of the north, Wales, and Scotland in open rebellion. Here as in *Richard II*, Shakespeare draws on Holinshed, which presents the reign of Henry IV as 'unquiet' because of 'the hatred of his people, the hartgrudgings of his courtiers'.[2] The King's speech to the rebellious Percies at the beginning of 1.3 insists on the dignity of his position:

> KING HENRY
> My blood hath been too cold and temperate,
> Unapt to stir at these indignities,
> And you have found me, for accordingly
> You tread upon my patience. But be sure,
> I will from henceforth rather be myself,
> Mighty and to be feared.   (1.3.1–6)

The King's 'self', as he presents it in these two speeches, is entirely a public façade, with any private feelings to be held in check, where the Prince's 'self' is defined by a deliberate refusal to concern himself with public affairs, the world of politics. As the father complains, confronting his son in 3.2, the Prince has abandoned his 'place in Council' and has become 'almost an alien' to King and court (3.2.32–5).

And yet, as the King's bitter criticism of his son clearly indicates, the two plots in *1 Henry IV* are in no way separable, but make up a single story, and the juxtapositions, parallels, and contrasts linking the 'history' plot and the comic plot reflect a complex relationship between these two sharply differentiated worlds – or between each of them and a third location, the battlefield, towards which the action moves halfway through the play. The structure of *1 Henry IV* is highly schematic: here, as in other history plays by Shakespeare, a clearly recognizable pattern is a way of making sense out of the chaos of history. There are two sons and two fathers, two young men who are set up from the very beginning of the play as potential rivals, and two old men who represent alternative father figures for the young prince. In 1.1, the King brings out the contrast and the implicit rivalry between the two young men explicitly, comparing a 'son who is the theme of honour's tongue . . . sweet Fortune's minion' with another whose visage is stained by 'riot and dishonour' (1.1.77– 85).

To the King, Hotspur, who has devoted his life to warfare and the pursuit of glory, is the soul of honour, where the prince's life, rejecting the father and all he stands for, is dishonourable. Anyone with any experience of plays or works of fiction will know that the two will inevitably have to meet in battle and fight out the supremacy.

What complicates this straightforward dramatic pattern is that *1 Henry IV* is not a single, free-standing play, but the first of two, followed by a sequel. Tillyard and Dover Wilson both 'treat the two parts as a single play' in ten acts, arguing that the action 'is patently incomplete at the end of the first part'.[3] And yet the title page of the 1598 Quarto gives no indication that *The Historie of Henrie the Fourth, With the battell of Shrewsburie [and] . . . With the humorous conceits of Sir John Falstalffe* is anything but an independent play (oddly, though the title page names the King, Falstaff, and Hotspur, it makes no mention of the Prince). The 1600 Quarto of *2 Henry IV* is avowedly a sequel, *The Second part of Henrie the fourth, continuing to his death, and coronation of Henrie the fift. With the humours of sir John Falstaffe, and swaggering Pistol.* In other Elizabethan and Jacobean two-part plays, the sequel is clearly an afterthought, rather than part of a premeditated design. The prologue to Marlowe's *Tamburlaine, Part Two* attributes the genesis of that play to market demands:

> The generall welcomes Tamburlaine receiv'd,
> When he arrived last upon our stage,
> Hath made our poet pen his Second Part.[4]

1 Henry IV is, paradoxically, both complete and incomplete. In 'The Structural Problem in Shakespeare's *Henry IV*', Harold Jenkins argues that the double plot in *1 Henry IV* sets up expectations of a double denouement:

> The plain fact is that in *Henry IV* two actions, each with the Prince as
> hero, begin together in the first act of Part I, though one of them ends
> with the death of Hotspur at the end of Part I, the other with the
> banishment of Falstaff at the end of Part II.[5]

Jenkins argues that, in effect, Shakespeare changed his mind in the course of writing *1 Henry IV*, finding that he had too much material for a single play. Furthermore, since *1 Henry IV* has as its central action the reformation of Prince Hal, where *2 Henry IV* at its outset appears to depict a Prince who is unreformed, and thus reduplicates what is already finished in the story of the Prince, in Jenkins's view the two plays are in some respects 'incompatible' (pp. 166–7, 171).

'When thou art king'

Part 2 thus serves as a commentary on, as well as a completion of, Part 1. *1 Henry IV* has a clearly defined structure, which can be brought out in performance. But we can also think of the two linked plays as having an overall structure, with Part 2 starting out where Part 1 leaves off – quite literally, in the Induction and 1.1, where Northumberland, hoping to hear of his son's triumph, is brought news of Hotspur's death in battle – and eventually completing the overall design. The rejection scene at the end of Part 2 is the inevitable climax of the whole. Falstaff assumes that the newly crowned King ('my royal Hal . . . my sweet boy . . . I speak to thee, my heart') is unchanged and that their relationship will continue, and the King's language and actions definitively refute these assumptions.

> KING HENRY
> I know thee not, old man. Fall to thy prayers.
> How ill white hairs become a fool and jester!
> I have long dreamt of such a kind of man,
> So surfeit-swell'd, so old, and so profane;
> But being awak'd, I do despise my dream.
>   (*2 Henry IV*, 5.5.41, 43, 46–51)

This conclusion is prefigured again and again throughout Parts 1 and 2. In the first of the scenes between the Prince and Falstaff in *1 Henry IV*, the words 'when thou art king' keep recurring.

> FALSTAFF
> But I prithee, sweet wag, shall there be gallows standing in England when thou art king? . . . Do not thou, when thou art king, hang a thief.
>
> PRINCE
> No, thou shalt.   (*1 Henry IV*, 1.2.55–60)

As this exchange suggests, Falstaff is aware that his ascendancy over the Prince may be only temporary, and, by his wit, seeks to deflect any possible criticism – the accusation, for example, that he is a bad influence on the young Prince, which he cleverly inverts and parodies.

> FALSTAFF
> O, thou hast damnable iteration, and art indeed able to corrupt a saint. Thou hast done much harm upon me, Hal, God forgive thee for it. Before I knew thee, Hal, I knew nothing; and now am I, if a man should speak truly, little better than one of the wicked. I must give over this life, and I will give it over. (1.2.87–92)

The question of what will happen when the Prince becomes King remains unresolved, with considerable suspense, until the final scene of Part 2. After the death of Henry IV, the assembled courtiers, awaiting the first appearance of the new monarch, are apprehensive, fearing that under his reign 'all will be overturned' (2 *Henry IV,* 5.2.19). But the conclusion of Part 2 is prefigured by the end of Part 1, in the death of Hotspur and the reconciliation of father and son. In the course of Part 1, Prince Hal moves away from the world and influence of Falstaff towards Hotspur and the King, as shown, for example, in the brief exchange on the battlefield in 5.3, when the Prince angrily reproves Falstaff, 'What, is it a time to jest and dally now?' (5.3.54). The climax of Part 1 occurs in 5.4, when Prince Hal stands between the dead body of Hotspur, his rival and enemy, whom he has just killed, and the seemingly dead body of Falstaff, his closest friend. His tribute to Hotspur is noticeably warmer than his lines directed at his 'old acquaintance':

> What, old acquaintance, could not all this flesh
> Keep in a little life? Poor Jack, farewell!
> I could have better spared a better man.
> O, I should have a heavy miss of thee
> If I were much in love with vanity.
>
> (5.4.101–5)

It is entirely characteristic of Falstaff that he jumps up a moment later, not dead at all, confounding expectations. In this play at least, though not in its sequel, Falstaff is irrepressible, not subject to the ordinary laws of nature.

The confrontation between father and son in 3.2 is the turning point of 1 *Henry IV.* Here the same points are at issue as in the play's opening scene: the father's disappointment at and disapproval of his son, the father's praise of young Hotspur, who by his deeds has gained 'never-dying honour':

> Now, by my sceptre, and my soul to boot,
> He hath more worthy interest to the state
> Than thou the shadow of succession.
>
> (3.2.97–9, 106)

In his opening speech, the King sees his son's behaviour as designed as punishment for him by an unforgiving God. The lines may reflect feelings of guilt at what, in a parallel scene in *2 Henry IV,* he calls the 'by-paths and indirect crook'd ways' by which he gained his crown, and they certainly reflect mutual distrust and hostility, a father and son at loggerheads.:

> KING HENRY
> I know not whether God will have it so
> For some displeasing service I have done,
> That in his secret doom out of my blood
> He'll breed revengement and a scourge for me;
> But thou dost in thy passages of life
> Make me believe that thou art only marked
> For the hot vengeance and the rod of heaven
> To punish my mistreadings.
>
> (3.2.4–11; *2 Henry IV*, 4.5.184)

Though he does not explicitly mention Falstaff, he characterizes the Prince's hedonistic life and his companions as 'mean' and 'low', 'rude society' unworthy of 'the greatness of thy blood', using terms which are simultaneously social and moral. The Prince is allowing himself to mingle indiscriminately with people of lower social status, and he is giving in to 'inordinate desires . . . barren pleasures' (3.2.12–16). Desires are to be resisted, and self-control is the secret of success in the world of affairs. His predecessor, Richard II, setting a bad example, compromised his position and ultimately lost power because he 'grew a companion to the common streets':

> That, being daily swallowed by men's eyes,
> They surfeited with honey and began
> To loathe the taste of sweetness, whereof a little
> More than a little is by much too much.
>
> (3.2.68, 70–3)

In recalling his own ascent to power, Henry IV takes pride in his political skills, his ability to read and master a situation, controlling others by calculated dissimulation. Following Machiavelli's advice, he creates the appearances most favourable to his advancement, making the most of any opportunity offered.

> And then I stole all courtesy from heaven,
> And dressed myself in such humility
> That I did pluck allegiance from men's hearts,
> Loud chants and salutations from their mouths,
> Even in the presence of the crownèd King.
>
> (3.2.50–4)

When the father seeks to shame his son as 'degenerate', capable of fighting on the side of his enemies 'under Percy's pay', Hal mounts a defence, wounded by these bitter insults (3.2.126–8). The Prince's last speech in the scene not only predicts the encounter of the two warriors, it also suggests that Hal is adopting a new set of values, competing with Hotspur on Hotspur's own terms, using Hotspur's language of honour and glory, proving oneself by combat.

> I will redeem all this on Percy's head,
> And in the closing of some glorious day
> Be bold to tell you that I am your son,
> When I shall wear a garment all of blood
> And stain my favours in a bloody mask,
> Which, washed away, shall scour my shame with it.
>
> (3.2.132–7)

No longer making excuses, Hal now sees his former behaviour entirely in terms of shame and indignity. Using a series of fiscal or legal metaphors, the son promises his father to bring about an 'exchange' in the forthcoming battle in which the King's 'unthought-of Harry' and Harry Hotspur, 'child of honour and renown', will change places. By a kind of magic, the Prince will become Hotspur, transferring all of Hotspur's accumulated glories to his own 'account' (i.e., turning debt into credit in a single transaction):

> For the time will come
> That I shall make this northern youth exchange
> His glorious deeds for my indignities.
> Percy is but my factor, good my lord,
> To engross up glorious deeds on my behalf;
> And I shall call him to so strict account
> That he shall render every glory up.
>
> (3.2.139, 141, 144–50)

The two plots in *1 Henry IV* are unified by the two rebellions – the Percies, challenging the king they had helped to the throne, and the Prince, under the influence of Falstaff – with Prince Hal, the disobedient son, the sinner promising reform, as the central figure, linking the tavern and the council chamber. The transformation in Hal is signalled in a speech by Vernon, one of the rebels, praising the magnificent spectacle of the Prince, 'gallantly armed', 'glittering' like 'the sun at midsummer'(*1 Henry IV*, 4.1.101–6). In the 1975 RSC production, the physical transformation of the Prince was beautifully made manifest in the golden armour of Alan Howard, in the battle scene and in the coronation scene of Part 2: the Prince becomes a different person, newly created by the clothes he wears. The political problem which the scene between father and son raises is the problem of succession, the future stability of the state, a recurrent concern in the final years of Queen Elizabeth's reign. Part 2 shows that the reconciliation of father and son is temporary, and that though the rebellion of the Percies continues only fitfully, the Prince is still 'inclin'd to mirth' and surrounded by his 'continual followers' in apparent 'headstrong riot' (4.4.38, 53, 62). A second confrontation is thus dramatically necessary between father and son in *2 Henry IV*, recapitulating both the estrangement and the reconciliation of Part 1. What is at issue in the triangular relationship of the Prince, Falstaff, and the King is the relationship, often uneasy, between the public man and the private man.

Questions such as this are raised in Hal's soliloquy at the end of 1.2. Immediately, in the switch from prose to verse, from friendly badinage with Falstaff and Poins to an entirely different tone, we become aware of aspects of the Prince not apparent earlier. His opening words 'I know you all' come as something of a shock.

> I know you all, and will awhile uphold
> The unyoked humour of your idleness.
> Yet herein will I imitate the sun,
> Who doth permit the base contagious clouds
> To smother up his beauty from the world,
> That, when he please again to be himself,
> Being wanted he may be more wondered at
> By breaking through the foul and ugly mists
> Of vapours that did seem to strangle him.
>
> (1.2.183–91)

No such inward dimension is apparent in the madcap Prince of *The Famous Victories of Henry the Fifth*, one of Shakespeare's principal sources, who blithely tells his companions 'my lads, if the old king my father were dead, we would all be kings' and then, later in the play, reforms in a instant: 'Even this day, I am borne new againe'.[6] In the soliloquy, Hal represents his sun-like kingly nature as inviolate, even if momentarily obscured from view, and his companions as excrescences, 'foul', 'ugly', and disease-ridden.

In this speech, Prince Hal shows himself to be his father's son. The emphasis on manipulation of appearances, on what will 'show more goodly', anticipates the King's narration of his own ascent to power in 3.2. Like his father, the son shows himself capable of dressing himself in whatever clothing is suitable for his purpose, exercising control over the image he presents to the world, with skilful dissimulation enabling him to 'falsify men's hopes' (1.2.199, 202). A Machiavellian in embryo, Hal seems quite cold and calculating in this speech. The speech is not one that encourages the audience to like Hal, especially in contrast with the warmth of Falstaff and the affection Falstaff has shown towards Hal earlier in the scene. In terms of the overall plot, the main question the speech raises is a practical one: as with Antony saying 'I must from this enchanting queen break off' (*Antony and Cleopatra*, 1.2.128), we don't know whether he can translate intention into practice. The appeal of Falstaff and the kind of life he leads is very great, after all, both to the prince and to the audience watching the play.

'The immortal Falstaff'

If in terms of their overall structure, the Prince is the central figure in the two plays, there is no doubt that Falstaff is the star part. In the seventeenth century, *1 Henry IV* was sometimes known as *The First Part of Sir John Falstaff*. There are nearly three times as many allusions to Falstaff in the seventeenth century as there are to any other Shakespearean character.[7] For at least two centuries, *1 Henry IV* was one of Shakespeare's most popular plays: seven Quarto editions were published between 1598 and 1622, more than for any other Shakespearean play, and Falstaff remained a favourite part for actors throughout the next three centuries.

Throughout the eighteenth and nineteenth centuries, critical commentary overwhelmingly singles out the character of Falstaff, as 'the summit of Shakespeare's comic invention': according to one critic, 'there is not a spectator who does not in Falstaff's humour forget, even love, his vices'.[8] Hazlitt in 1817 is one of a number of critics who show a distinct preference for Falstaff as compared to the prince who rejects him, arguing that 'Falstaff is the better man of the two' (Variorum, p. 419). A. C. Bradley in 'The Rejection of Falstaff' (1909) sees 'the immortal Falstaff' as a source of 'sympathetic delight' to the audience in 'his humorous superiority to everything serious', where Prince Hal shows a 'readiness to use other people as a means to his own ends'. When Falstaff is harshly and decisively rejected, 'we feel . . . a good deal of pain and some resentment':[9] According to Bradley, Falstaff triumphs over the ostensible morality of the play.

Harold Goddard in 1951 and Harold Bloom in 1999 argue essentially the same position as Bradley. To Goddard, the Prince is 'coldly ambitious', unloving, and Falstaff is the embodiment of freedom, 'a symbol of the supremacy of imagination over fact'.[10] Bloom, like Goddard, sees Falstaff as 'the representative of imaginative freedom, of a liberty set against time, death, and the state, which is a condition that we crave for ourselves', adding a Freudian touch with 'freedom from censoriousness, from the superego, from guilt'. To Bloom, Falstaff eventually 'dies a martyr to ... his unrequited affection for his displaced son, Prince Hal'.[11] Like earlier romantic critics of Shakespeare, Bloom celebrates Falstaff as an archetype, 'the image of life itself', transcending his immediate dramatic context (p. 284).

Bloom and Goddard are consciously reacting against the influential school of criticism that treats Falstaff with severe moral disapproval, seeing the structure of the two *Henry IV* plays as essentially that of a medieval morality play. To J. Dover Wilson in *The Fortunes of Falstaff* (1943) and Tillyard in *Shakespeare's History Plays* (1944), Falstaff is the embodiment of riot and disorder, the theatrical heir of 'the Devil of the miracle play, the Vice of the morality, and the Riot of the interlude', a bad influence on the young Prince.

> Shakespeare's audience knew, from the beginning, that the reign of this marvellous Lord of Misrule must have an end, that Falstaff must be rejected by the Prodigal Prince, when the time for reformation came. And they no more thought of questioning or disapproving of that finale, than their ancestors would have thought of protesting against the Vice being carried off to Hell at the end of the interlude.[12]

In Tillyard's reading of *1 Henry IV*, the Prince is idealized even more than Falstaff is idealized by Goddard and Bloom: he is 'from the very first a commanding character, deliberate in act and in judgement, versed in every phase of human nature', and the embodiment of 'the abstract Renaissance conception of the perfect ruler' (p. 277).

To Dover Wilson as to C. L. Barber in *Shakespeare's Festive Comedy* (1959), Falstaff is an archetypal figure, a Lord of Misrule. Barber is more alert to Falstaff's appeal than either Dover Wilson or Tillyard, less partisan in his approach. The basic pattern he finds in the *Henry IV* plays is not the medieval morality play but myth and ritual, in the relation of holiday to everyday.

> If all the year were playing holidays,
> To sport would be as tedious as to work;
> But when they seldom come, they wished-for come,
> And nothing pleaseth but rare accidents.
>
> (1.2.192–5)

According to festive or Carnival theory, as explored by Barber, the reign of disorder and appetite under the aegis of a Lord of Misrule, 'one appointed to make sport' in a court or in a rural community, can only be a temporary interlude, a relaxing of the normal constraints in a period of 'liberal feasting' of the senses, to fortify the celebrants for the long cold months ahead.[13] Unlike Tillyard and Dover Wilson, Barber concedes that Falstaff 'does indeed care for Hal' and that in Falstaff's 'burlesque and mockery' he displays 'an intelligence of the highest order'. To Barber as to Goddard and Bloom, Falstaff as representative of the spirit of freedom associated with Carnival gives the impression of 'life overflowing its bounds by sheer vitality' (p. 204).

What everybody remembers about Falstaff, of course, is his enormous girth, his great belly, combined somewhat unexpectedly with quick and agile wit. As a figure of Carnival abundance and gluttony, he is 'that huge bombard of sack, that stuffed cloak-bag of guts', a 'fat paunch', compared again and again to a 'hogshead', 'fat meat', 'sweet beef', 'as fat as butter'.[14] The exchange of witty insults with Hal in 2.4 is overtly a Battle of Carnival and Lent: in answer to the Prince's jokes at the expense of his grotesque size, Falstaff, not to be outdone, unleashes an inexhaustible stream of comparisons, portraying the Prince as comically thin:

> PRINCE HENRY
> I'll be no longer guilty of this sin. This sanguine coward, this bed-presser, this horse-backbreaker, this huge hill of flesh –
>
> FALSTAFF
> 'Sblood, you starveling, you eel-skin, you dried neat's tongue, you bull's pizzle, you stockfish! O for breath to utter what is like thee, you sheath, you bow-case, you vile standing tuck.   (2.4.234–40)[15]

Barber sees the ultimate rejection of Falstaff in Part 2, in the terms of myth and ritual, as 'purification by sacrifice': 'The ritual analogy suggests that by turning on Falstaff as a scapegoat . . . the prince can free himself from the sins, the "bad luck", of Richard's reign and of his father's reign' (pp. 206–7). For all Falstaff's attractiveness, to Barber he must be rejected, both on political and on personal grounds, for the stability of the state and as an inevitable process in Hal's maturation, as he achieves adulthood and gains independence from one who has been 'the tutor and the feeder of my riots' (*2 Henry IV*, 5.5.62).

Greenblatt in 'Invisible Bullets' argues a position in many ways similar. Like Barber, he presents Falstaff as in some respects deeply subversive, representing 'a radical challenge to accepted ideas' and pointing up 'the potential instability of the structure of power' in the England of Henry IV.[16] Greenblatt resembles such romantic critics as Goddard and Bloom in strongly preferring Falstaff to

Hal, whom he characterizes as a 'counterfeit companion', intent 'to deceive . . . to betray', reliant on 'the subtle manipulation of appearances' (pp. 41–2). In keeping with the spirit of Carnival, Falstaff introduces into the play a colloquial popular voice, puncturing pretensions, destabilizing hierarchy. And yet for Greenblatt as for Barber, the potentially subversive forces Falstaff embodies are *contained*. Ultimately, like Tillyard, Greenblatt sees *1* and *2 Henry IV*, along with Shakespeare's other history plays, as fundamentally conservative, upholding the established order. 'The subversive voices are produced by and within the affirmations of order; they are powerfully registered, but they do not undermine that order' (p. 52).

The New Historicist position Greenblatt is arguing here rests on a paradox: those in power produce opposition in order to be able to control it. Elizabethan and Jacobean drama is the servant of the state. Where Tillyard and Dover Wilson see the ruling order as benevolent, and Shakespeare's history plays as expressing 'a universally held and still comprehensible view of history', with 'order as the norm to which disorder, though lamentably common, was yet the exception', Greenblatt, in contrast, sees the *Henry IV* plays as illustrating 'the Machiavellian hypothesis that princely power originates in force and fraud'.[17] In Greenblatt's bleak assessment, Prince Hal rises to power by betraying and abandoning his friend, and in *2 Henry IV*, there is nothing but 'predation and betrayal', public and private (p. 47).

A less dark and pessimistic view of the two plays can be found in several recent critics who employ Bakhtinian Carnival theory in commenting on the relationship of Falstaff and the Prince. Rather than being a safety valve provided by and under the control of the rulers of the state, the Carnivalesque is, according to Bakhtin, a 'second life', popular or plebeian, which is not only independent of but 'existentially prior to the state and its administrative apparatus'. As a Carnivalesque figure to whom 'material, physical life' is 'the ultimate reality', Falstaff's 'attitude toward authority is always parodic and satirical: he mocks authority, flouts power', is scornful or indifferent to 'the pressures of social duty and civic obligation'.[18] As clown, Falstaff in some ways exists outside history and its moral patterning, engaging in a running dialogue with the audience, anchored in the theatrical present. The clown, disruptive of social hierarchy, speaks 'the language of the audience' in witty, irreverent prose, contesting the hegemony of the elevated blank verse of kings and barons.[19]

When Warwick in *2 Henry IV* tries to reassure the King that his son's behaviour does not constitute 'unguided . . . headstrong riot' but instead represents a conscious attempt to turn 'past evils to advantages', he argues a version of containment theory, hegemonic control:

WAR.
The Prince but studies his companions
Like a strange tongue, wherein, to gain the language,
'Tis needful that the most immodest word
Be look'd upon and learnt; which once attain'd,
Your Highness knows, comes to no further use
But to be known and hated.

(2 Henry IV, 4.4.59, 62, 68–73, 78)

Carnival licence, in this formulation, is indulged in only for the sake of being rejected: the prince dips himself in filth in order to be seen to come out spotless. Yet Falstaff resists moral straitjackets as, in Part 1, he resists the ordinary restrictions of time and ageing. Hal's epithets for Falstaff, 'thou latter spring... All-hallown summer' (1.2.150–1), invoke the spirit of Carnival, with Falstaff as life force, irrepressible, in constant renewal. Falstaff, in this view, embodies 'the heterogeneity that will not be made one', comic energy, 'exuberance and excess', which refuse to be incorporated or contained.[20]

'This chair shall be my state'

In the 1975 RSC production of the two plays, directed by Terry Hands, the emphasis was very much on the maturation of the young prince. The programme, festooned with several pages of quotations from the psychologists Erving Goffman, Eric Berne, and others, presented *1 Henry IV* as the first part of 'a trilogy about the education of a king', with Prince Hal as the hero of a *bildungsroman*. Alan Howard's troubled, insecure Prince clearly preferred the company of Falstaff to that of his snarling, unloving father ('a father any son would be glad to escape', according to one reviewer) in the tortured, harsh performance of Emrys James.[21] Howard's prince, affectionate in his scenes with the benevolent, dignified Falstaff of Brewster Mason, was aware throughout of his destiny as future king – the trumpet tones of his voice suggested the future Henry V.

Orson Welles's film *Chimes at Midnight* (1966), a condensed and rearranged version of the two *Henry IV* plays, is dominated by the massive presence of Welles as Falstaff. Welles treats Falstaff as a figure with tragic dimensions, the hero of 'a very sad story', aware that he must inevitably be rejected: 'I directed everything, and played everything, with a view to preparing for the last scene.' In a film which includes interpolated wordless battle scenes, presenting the Battle of Shrewsbury as meaningless slaughter, Falstaff is a wholly sympathetic,

4. Alan Howard as Prince Hal, Brewster Mason as Falstaff, *Henry IV, Part 1*, Royal Shakespeare Company, 1975, directed by Terry Hands.

even admirable figure.[22] John Gielgud's King Henry IV, austere and remote, filmed in an echoing hall with rays of light streaming from impossibly high windows, is juxtaposed by cross-cutting with Welles's fatherly Falstaff and the crowded, bustling life of the tavern. This version, as Welles recognized, was not particularly comic: 'the more I studied the part, the less funny he seemed to be' (p. 261).

Michael Bogdanov's iconoclastic touring production for the English Shake-speare Company in 1986–7 featured an unsympathetic Prince Hal, cynical and manipulative, in the performance of Michael Pennington. This Hal, who 'did not love anybody', in some ways resembled the Machiavellian prince of Green-blatt's 'Invisible Bullets', published the previous year.[23] Bogdanov's production stripped all heroism from the single combat between Hal and Hotspur. Here Hotspur easily overcomes his opponent, chivalrously returns his sword after disarming him, and then is stabbed in the back by Hal.

The ESC production had as its central figure the charismatic Falstaff of John Woodvine, probably the best Falstaff (and certainly the funniest) I have ever seen. Woodvine's Falstaff was not a cuddly, lovable Santa Claus, but formidable in his intelligence, vitality, and force of character. Unlike Welles, Woodvine avoided sentimentality in his performance, and yet the rejection scene was extremely moving. Like Desmond Barrit, another excellent Falstaff, Woodvine brought out the character's darker side while showing the power of his appeal over the prince and over the audience – maintaining the 'balance between Falstaff's ability to inspire affection . . . and the frequent unscrupulousness of his self-interest'.[24]

Michael Attenborough's 2000–1 production for the RSC had three strong performances in Barrit's Falstaff, William Houston's Hal, and David Troughton's guilt-ridden King. Houston's Prince, more enigmatic but not more likable than Pennington's, according to one reviewer combined 'vulpine energy and cold calculation . . . exploitative ruthlessness'. Reviewers mentioned the 'vulnerability' of Barrit's 'surprisingly gentle' Falstaff, who 'never roared or gave way to a false joviality' and, without overtly playing for sympathy, suggested a 'need for Hal's love, which we know will never be returned'.[25]

Barrit's Falstaff was visibly old and sick, 'facing up to his own physical decay', in a Part 2 'infinitely more melancholy than Part One'.[26] One of the strengths of this performance was that, especially in Part 2, it brought out Falstaff's less attractive qualities – callousness, egotism, a willingness to exploit others. The production caught the moral ambiguities in the *Henry IV* plays effectively, making Falstaff's eventual rejection seem both painful and justified.

Michael Gambon's Falstaff in the 2005 NT production, less comic and less sympathetic than either Barrit or Woodvine, was unusually disreputable and down at heel – almost a version of Pinter's tramp in *The Caretaker*. This was a Falstaff 'utterly out for himself', with a 'predatory cruelty' towards most of those he encounters.[27] Like several of the reviewers, I found little evidence of an affectionate bond between Falstaff and the Prince, played by Matthew MacFadyen. The high point of the production was the painful confrontation in Part 2 between David Bradley's cadaverous, agonized father and a son he seemed to loathe, and here MacFadyen came to life. With its emphasis on disease and decrepitude in Part 2 and on duplicity and betrayal throughout, this was the darkest production of the two plays I can remember.

In nearly all productions and in many critical accounts, a key episode is the 'play extempore' in 2.4, in which Hal and Falstaff rehearse the Prince's anticipated meeting with his father. The scene is a play-within-a-play, a performance before an appreciative onstage tavern audience, in which each of the actors takes pride in his acting ability, assuming a voice other than his own. This aspect of the scene is brought out in the Hostess's interjections towards the beginning of the scene, and comes across particularly well in *Chimes at Midnight,* where the tavern suddenly fills up with a delighted audience, watching Falstaff's performance.

HOSTESS

O Jesu, this is excellent sport, i'faith!

FALSTAFF

Weep not, sweet queen, for trickling tears are vain.

HOSTESS

O the Father, how he holds his countenance!

FALSTAFF

For God's sake, lords, convey my tristful queen,
For tears do stop the floodgates of her eyes.

HOSTESS

O Jesu, he doth it as like one of these harlotry players as ever I see!

(2.4.377–83)

Falstaff's blank verse here, like his prose a moment later, is an impromptu parody – in this case, of the theatrical vocabulary of an earlier generation, and, later, of the elaborate verbal patterns of Euphuism ('not in words only, but in woes also'). In parodying the pompous sententiousness of elderly moralists, Falstaff implies that this kind of severe moral stance is itself a performance, a mask put on to suit an occasion, just as, with 'this chair shall be my state', he had suggested that monarchy is itself performance (2.4.365, 402).

In satirizing the objections that have been raised against his influence on the Prince, Falstaff is shoring up his own position. As the scene progresses, he turns his parodic wit to more direct defence, assuming the stance not simply of moral orthodoxy, but of Scripture-quoting religiosity.

> And yet there is a virtuous man whom I have often noted in thy
> company, but I know not his name . . . and now I remember me, his
> name is Falstaff. If that man be hardly given, he deceiveth me; for, Harry,
> I see virtue in his looks. (2.4.402–4, 410–12)

In the play-within-a-play, Falstaff disarms possible objections against his behaviour and influence by presenting his physical characteristics in favourable terms, as symptoms of health rather than disease and excess, suggesting a natural abundance that observes decorum.

FALSTAFF

A goodly portly man, i'faith, and a corpulent; of a cheerful look, a
pleasing eye, and a most noble carriage; and, as I think his age some fifty,
or, by'r lady, inclining to threescore . . . There is virtue in that Falstaff.
Him keep with, the rest banish. (2.4.407–11, 414–15)

Barrit comments on how, in the play-within-a-play and elsewhere, 'Falstaff keeps harping on the question of his own banishment'.[28] In the role of the King and, after they switch parts, in the role of the Prince, he is always defending 'plump Jack'. When the Prince takes on the persona of his father, the tone of the scene changes. In assuming his father's voice, Hal is in a sense becoming his father, unleashing his feelings of anger and resentment, in what is virtually an exorcism, casting Falstaff as the World, the Flesh, the Devil. His opening words maintain the pretence of the father castigating his son, and adopt the tone of orthodox Christian morality, a strict asceticism, anticipating the father's own emphasis on 'the hot vengeance and the rod of heaven' in 3.2. The deity invoked here is a God of wrath, unforgiving towards offenders.

> PRINCE HENRY
> Swearest thou, ungracious boy? Henceforth ne'er look on me. Thou art
> violently carried away from grace.   (2.4.429–31; 3.2.10)

In the rest of this speech, the fiction of the play-within-a-play (Falstaff as the prince, Hal as the king) is virtually abandoned, as Hal directly attacks Falstaff, piling up the charges in a cumulative indictment. In nearly all the productions I have seen, the lines are spoken with great bitterness and force, suggesting that Hal is expressing his own feelings through the mask. The case against Falstaff could hardly be made more strongly:

> There is a devil haunts thee in the likeness of an old man; a tun of man is
> thy companion. Why dost thou converse with that trunk of humours,
> that bolting-hutch of beastliness, that swollen parcel of dropsies, that
> huge bombard of sack, that stuffed cloak-bag of guts, that roasted
> Manningtree ox with the pudding in his belly, that reverend Vice, that
> gray iniquity, that father ruffian, that vanity in years?   (2.4.431–8)

The standards of judgement, as Dover Wilson and Tillyard have said, are explicitly those of the medieval morality play: Falstaff is identified with the allegorical figures Vanity and Iniquity, the Vice who, though we may laugh at him, is a servant of Satan. Rather than behaving in the dignified way appropriate to his age, he sets the worst possible example, giving himself over to 'villainy' and 'beastliness' (2.4.441–2). This unforgiving portrait of Falstaff as tempter, emissary of evil, reaches its culmination in 'That villainous abominable misleader of youth, Falstaff, that old white-bearded Satan' (2.4.445–6).

In Hal's indictment of Falstaff, his physical appetites and great size are consistently presented in pejorative terms as signs of disease and self-indulgence, rather than as natural abundance. If the Carnivalesque is invoked here, it is stripped of any favourable aspects: Falstaff is swollen, bestial, monstrous. In the reading of Dover Wilson and Tillyard, this is the final verdict on Falstaff, the perspective by which he must be judged and found wanting. But Shakespeare allows Falstaff to answer these charges, finding 'much to say on behalf of that Falstaff', reinterpreting the physical facts in an entirely different way.

> FALSTAFF
> My lord, the man I know.
>
> PRINCE HENRY
> I know thou dost.
>
> FALSTAFF
> But to say I know more harm in him than in myself, were to say more than I know. That he is old, the more the pity, his white hairs do witness it; but that he is, saving your reverence, a whoremaster, that I utterly deny. If sack-and-sugar be a fault, God help the wicked! If to be old and merry be a sin, then many an old host that I know is damned. If to be fat is to be hated, then Pharoah's lean kine are to be loved.
>
> (2.4.447–56, 465–6)

Falstaff is saying here that the moralistic perspective, searching for sin and finding damnation around every corner, is not only one-sided but inadequate. The appetites are not corrupt, but natural, healthy, God-given. Charity and generosity of spirit, he implies, constitute true virtue, where censoriousness and hate do not. The lines that follow are more naked in their appeal for sympathy, without breaking comic decorum, and, in their incantatory quality, are always effective in performance.

> No, my good lord, banish Peto, banish Bardolph, banish Poins; but for sweet Jack Falstaff, kind Jack Falstaff, true Jack Falstaff, valiant Jack Falstaff, and therefore more valiant being as he is old Jack Falstaff; banish not him thy Harry's company, banish not him thy Harry's company – banish plump Jack, and banish all the world.   (2.4.456–62)

When the Prince responds 'I do, I will' (2.4.463), foreshadowing the ultimate, unanswerable rejection at the end of Part 2, Shakespeare is, characteristically, contrasting two imperatives, both in their own ways incontestable. For the future King of England, to 'banish plump Jack' is a necessity, personal and political. But to do so is, as Shakespeare strongly suggests, to 'banish all the world', to cut off an entire area of experience, to opt for emotional poverty rather than wealth, to banish part of himself, forswearing love for the pursuit of power.

Honour

In *1 Henry IV,* Hotspur is consistently seen as 'the king of honour' (4.1.10). Scornful of 'bare and rotten policy' and of courtly flattery, Hotspur conceives of honour as an absolute, to be given unquestioning allegiance:

> HOTSPUR
> Send danger from the east unto the west,
> So honour cross it from the north to south,
> And let them grapple. O, the blood more stirs
> To rouse a lion than to start a hare!
>
> (1.3.108, 195–8)

Impatient for the chance of 'some great exploit' (1.3.199), most at home on the battlefield, astride a horse, Hotspur sees risk as a spur to action. When he learns, on the eve of the battle, that Northumberland and Glendower have failed to send troops, his reaction is that he and his army will gain greater glory by a victory against the odds.

In his impetuosity, idealism, and liveliness, Hotspur is an attractive figure. Again and again, he is contrasted with his worldly, Machiavellian father and uncle, self-seeking politicians who are quite willing to behave dishonourably when it suits them. Worcester, who lies to Hotspur about 'the liberal and kind offer of the King' before the battle (5.2.2), is critical of his nephew as hotheaded and impractical, but uses Hotspur in furtherance of his own designs. The domestic scene with Lady Percy, like his teasing of Glendower and his satiric remarks on the epicene courtier in 1.3, illustrates Hotspur's attractiveness and his limitations. He has a sense of humour, and is impatient with pomposity, boasting, and cant.

> GLENDOWER
> I can call spirits from the vasty deep.
>
> HOTSPUR
> Why, so can I, or so can any man;
> But do they come when you do call for them?
>
> (3.1.51–3)

And yet the scene with Lady Percy, for all the signs of affection between the couple, shows that his conscious choice of a masculine world of 'fields and blows and groans' (1.3.300) is at considerable cost. His nightmares, as, 'the fresh blood' drained from his cheeks, he talks in his sleep of 'palisadoes, frontiers, parapets', betray inner doubts, a 'spirit within . . . at war' with itself. Lady

Percy's complaint that she has 'this fortnight been / A banished woman from my Harry's bed' is reinforced by Hotspur's half-joking renunciation of love and female companionship for a world of male violence, sterile and friendless:

> HOTSPUR
> Away, away, you trifler! Love? I love thee not;
> I care not for thee, Kate. This is no world
> To play with mammets and to tilt with lips.
> We must have bloody noses and cracked crowns,
> And pass them current too.
>   (2.3.35–6, 41, 49, 52, 86–90)

The code of honour by which Hotspur lives is presented in the play as anachronistic, appropriate to a feudal society. The Percies were powerful regional magnates, enjoying virtual autonomy in the north of England and challenging the centralized rule of the monarchy.[29] In refusing to surrender prisoners to the King in 1.1, Hotspur is asserting his feudal rights, as well as his pride in his individual achievements and his scorn for Henry IV as a 'vile politician' (1.3.240). When Worcester openly cites self-interest as a motive for rebellion ('to save our heads by raising of a head'), Hotspur makes it a matter of principle, setting honour and the verdict of history against 'shame'.

> Shall it for shame be spoken in these days,
> Or fill up chronicles in time to come,
> That men of your nobility and power
> Did gage them both in an unjust behalf[?]
>   (1.3.170–3, 282)

For Hotspur, honour is a value worth pursuing for its own sake. A hero is one who is aware that he may die at any moment, and acts in accordance with the belief that 'a man of honor should alwaies preferre death, before infamous saftie'.[30]

> O gentlemen, the time of life is short!
> To spend that shortness basely were too long
> If life did ride upon a dial's point,
> Still ending at the arrival of an hour.
>   (5.2.81–4)

The most dishonourable act in the two plays is the treachery of Prince John of Lancaster in cynically breaking his word towards the rebels at Gaultree Forest. Prince John, negotiating a truce with the rebels on behalf of the King, gives them his word of honour that the King will redress the grievances of which they complain, once they have agreed to dismiss their troops, avoiding a battle. In chivalric tradition, an oath 'by the honour of my blood' (4.2.55) is considered sacred, and the Archbishop, leader of the rebel forces, immediately responds 'I take your princely word for these redresses' (4.2.66). But Prince John, behaving in accordance with Machiavelli's advice that princes should keep their word only when it is to their advantage to do so, orders the arrest of the rebel leaders as soon as 'the word of peace' (4.2.87) is proclaimed and the rebel army is dispersed. When the Archbishop and Mowbray upbraid him for violating accepted principles of honourable conduct, his response is curt: now that he has the upper hand, he can dispense with formulae of courtesy, gloating over them for having behaved 'foolishly' (4.2.119). Though conservative critics have argued that 'almost any trickery was justified in dealing with rebels', Greenblatt seems to me accurate in seeing Prince John's behaviour here as predatory 'betrayal', Machiavellian cunning in a world where power alone rules.[31]

Falstaff, who sees Prince John as a 'young sober-blooded boy' who neither drinks wine nor laughs (4.3.75–7), rejects the code of honour outright. Military glory, he says on several occasions, is fraudulent. During the later acts of *1 Henry IV*, he keeps up a running commentary, puncturing the heroic pretences of others – as for example, in his response to Hal's call to arms at the end of 3.3:

> PRINCE HENRY
> The land is burning. Percy stands on high,
> And either we or they must lower lie. *Exit.*
>
> FALSTAFF
> Rare words, brave world! Hostess, my breakfast, come!
> O, I could wish this tavern were my drum!
>
> (3.3.195–8)

Life is preferable to honour, if the pursuit of honour brings one death on the battlefield, as with the 'gallant knight' Sir Walter Blunt. Self-preservation, as Falstaff sees it, is a better guide than foolish idealism: an honourable reputation after one's death provides cold comfort.

> FALSTAFF
> Soft, who are you? Sir Walter Blunt. There's honour for you . . . I like not such grinning honour as Sir Walter hath. Give me life, which if I can save, so; if not, honour comes unlook'd for, and there's an end.
>
> (5.3.20, 31–2, 57–60)

Falstaff's most comprehensive verdict on honour comes in his soliloquy in Act 5. In some respects, Falstaff's case against honour in this mock catechism is unanswerable. On the materialist principles he argues, honour, as an empty abstraction, can have no existence: compared to solid physical realities, it is, in a literal sense, nothing, mere air.

Can honour set to a leg? No. Or an arm? No. Can it take away the grief of a wound? No. Honour hath no skill in surgery, then? No. What is honour? A word. What is in that word honour? What is that honour? Air. A trim reckoning. Who hath it? He that died o' Wednesday. Doth he feel it? No. Doth he hear it? No. 'Tis insensible, then ? Yea, to the dead. But will it not live with the living? No. Why? Detraction will not suffer it. Therefore I'll none of it. Honour is a mere scutcheon. And so ends my catechism.   (5.1.131–40)

These lines are likely to appeal to anti-war sentiments in a modern audience. In Welles's *Chimes at Midnight*, Falstaff's soliloquy is followed by a long battle sequence of hand-to-hand combat, with the mud-streaked soldiers seen as victims, in a desperate struggle for survival.[32] Barrit comments on the way the convention of direct address in this soliloquy encourages an appeal to kindred feelings about war and its wastefulness in a modern theatrical audience:

> I used to play the 'honour' soliloquy as a sort of dialogue with the audience . . . Falstaff is here placing himself, I think as an intermediary between the war and the audience, forcing them to wonder why men go to war at all, asking, and answering, the questions that are in their minds. (*Players* 6, pp. 136–7)

Falstaff's preference for life over honour has its less attractive aspects. Given the responsibility of raising troops for the King's army, he shamelessly turns this to his own advantage by taking bribes from prospective candidates unwilling to serve. Conservative critics like Dover Wilson are sternly disapproving of his behaviour, though in production, any moral judgement of his blatant cynicism is balanced against pleasure in the comic energy of Falstaff's language. His description of his troop of 'scarecrows' (4.2.36) violates any accepted principles of heroism or dignity in warfare, but it is also very funny, and so is the extended scene in Part 2, where Falstaff and Bardolph are seen in action at a muster of the troops, rejecting the 'likeliest men' and accepting only those who cannot pay a bribe. And yet the woman's tailor Feeble, in appearance an unlikely soldier, can state principles of conduct more in keeping with the chivalric ethos, standards by which Falstaff's cynicism appears shabby.

FEEBLE
By my troth, I care not, a man can die but once, we owe God a death. I'll ne'er bear a base mind . . . No man is too good to serve's prince, and let it go which way it will, he that dies this year is quit for the next.

(*2 Henry IV*, 3.2.229–33, 250)

When Falstaff characterizes his soldiers to Hal as 'food for powder', able to 'fill a pit as well as better' (*1 Henry IV*, 4.2.63), he seems callous, all the more so when we are told that nearly all of them have been killed in battle.

> FALSTAFF
> I have led my ragamuffins where they are peppered. There's not three of my hundred-and-fifty left alive, and they are for the town's end, to beg during life. (5.3.35–8)

Even if we don't interpret this speech, as Bevington does, as suggesting that he has deliberately led the troops into dangerous positions in order to pocket their pay,[33] Falstaff's action here shows an indifference to the welfare of the soldiers under his command, looking after his own interests at the expense of others.

Falstaff's behaviour at the end of Part 1, where he wounds the dead body of Hotspur and then claims to have killed him, are not so much a challenge to the chivalric ideal as an attempt, quite illegitimate, to acquire concrete honours and rewards for deeds he has not performed, 'a bogus military reputation'.[34] His motives here are wholly selfish: 'I'll follow, as they say, for reward' (5.4.157). Rather than serving as an ironic commentary on the duel, a moment earlier, between Prince Hal and Hotspur, Falstaff's action in stabbing the dead Hotspur seems a desecration, not comic but base and ugly, showing Falstaff's darker side.

> Therefore I'll make him sure; yea, and I'll swear I killed him. Why may not he rise as well as I? Nothing confutes me but eyes, and nobody sees me. (5.4.122–5)

Part 2: old age, disease, and death

A recurrent motif in Part 2 is disease. Recent productions emphasize the physical change in Falstaff between Parts 1 and 2, with the pox and gout visibly apparent in Falstaff's 'crumbling' body.[35] Again and again in Part 2, the commonwealth is represented as diseased. The Archbishop of York claims that he has raised an army to 'purge th'obstructions which begin to stop / Our very veins of life':

> We are all diseas'd,
> And with our surfeiting, and wanton hours,
> Have brought ourselves into a burning fever,
> And we must bleed for it. (4.1.54–7, 65–6)

The King, infected with the disease of sleeplessness and visibly declining in his two appearances in the play, uses very similar imagery of a kingdom afflicted with 'rank diseases' (3.1.39), though of course he does not see himself as the source of the infection.

An extraordinary number of characters in *2 Henry IV* are old men: Falstaff, the Lord Chief Justice, Northumberland, Shallow, Silence, the King. In Part 1, Falstaff manages somehow to ignore his age, shouting 'Young men must live' and 'They hate us youth' in the Gadshill episode (*1 Henry IV*, 2.2.83,88), but in Part 2, he and the audience are constantly reminded of it. The Lord Chief Justice, Falstaff's implacable antagonist, scornful of his 'manner of wrenching the true cause the false way', dismisses Falstaff's wit as no more than a 'throng of words . . . impudent sauciness'. Attempting to shame Falstaff into acting more in accordance with his actual age, the Lord Chief Justice paints a vivid portrait of physical decline and decrepitude:

> CH. JUST.
> Do you set down your name in the scroll of youth, that are written down old with all the characters of age? Have you not a moist eye, a dry hand, a yellow cheek, a white beard, a decreasing leg, an increasing belly? Is not your voice broken, your wind short, your chin double, your wit single, and every part of you blasted with antiquity? And will you yet call yourself young? Fie, fie, fie, Sir John! (1.2.177–85, 2.1.108–11)[36]

Old age in *2 Henry IV* is consistently associated with approaching death. In the tavern scene, with the whore Doll Tearsheet sitting on his knee, Falstaff admits for the first time in the two plays, 'I am old, I am old'. The 'flattering' kisses of Doll are presented, in this brief interlude of tenderness, as a stay against mortality.

> DOLL
> Thou whoreson little tidy Bartholomew boar-pig, when wilt thou leave fighting a-days, and foining a-nights, and begin to patch up thine old body for heaven?
>
> FALSTAFF
> Peace, good Doll, do not speak like a death's-head, do not bid me remember mine end. (2.4.227–32, 266–8)

In its reminder of the inevitability of death, this exchange is another version, very different in tone, of Falstaff's encounter with the Lord Chief Justice earlier in the play.

Ageing and death are constant presences in the Gloucestershire scenes, in the discourse of Justice Shallow and his neighbour Silence, though here old age is made comic rather than pathetic. As a comic turn, the double act of Shallow and Silence provides the actors with a splendid opportunity for comic business, and recent productions have included Silences falling asleep at every moment, stammering, or bursting into feeble song, and pompous, self-deluding Shallows. Justice Shallow is full of reminiscences about 'the wildness of his youth', with 'every third word a lie'. In the dialogue of Shallow and Silence before Falstaff comes onstage, scraps of memory, *sententiae* about mortality, and practical observations about farming business jostle together.

> SHAL.
> Jesu, Jesu, the mad days that I have spent! And to see how many of my old acquaintance are dead!
>
> SIL.
> We shall all follow, cousin.
>
> SHAL.
> Certain, 'tis certain, very sure, very sure. Death, as the Psalmist saith, is certain to all, all shall die. How a good yoke of bullocks at Stamford fair?   (3.2.32–8, 299–301)

The coupling of the price of bullocks and of 'a score of ewes' (3.2.49–51) with the tolling of the bells of mortality suggests an enduring life in nature, with death part of the natural cycle. But in his reminiscences – old Double, who once 'drew a good bow' (3.2.43) at archery, the ancient beauty Jane Nightwork, his own imagined feats in his youth – Justice Shallow widens the gap between youth and age, one remembered inaccurately and the other inescapable.

Welles, taking his title *Chimes at Midnight* from the Gloucestershire scenes, infuses these scenes with melancholy, setting Shallow's musings in a wintry landscape. One effect of the exchanges about a half-invented past is to blur the distinctions between the gull Shallow and the manipulative Falstaff, two old men subject to the ravages of time. For all the comedy in the Gloucestershire scenes, the sense of time's omnipresence, that 'nothing stands but for his scythe to mow', helps prepare the audience for Falstaff's rejection and ultimate death.[37]

In the play's climactic scene, Falstaff's hopes that with the death of the old king he will be able to reward his friends and punish his enemies, boasting that 'the laws of England are at my command', are shattered. Instead, the newly crowned king humiliates him in public, in uncompromising terms that are overtly religious, proclaiming the death of their friendship.

> Make less thy body hence, and more thy grace;
> Leave gormandizing; know the grave doth gape
> For thee thrice wider than for other men.
>
>   (5.3.126–7, 132–4; 5.5.52–4)

In Part 2, we rarely see Falstaff and Hal together: before the rejection scene, there is only one scene with the two of them onstage at once. Hal's most significant relationship in Part 2 is with his father, not with Falstaff. This is apparent in the powerful scene of confrontation, with the King near death. Following Holinshed and *Famous Victories*, Shakespeare depicts the King grievously ill, falling asleep with the crown on his pillow, and his son, thinking his father dead, picks up the crown and walks off with it.[38] Shakespeare's version immediately focuses on the problem of succession, the 'lineal honour' (4.6.45) passing from father to son, and on the father's distrust of his son and fears about what may happen after his death. When the King wakes, his reaction is bitter anger at a son who, he thinks, longs for his death, showing him neither love nor respect.

After the Prince returns, his father accuses him of stealing the crown, seeking prematurely to invest himself with his father's honours while the father still lives. Extrapolating from the Prince's past behaviour and thinking the worst of him in all respects, the King predicts the reign of chaos after his death, with appetite run wild. As David Troughton says, the King's 'language is extraordinarily fierce and passionate', an outburst of anger and disappointment, by a father fearing that all he has worked for will be brutally discarded after he dies.[39] In the 2000 and 2005 productions, this nightmare vision of a commonwealth turned into a 'wilderness . . . peopled with wolves' was projected with great dramatic power.

> Have you a ruffian that will swear, drink, dance,
> Revel the night, rob, murder, and commit
> The oldest sins the newest kind of ways?
> . . .
> England shall give him office, honour, might:
> For the fifth Harry from curb'd licence plucks
> The muzzle of restraint, and the wild dog
> Shall flesh his tooth on every innocent.
> O my poor kingdom, sick with civil blows!
>
> (4.5.124–33, 136–7)

As the scene continues, the Prince defends himself, professing his 'most inward true and duteous spirit' towards his father, as he kneels before him in token of his obedience (4.5.147). Accepting this apology, the dying King, now reconciled with his son, gives the Prince heartfelt 'counsel' from his deathbed, reflecting on his accession to power and the troubles of his reign. Admitting the uncertainty of his title to the crown and the endless challenges to his authority resulting from that uncertainty, the King expresses the hope that his son will enjoy a peaceful, unchallenged reign, with the crown descending to him 'with better quiet, better opinion' (4.5.182, 187–8). Where the father seized the throne, the son would inherit the position of king by primogeniture and succession. Any stain will be washed away at the King's death.

> And now my death
> Changes the mood, for what in me was purchas'd
> Falls upon thee in a more fairer sort;
> So thou the garland wear'st successively.

> (4.5.198–201)[40]

A practical politician to the end, the King goes on to give his son advice, on sound Machiavellian principles, on how to hold onto his power. Don't trust professed friends or former enemies, but find ways of securing their allegiance to you; don't allow anyone to 'look / Too near unto' your 'state'. Provide a useful distraction in foreign wars, to lessen the danger of new civil wars.

> Therefore, my Harry,
> Be it thy course to busy giddy minds
> With foreign quarrels, that action hence borne out
> May waste the memory of the former days.

> (4.5.211–15)

As we will see, this is precisely what happens in *Henry V,* as the young King, following his father's advice, leads his army to victories in France.

Chapter 8

Band of brothers: *Henry V*

The reformed Prince

The most striking difference between *Henry V* and the two *Henry IV* plays is the absence of Falstaff. In the epilogue to *2 Henry IV*, Shakespeare promises to 'continue the story, with Sir John in it' (Epilogue, 28), and also mentions that Falstaff will 'die of a sweat' (l. 30) in the new play. When he sat down to write *Henry V*, Shakespeare decided to leave Falstaff out, though Falstaff's tavern companions play prominent roles in the play. There are comic scenes in *Henry V* alternating with the serious plot, and, as in *1* and *2 Henry IV*, these scenes are integrated into a clearly unified whole. In this play and generally in Shakespeare, the comic scenes are in prose, and in the Shakespearean acting company, the roles of Pistol, Bardolph, Nym, and also Fluellen were probably played by the company's clowns, specialists in comic roles.

In *Henry V* as well as in *1* and *2 Henry IV*, the comic scenes often provide a realistic or anti-idealistic counterpoint to the high sentiments and inflated rhetoric of the princes and noblemen in the main plot. The relationship between comic subplot and heroic main plot is often one of parody, conveying 'a half-secret doubt about the value of kings and their quarrels'.[1] In *Henry V*, the King's impassioned address to the soldiers at the siege of Harfleur ('Once more unto the breach, dear friends') is followed immediately by a scene with the clowns. The two consecutive scenes (3.1 and 3.2 in the received text) are a characteristic Shakespearean juxtaposition of opposites. King Harry's rousing speech, urging the 'noble English' to make common cause, show 'that you are worth your breeding' and can act bravely as part of a coherent unit (3.1.1, 17, 28), is met with a double response. In the Laurence Olivier and Kenneth Branagh films, as in every stage production I have seen, the lines are addressed to an onstage audience of soldiers, who respond by charging, resuming the battle. Yet Pistol and his fellow clowns provide concrete evidence that several among those addressed resist the call, preferring to save their own skins.

NYM
Pray thee, Corporal, stay; the knocks are too hot, and for mine own part
I have not a case of lives . . .

PISTOL
Knocks go and come, God's vassals drop and die . . .

BOY
Would I were in an alehouse in London! I would give all my fame for a
pot of ale and safety.   (3.2.3–4, 8, 12–13)

In a sense, Nym and the others refute the words of King Harry: they are the
ordinary soldiers, who aren't in the least motivated by heroism, but would
rather be somewhere else. The episode is a classic example of 'negative capability' – both positions (the appeal to courage and patriotism and the appeal
to self-preservation) are true, according to the speakers' separate perspectives.

And yet I think there is a significant difference between the tone of the comic
scenes here and in the *Henry IV* plays, and in the way the comic characters are
presented. Fluellen at the end of this scene berates them for cowardice, beating
them into the breach, and later in the play beats Pistol again, humiliating
him and exposing him as 'a counterfeit cowardly knave' (5.1.70). Again and
again, Pistol and his fellow 'sworn brothers in filching' (3.2.44–5) are judged
and found wanting. In a comic soliloquy, the Boy gives a wholly negative
assessment of the men he serves: they are cowards, liars, and thieves, who
will 'steal anything', behaving constantly in ways he defines as contrary to any
principle of 'manhood':

BOY
As young as I am, I have observed these three swashers . . . for indeed
three such antics do not amount to a man. For Bardolph, he is
white-livered and red-faced, by the means whereof 'a faces it out but
fights not. For Pistol, he hath a killing tongue and a quiet sword . . . I
must leave them and seek some better service; their villainy goes against
my weak stomach, and therefore I must cast it up.   (3.2.28–34, 49. 51–3)

These are far less attractive figures than Falstaff. Throughout *Henry V*
Shakespeare emphasizes the distance between the King and his former tavern
companions. On the one occasion when the King and Pistol share the stage
(4.1.35–64), Pistol claims former acquaintance and the King denies it. There is
no possibility that the reformed King Henry V, as he is presented in this play,
would relapse or that he would want to spend his time in the company of Pistol
and Pistol's disreputable companions.

In the early scenes of *Henry V*, much is made of the King's reformation, and especially its suddenness, the sharp, unexpected difference between the wildness and apparent indiscipline of his conduct as Prince and the gravity and dignity of his behaviour as King. In 1.1 the Archbishop of Canterbury comments approvingly of how his reformation appeared to come 'in a flood ... all at once', presenting it as a religious conversion, a rebirth:

> The breath no sooner left his father's body
> But that his wildness, mortified in him,
> Seemed to die too; yet, at that very moment,
> Consideration like an angel came
> And whipped th'offending Adam out of him,
> Leaving his body as a paradise.
>
> (1.1.25–30, 33, 36)

The Dauphin's insulting gift of tennis balls (an incident taken from the chronicles) is based on the erroneous assumption that the King is unchanged since his 'wilder days' (1.2.268). In a later exchange between the Dauphin and the Constable of France, the Dauphin contemptuously dismisses any threat posed by England because 'she is so idly kinged, / Her sceptre so fantastically borne / By a vain, giddy, shallow, humorous youth' (2.4.26–8). The Constable answers 'You are too much mistaken in this king', whose 'vanities forespent' hid his true nature, now revealed (2.4.30, 36).

The Prince's seemingly miraculous transformation is of course central to the action of the two parts of *Henry IV*. In Acts 4 and 5 of *2 Henry IV*, King Henry IV, the Lord Chief Justice, Prince John of Lancaster, the Earl of Warwick, Falstaff, Pistol, and Bardolph are all convinced that the young Prince, heir to the throne, is unreformed, and look forward to his reign after his father's death, either with apprehension or, like Falstaff and Pistol, with eager anticipation. None of these characters has had the advantage of hearing the Prince's soliloquy in Act 1 of *1 Henry IV*, or of reading critical essays on the *Henry IV* plays. They assume, like the dying King Henry IV, that the coronation of Henry V will give licence to misrule:

> KING
> Pluck down my officers; break my decrees;
> For now a time has come to mock at form –
> Harry the fifth is crown'd! Up, vanity!
> Down, royal state! All you sage counsellors, hence!
> And to the English court assemble now
> From every region, apes of idleness!
>
> (*2 Henry IV*, 4.5.117–22)

The new king's address to the Lord Chief Justice and the assembled courtiers in *2 Henry IV* uses the language of 'seeming' and 'opinion' – falsifying men's hopes, showing more goodly – that he had previously used in the soliloquy with which he announced his intentions to the audience. After the death of the old king, the new king reassures his anxious courtiers that they have been mistaken in their assessment of his character, and that his previous behaviour would in no way be indicative of what he would be like as king. His wildness would be buried with his father.

> My father is gone wild into his grave,
> For in his tomb lie my affections;
> And with his spirits sadly I survive
> To mock the expectation of the world,
> To frustrate prophecies, and to raze out
> Public opinion, which hath writ me down
> After my seeming.
>
> (*2 Henry IV*, 5.2.123–9)

One problem with *Henry V* is that the unreformed Prince (or the Prince who has not yet fulfilled prophecies and for whom 'the expectation of the world' remains problematical) is a more interesting and complex character than the reformed King. Gary Taylor points out in his introduction to the Oxford edition that the play has never been as popular as *Richard III* or the two *Henry IV* plays, and many critics have been hostile in their assessment of the play.[2] Michael Quinn's *Casebook*, published in 1969, is full of extracts from critics who dislike *Henry V* or its principal character: Hazlitt, disdainfully characterizing the warrior king as 'a very amiable monster' with 'no idea of any rule of right or wrong, but brute force, glossed over with a little religious hypocrisy'; John Masefield dismissing the play as one which 'bears every mark of having been hastily written . . . to fill a gap in the series of historical plays'; Mark Van Doren objecting to 'a direct and puerile appeal to the patriotism of the audience' in language which 'struts on tiptoe'.[3] Tillyard's account of the play is particularly interesting in this respect, since the play has a prominent place in Tillyard's overall scheme, as illustrative of unity rather than the divisiveness of civil war and as constituting the 'epic of England', an appeal to patriotic sentiments. And yet he finds the play deeply unsatisfactory, seeing the presentation of 'Henry in his traditional part of perfect king' as dutifully fulfilling requirements and little else. To Tillyard, the 'simple forthright energetic man' depicted in *Henry V* is 'utterly inconsistent with his old self' as Prince Hal.

Shakespeare came to terms with this hopeless situation by jettisoning the character he had created and substituting one which, though lacking all consistency, satisfied the requirements both of the chroniclers and of popular tradition. No wonder if the play constructed round him shows a great falling off in quality.[4]

The Henry V of Shakespeare's play is pre-eminently a warrior, at home on the battlefield. In the wooing scene in Act 5, he describes himself in terms which would be suitable for Hotspur: 'I speak to thee plain soldier . . . a fellow of plain and uncoined constancy', incapable of dissembling and untutored in courtly ways:

> If I could win a lady at leapfrog, or by vaulting into my saddle with my armour on my back, under the correction of bragging be it spoken, I should quickly leap into a wife.   (5.2.137–40, 149–50, 153–4)

Tillyard overstates his case in claiming that Shakespeare has jettisoned his earlier character. But there is no question that Henry V, on the surface at least, seems to be a more straightforward, simpler figure than in his previous incarnation as Prince Hal. If in *1* and *2 Henry IV*, we are conscious throughout of a tension between the public and private man, here King Henry, as presented, is entirely a public man, who can have no private life. Only in one scene, where, in the night before battle, he disguises himself, casting off the garments of monarchical power, are we aware of an inward dimension, a sense of strain behind the façade. At all other times, including the scene in Act 5 in which he is shown negotiating for an arranged marriage with the French princess after defeating the French in battle, he is always aware of his position and responsibilities as King. To an unusual extent, the play's leading character is opaque, giving us very little access to his inner feelings. Productions in recent years have often tried to bring out 'fissures in his public self', tensions in the reformed prince, finding or creating a subtext.[5]

War and politics

If *Henry V* has had a rough ride with critics, it is partly because patriotic and nationalistic sentiments, of the kind expressed throughout the play, can seem embarrassing to those encountering the play in an age suspicious of such sentiments. When the Chorus calls on the theatrical audience to join in the celebrations, to embark with the 'brave fleet' by the power of imaginative empathy, rejoicing in the glorious spectacle, it is possible to resist the siren call as well as to succumb to it:

> Now all the youth of England are on fire,
> And silken dalliance in the wardrobe lies.
> Now thrive the armourers, and honour's thought
> Reigns solely in the breast of every man.
>   (2. Cho.1–4, 3 Cho.5)

Anti-war sentiments are likely to meet with a more sympathetic response from a twentieth- or twenty-first-century audience than the glorification of war in a play whose climax is the triumphant battle of Agincourt.

A number of critics, repelled by what they consider 'windy chauvinism' or 'mingled brutality and hypocrisy' in some of the speeches, have argued that the play is ironic in intent, 'a satire on monarchical government, on imperialism, on the baser kinds of "patriotism", and on war'. To Gerald Gould, writing in 1919, in the aftermath of the senseless slaughter of trench warfare, and to Harold Goddard in 1951, it was inconceivable that Shakespeare could have intended anything other than a 'pitiless exposure of the hollowness and rottenness of power'.[6] To Gould and to Goddard, the play's secret meaning is an 'indictment of Henry' as Machiavel and hypocrite: 'Through the Choruses, the playwright gives us the popular idea of his hero. In the play, the poet tells the truth about him.'[7] The commentary on the play in Greenblatt's *Shakespearean Negotiations* similarly emphasizes internal contradictions and ideological faultlines in the text, but does not enlist Shakespeare as an ally. In this New Historicist reading of *Henry V*, the critic is bitingly ironic at the expense of the conventional Elizabethan ideological attitudes he finds in the play, seeing Shakespeare as not himself being ironic, but as registering a fundamental ambivalence inherent in the exercise of power, which the critic is able to deconstruct.

Among the paradoxes Greenblatt cites is Fluellen's praise of the 'gallant king' for having killed his 'best friend', as Alexander the Great had done (4.7.10, 38, 44–7). As Greenblatt says, this reminder of Falstaff's rejection is 'potentially devastating': 'Hal's symbolic killing of Falstaff – which might have been recorded as a bitter charge against him – is advanced by Fluellen as the climactic manifestation of his virtues.' Here and elsewhere in the play, Greenblatt argues, 'the very doubts that Shakespeare raises serve not to rob the king of his charisma but to heighten it, precisely as they heighten the theatrical interest of the play'.[8] Dollimore and Sinfield, in a variant on Greenblatt's 'containment' thesis, argue that 'the drive for ideological coherence' in the play leads to an effacing or erasure of potentially discordant elements: 'systematically, antagonism is reworked as subordination or supportive alignment.' The existence of 'idle and implicitly disaffected people at home' in England – the 'ten thousand of those men in England / That do no work today', or the conspirators who, rather than being 'kind and natural' subjects, accept French bribes – is 'converted into a pretext for the King to insist upon his army as a "band of brothers"'.[9] Though the play 'betrays inherent instability' in the ideology it subserves, its fundamental aim, as Dollimore and Sinfield see it, is 'the legitimation of warfare' and the authoritarian state (p. 212).

Holderness in *Shakespeare Recycled* (1992) finds considerable ideological ambivalence within Shakespeare's text. The view that the play embodies an 'ideology of patriotism, national unity, and just war', Holderness argues, is a 'reconstruction' or appropriation by later critics who 'found in Shakespeare's play a ruling ideology of order because that is precisely what they wanted to find'.[10] Holderness's account of *Henry V* emphasizes 'the aesthetic devices which work within Shakespeare's drama to undermine the play's traditionalist and official ideology' (pp. 186–7). Annabel Patterson in *Shakespeare and the Popular Voice* (1989) points out that the Quarto version of *Henry V* (Q1, 1600) is far more conducive to a reading of the play as expressive of a 'simpler patriotism' supportive of authority than the Folio text. In the Quarto text, 'the justice of the war' against France is never questioned, since the scene of the King's encounter with the soldiers Bates and Williams is radically shortened, and the Harfleur episode, with its threats of rape and murder, 'waste and desolation' (3.3.10–43), is cut to eighteen hurried lines. The scene with the quarrelling Welsh, Irish, and Scottish captains is excised entirely, as is the eloquent speech of the Duke of Burgundy in Act 5 describing the destructive effects of war on the French countryside (5.2.34–67), and the scene at the very beginning of the play in which the cynical, worldly Archbishop reveals the selfish motives underlying the war.[11] The Quarto text is thus one from which nearly all of the problematical elements, the complex 'representational instability that Shakespeare has introduced into *Henry V*', have been removed (p. 86).

Norman Rabkin's *Shakespeare and the Problem of Meaning* has commented on the tendency of critics of *Henry V* to divide into 'rival camps', two opposed interpretations which seem incompatible. Rabkin argues that 'no real compromise is possible between the extreme readings the play provides': some critics see the play as 'infectiously patriotic' and its hero 'an exemplary monarch', where for others its protagonist is a ruthless Machiavel, whose characteristic action is the gratuitous command 'Then every soldier kill his prisoners' (4.6.37).[12] In a variant on Rabkin's view of the play, Shapiro argues that *Henry V* 'consistently refuses to adopt a single voice or point of view about military adventurism', but consists largely of 'scenes in which opposing voices collide over the conduct of the war'. According to Shapiro, 'it wasn't a pro-war play or an anti-war play but a going-to-war play'.[13]

5. Laurence Olivier as Henry V, *Henry V*, directed by Laurence Olivier, 1945.

Productions on stage and screen tend to polarize. Either, like Olivier's 1944 film, they are celebrations of the English spirit triumphing over obstacles, or they seek to undermine conventional ideas of heroism and patriotism, bringing out the ugliness of war. Several productions in recent years, including Branagh's 1989 film, Edward Hall's RSC production of 2000, and Nicholas Hytner's NT production of 2003, have sought to bring out the darker elements in Shakespeare's play, seeing the potential for demystification of war and political power. Olivier's film, an enormous popular success filmed during the war against Hitler, explicitly appeals to the desire of the audience to find and identify with a hero. Olivier commented on his adaptation, presenting himself as Shakespeare reincarnated: 'I had a mission . . . my country was at war; I felt Shakespeare within me. I felt the cinema within him. I knew what I wanted to do, what he would have done.' Branagh's film, nearly half a century later, could hardly be more different. The emphasis throughout is on the horrors of war, rather than military glory or 'pageantry and chivalric splendour'.[14] The battle scenes in Branagh's film, additions to the Shakespearean text, are violent, prolonged, and bloody, with bodies pierced with arrows or hacked to pieces, falling ignominiously in the mud. No one is killed on screen in Olivier's choreographed Agincourt (with echoes of the cavalry in countless Western films), aside from the Boy, Pistol and Bardolph's companion, and the Constable of France, killed by King Harry in knightly single combat. In Branagh's film the battlefield is littered with dead bodies, given a loving requiem (including Pistol, weeping over the body of Nym in a *pietà*).

The 2000 and 2003 productions, like Branagh's film, tried to bring out problematical aspects of Shakespeare's play, its latent anti-war sentiments. Where Olivier's Chorus set the film's basic tone – a celebration of English courage and a celebration of the possibilities of the cinema medium – and Branagh's Chorus, stalking through the film in a heavy overcoat, provided Brechtian alienation effects, Edward Hall in 2000 divided up the speeches of the Chorus among the soldiers, in battle fatigues, who filled the stage, dominating the production. As Russell Jackson says, the effect was 'as though the likes of Bates and Williams were presenting the whole play'. A markedly unheroic King Henry, played by William Houston (earlier in the season a cold, calculating Prince Hal), and an almost total absence of 'royal pageantry' fitted the unglamorous tone of the production.[15] In Hytner's 2003 production, the Chorus was a female spin-doctor, in cardigan and spectacles, providing one of many ways of ironizing the action.

Hytner's production, even more than Branagh's film, set out 'to undercut the rhetorical glamour surrounding war', and was satiric in its overall approach, with many explicit parallels to contemporary events. Rehearsals began in the period leading up to the Iraq war, and the play opened shortly after Bush announced victory. 'As the war finished and as scepticism returned and we were looking at it with cooler heads', Hytner said in an interview, 'that which is propagandistic about the play and that within the play which is hagiographic about the king felt very familiar'.[16] The frequent use of video clips, reruns of inspirational or bellicose speeches for public consumption, and the presence on stage of 'embedded' TV cameramen recording the progress of the war, constituted 'an ingenious re-imagining of the play into a world of television news-management'.[17]

Hytner's interview emphasizes Shakespeare's 'doubleness', the way the action on stage will often 'completely undercut what the Chorus tells you you're about to see': 'Moment by moment, you believe everything that's being told to you; it's the juxtaposition that you're left to work out for yourself.'[18] What makes *Henry V* a perennially interesting, problematical play is that it is open to such widely varying interpretations, containing within it both an anti-war and a pro-war play. Olivier and Branagh, in order to present coherent, opposed readings, each cut nearly half of Shakespeare's text, and most critical interpretations of the play are no less selective, carving out their own versions and leaving out bits that are less digestible.

The death of Bardolph: rewriting *Henry V*

One of the most striking moments in Branagh's film of *Henry V*, the death of Bardolph, does not occur in Shakespeare's text.[19] In 3.6 of Shakespeare's play, King Henry, entering with his soldiers, asks Fluellen if there have been any casualties in the recent fighting, and Fluellen answers 'the Duke hath lost never a man, but one that is like to be executed for robbing a church, one Bardolph, if your majesty know the man' (ll. 99–101). Though the King of course does 'know the man', his next speech makes no mention of any previous association with Bardolph, and has no element of personal warmth.

> KING HENRY
> We would have all such offenders so cut off: and we give express charge
> that in our marches through the country there be nothing compelled
> from the villages, nothing taken but paid for, none of the French
> upbraided in disdainful language; for when lenity and cruelty play for a
> kingdom, the gentler gamester is the soonest winner.   (3.6.106–12)

In Shakespeare's text, the King is not directly responsible for the death of Bardolph. But the King's speech endorses the sentence, citing the need for discipline. The passage is one illustration among many of the King's miraculous reformation, further proof that, as he says in his rejection of Falstaff:

> For God doth know, so shall the world perceive,
> That I have turned away my former self;
> So will I those that kept me company.
> (*2 Henry IV*, 5.5.57–9)

Olivier's film omits the episode entirely, just as it omits the sequence in 2.2 where the King outwits and sentences to death three English noblemen (one of them a former close friend) who were plotting treason against him, in the pay of the French. Branagh makes the 'dangerous treason' episode seem quite sinister, suggesting the power of the authoritarian state, with its machinery of surveillance, rather than any threat of rebellion, as Branagh's King plays with the conspirators like a cat with a mouse. Branagh uses tight close-ups and expressionist lighting to convey an atmosphere of Machiavellian intrigue and *Realpolitik* in scenes early in the film involving the clerics Canterbury and Ely. Olivier treats these scenes as broad comedy, with papers fluttering to the ground and characters forgetting their lines. There is a good deal more comedy in Olivier's film than in Branagh's, which is much darker, even in the scenes with the clowns, Pistol, Bardolph, and Nym. In the Olivier film, they are introduced on the stage of the Globe, with reaction shots from the appreciative Elizabethan audience, firmly establishing their status as clowns in the Shakespearean acting company, and once the action opens out to be avowedly cinematic, the actors playing Pistol and Bardolph continue to give the same kind of performance, self-consciously theatrical and playing for laughs. The same pattern holds throughout: where Olivier maintains a distinction in genre between main plot and subplot, while taking every opportunity to lighten the tone with touches of humour, Branagh maintains more or less the same mood throughout, and it is neither heroic nor comic.

The interpolated scene of the death of Bardolph in Branagh's film begins, as in Shakespeare's 3.6, with an encounter between Pistol and Fluellen, in which Pistol pleads with the Welsh captain to use his influence to save the condemned Bardolph. There is not an ounce of humour in Branagh's version of the scene: Pistol is no swaggerer, but a battered, unshaven soldier, close to tears, while Fluellen is cold-eyed, ramrod-straight, fanatical. The exchange between Gower and Fluellen, in which Pistol is characterized as 'an arrant counterfeit rascal . . . a bawd, a cutpurse' (3.6.60–1) is cut, and then King Harry rides up through the mist, followed by a procession of men accompanying a bloodstained Bardolph, dejected, on a cart with a rope around his neck. With the words 'one Bardolph, if you know the man', there are close-ups of the faces of the King and Bardolph, followed by a flashback of the two drinking and laughing together in the Boar's Head tavern, with an exchange adapted from lines of Falstaff and Prince Hal in *1 Henry IV*:

> BARDOLPH
> Do not thou when thou art King hang a thief.
>
> KING
> No, thou shalt.

The King's eyes are filled with tears as, with a gesture, he orders his friend's execution. Branagh's screenplay speaks of 'the young king's intense isolation at this moment'.[20] The King speaks his next lines through clenched teeth, and Bardolph's body is left swinging from a tree at the end of the scene, as the English army trudges off in the rain, on their way to Agincourt.

As with King Harry's speech at the siege of Harfleur, also absent from the Olivier film, the scene of Bardolph's death is an attempt by the director to find elements of conflict and complexity in the characterization of the warrior King. Branagh's interpretative strategy necessitated underplaying the comic elements of the play in pursuit of a unity of tone, where Olivier saw the comic scenes as integral to the play and to his overall purpose. In the Olivier film, the French King is a buffoon, in no way formidable, and the French lords, aside from the Constable and the herald Montjoy, are foppish and effete. An audience in 1944 was encouraged to make a straightforward substitution, France = Hitler Germany (I remember a wartime Walt Disney cartoon, *Der Führer's Face*, in which Donald Duck stood in for Hitler). Branagh, on the other hand, cast Paul Scofield, dignified and sorrowing, with eyes that had seen everything, as a tragic King of France, suggesting (as in Owen's *Strange Meeting* or *All Quiet on the Western Front)* that suffering knew no national boundaries, that French and English were alike victims.

In keeping with Branagh's overall interpretation of *Henry V*, Pistol is presented as a casualty of war, a victim cast off by the King, his old companion, and one of many ragged, mud-covered soldiers, but not as coward, a braggart – or indeed, as a Shakespearean clown.[21] In Olivier's film, Pistol and Fluellen are a comic double act, like Kemp and Cowley in the Shakespearean acting company, Nokes and Leigh on the Restoration stage, Morecombe and Wise, Abbott and Costello, Peter Cook and Dudley Moore. Shakespeare's Pistol is a monument to intertextuality, spouting half-remembered quotations from old plays, which (as with the Player King in *Hamlet*) parody the pre-Shakespearean drama, Marlowe and the repertory of the Queen's Men. Robert Newton in Olivier's *Henry V*, given top billing after Olivier, brings out this aspect of Pistol in a self-consciously metatheatrical performance ('I am an actor and this is a play'), with deliberate echoes of his Long John Silver, and anticipation of his Bill Sykes. Fluellen in Olivier's film is a comic Welshman, a lovable eccentric with a funny accent – another performance which is deliberately exaggerated, far distant from any norm of cinematic realism.

The scene with the quarrelling Welsh, Irish, and Scottish captains, a favourite with post-colonial and New Historicist critics, is treated by Olivier as broad comedy, with a blubbering, babyish Macmorris, and with Fluellen and Jamy relishing the joke. In Branagh's film, the quarrel is in deadly earnest, with mud-streaked, exhausted soldiers crouching in a fox-hole, the sound of explosions in the background. Shakespeare's text in this passage presents the Irishman Macmorris as angry and resentful, bridling at Fluellen's 'there is not many of your nation', which he evidently takes as an insult:

> MACMORRIS
> Of my nation? What ish my nation? Ish a villain, and a bastard, and a knave, and a rascal? What ish my nation? Who talks of my nation? . . .
> I do not know you so good a man as myself. So Chrish save me, I will cut off your head. (3.2.124–6, 134–5)

Branagh's version of this scene is in keeping with his anti-heroic agenda, his attempt (as he says in the introduction to his screenplay) to present 'an

6. Robert Stephens as Pistol, Geoffrey Hutchings as Nym, *Henry V*, directed by Kenneth Branagh, 1989.

uncompromising view of politics and a deeply questioning, ever-relevant and compassionate survey of people and war'.[22] Like a good New Historicist, Branagh sets out here to undermine the view of King Harry's army as a 'band of brothers' united in a common enterprise, by bringing out tensions and animosities, not easily resolved.

In Branagh's film (after Macmorris's 'I will cut off your head' and without the Englishman Gower's ineffectual intervention 'Gentlemen both, you will mistake each other'), the King's bellicose speech before Harfleur follows immediately. This speech is cut entirely by Olivier, and Harfleur falls without a shot being fired or a threat being uttered. Branagh leaves out a few lines, but the full horrors of war are present, emphasized by the King's desperate tone, his 'almost uncontrollable rage',[23] and the reaction shots of grim, heavily armed soldiers and frightened citizens.

> look to see
> The blind and bloody soldier with foul hand
> Defile the locks of your shrill-shrieking daughters;
> . . .
> Your naked infants spitted upon pikes.
> (3.2.135–6; 3.3.33–8)

As Branagh shoots the scene, there is no doubt that the threat is a genuine one, and he adds a sequence making explicit the King's relief that this sentence will not be carried out, showing him visibly moved, physically exhausted by the tension, and almost fainting at the end of the scene. By the added, non-textual emphasis on the King's reaction to the surrender of Harfleur, Branagh is able to hold in balance the threat of violence, wreaked on a helpless civilian population, and the possibility of a harmonious reconciliation, an opening up of the gates of mercy.[24] The Shakespearean line 'Whiles yet the soldiers are in my command' (3.3.29), omitted by Branagh, expresses a similar ambivalence. By shooting the scene from King Harry's point of view, bringing out an emotional sub-text, Branagh allows for a reconciliation of the heroic and the anti-heroic, a warrior with conscience.[25]

One of the passages in the text most expressive of an ideology of unity and brotherhood is the King's 'Once more unto the breach' speech, which both Olivier and Branagh film effectively, in different ways. Olivier begins with close-ups of the warrior prince, a romantic figure on horseback, and in the course of the speech the camera gradually draws backward, until by the end it becomes a long-shot, with King Harry incorporated into the body of his soldiers, and backs of anonymous soldiers bearing pikes in the foreground. The effect is to implicate the screen audience, encouraging them to feel that the words of King Harry's appeal are directed at them in a time of national crisis, in the war against Hitler Germany – 'Be copy now to men of grosser blood / And teach them how to war'. As with the St Crispin's Day oration later, King, noblemen, common soldiers (the 'good yeomen / Whose limbs were made in England'), and cinematic audience are all enrolled in a 'band of brothers', transcending class and regional divisions:

> For there is none of you so mean and base
> That hath not noble lustre in your eyes.
> (3.1.24–30)

Branagh's oratory is specifically directed at the soldiers around him, who are initially photographed running away from the breach and its fire and smoke, and need encouragement to resume the assault. Close-ups of a sweat-stained prince, with a note of desperation in his voice, are alternated with individual close-ups of sombre, grimy soldiers, weary with battle, and only towards the end of the speech do they respond to their commander's pleas to charge once again. In this scene, as in recent stage productions by Hytner and Hall, the ordinary soldiers, the infantrymen of the First World War, the Second World War, and Vietnam, are brought into the foreground, and this is even more the case in the night scene before Agincourt, in which three named soldiers are singled out from anonymity.

The night-time encounter between the disguised King and three ordinary soldiers, Williams, Bates, and Court, is interpreted very differently by Olivier and by Branagh. Olivier films it as 'a little touch of Harry in the night' (4.Cho.47), showing him, as in the Chorus's introductory remarks, as heroic, noble yet (within limits) democratic, passing among his troops 'with a modest smile' (l. 33), to encourage them and listen to what they have to say. The soldiers, rarely shown in close-up, and mostly in semi-darkness, are not individualized, and Williams's longest speech is reassigned to Court, presented as a fresh-faced recruit. Branagh films this scene as a debate among equals, not tilting the balance or choosing sides, with alternating close-ups of the King, his face partly hidden by a cloak, and an utterly sincere, grizzled Williams (Michael Williams) speaking his lines with conviction, seemingly out of experience. In Shakespeare's text, Bates and Williams both say things to the disguised King which they would not dream of saying in the presence either of the King or of a superior officer:

> KING
> By my troth, I will speak my conscience of the King. I think he would not wish himself anywhere but where he is.
>
> BATES
> Then I would he were here alone; so should he be sure to be ransomed, and many a poor men's lives saved . . .
>
> KING
> Methinks I could not die anywhere so contented as in the King's company, his cause being just and his quarrel honourable.
>
> WILLIAMS
> That's more than we know. (4.1.118–29)

As in the play-within-a-play at the Boar's Head tavern (*1 Henry IV*, 2.4), the prince is playing himself while holding himself at a distance ironically, trying out various roles in what is partly a game. Williams and Bates, without any disguise, are entirely in earnest, and Branagh's film brings this out effectively.

> WILLIAMS
> But if the cause is not good, the King himself hath a heavy reckoning to make when all those legs and arms and heads chopped off in a battle shall join together at the latter day and cry all 'We died at such a place', some swearing, some crying for a surgeon, some upon their wives left poor behind them, some upon the debts they owe, some upon their children rawly left. I am afeard there are few die well that die in a battle, for how can they charitably dispose of anything when blood is their argument? (4.1.134–43)

Both Branagh and Olivier make some cuts in the King's answer to Williams, though both films represent his argument fairly, ending with the line 'Every subject's soul is his own' (4.1.175–7). The King's argument is that a king bears no more responsibility for the actions of his soldiers than a father for the actions of his son, or a master for the actions of his servants: 'So that if a son that is by his father sent about merchandise do sinfully miscarry upon the sea, the imputation of his wickedness, by your rule, should be imposed upon his father that sent him' (4.1.147–50).[26] In Branagh, the common soldiers Bates and Williams are much more forceful, with real anger in Williams's bitter 'You pay him then!' (4.1.195), omitted by Olivier. As in the scene with the quarrelling captains, the disunity among the English troops is more apparent than any longed-for unity. The King's 'God of battles' speech, impassioned in Branagh's delivery, is cut severely by Olivier, who omits all mention of a desire to expiate 'the fault / My father made in compassing the crown' (4.1.190–1).

King Harry's St Crispin's Day speech to the troops is effectively presented in both films. Olivier in this scene is handsome, heroic, glamorous, surrounded by a crowd of admiring extras, and he uses the camera trick once again of a backwards zoom, so that by the end of the speech the King seems one of the 'band of brothers', yet still, by his oration, the dominant figure. Here and in the battle scene that follows, Olivier's King Harry is spotless, the mirror of chivalry, leading his army against effete and arrogant adversaries (as illustrated, memorably, by the wordless scene where a French nobleman, weighed down by heavy armour, is hoisted onto a horse). In sharp contrast, Branagh and his troops are grimy and battle-worn, and in the St Crispin's Day speech he uses alternating close-ups of the King and the listening soldiers, in leading up to a protracted battle sequence of desperate, violent hand-to-hand combat (much of it in blood-spattered, effortful slow motion), where the issue seems in doubt up to the end.

By their cuts and additions Olivier and Branagh create two cinematic versions of Shakespeare's play that have little in common: even Branagh's conscious echoes of Olivier are often in a spirit of rivalry. Critics, assuming their own perspectives to be ideology-free, often, from a position of knowing superiority, triumphantly unearth ideological faultlines in a play or a film. But both Olivier and Branagh seem to me to be responding to elements present in Shakespeare's complex and problematical play, and providing coherent interpretations, making Shakespeare's *Henry V* available to a wide audience.[27] Each interpretation is legitimate, each is appropriate to its time, and each, with great skill, brings out aspects of the Shakespearean text which are both latent and overt. By seeking to humanize the story-book prince in the St Crispin's Day speech and the death of Bardolph, Branagh, like Olivier before him, is in effect answering those legions of critics, beginning with Tillyard, who find the play boring, an unconvincing, mechanical recapitulation of the Tudor myth. But the two film versions also provide support for Rabkin's view that its discordant elements are difficult to reconcile in a single coherent interpretation.

Imaginary forces

The opening Chorus calls on the audience in the theatre to use their imaginations in a collaborative enterprise. Since it is impossible literally 'to bring forth / So great an object' as 'the vasty fields of France' or the troops massed for battle at Agincourt on the stage, then it is necessary to pretend, to 'suppose':

> And let us, ciphers to this great account,
> Upon your imaginary forces work.
> . . .
> Think, when we talk of horses, that you see them
> Printing their proud hoofs i'th' receiving earth.
> For 'tis your thoughts that now must deck our kings,
> Carrying them here and there, jumping o'er times,
> Turning th'accomplishment of many years
> Into an hour-glass.
>
> (Prologue, 10–12, 17–19, 26–31)

Though the passage uses a number of apologetic formulae ('pardon, gentles all', 'flat unraised spirits', 'unworthy scaffold', 'ciphers'), its overall effect is not to stress the limitations of the Elizabethan stage, but its potentialities. On a bare platform stage, with no scenery and minimal props, it is possible to represent any scene, however great. Rather than putting live horses on stage, rather than crowding the stage with a hundred extras marching around in front of elaborate pictorial scenery (as in nineteenth-century productions of Shakespeare), the dramatist paints pictures in words, enlisting the cooperation of the audience.

Shakespeare's pun in 'imaginary forces' contrasts actual, literal armies with the armies in the mind. The addresses of the Chorus suggest something like a contractual arrangement between poet or players and audience, even at one point joking about the way those sitting in the playhouse can be carried from London to Southampton and then to France, without any danger of becoming seasick (2.Cho.37–40). The imagination is presented as able to obliterate both space and time. On the Elizabethan platform stage, the same stage space can in successive scenes, with no interval between, represent a tavern in London and the French court – as is the case today in productions staged in venues like the Swan and Courtyard in Stratford or the Globe in London, modern imitations of the Elizabethan playhouse. A theatre audience willingly accepts the convention.

Emrys James, who played the Chorus in Terry Hands's 1975 production, commented that his role kept him 'separated . . . from the rest of the action' and from the other actors.

> It seems to me that the main relationship the Chorus has, is with the audience. You are their guide: it's the duty of the Chorus to lure the audience into the play, to be friendly, to relax them, so that their imaginations can start working on the scene they're about to see . . . In order to do this, you have to win the audience's confidence.[28]

This production began with actors in rehearsal clothes, on a bare stage: the actors, according to the designer Farrah, were thus 'stripped . . . of the usual comforting stage accoutrements'. No scenery was introduced until the Chorus of Act 2, when, at a signal from the actor playing the Chorus, 'the full apparatus of proscenium theatre goes into action':

> Music plays, a giant heraldic canopy billows over the stage, a huge cannon on its trailer is swept into position, the actors gather about it and begin dressing and arming for war.
>
> (Beauman, *The RSC Henry V*, pp. 31, 119)

In the Olivier film, even more than in this production, the appeal to the imagination of the audience is turned into an appeal to the ingenuity and technical skill of the scene designer and director. Olivier uses the Chorus to Act 3, paradoxically contradicting the words uttered, to show what the cinema as a medium, with all the resources at its disposal, can do, excelling the 'flat unraised spirits' (Prologue, 9) of the Elizabethan stage.

> Play with your fancies, and in them behold
> Upon the hempen tackle ship-boys climbing;
> Hear the shrill whistle which doth order give
> To sounds confused; behold the threaden sails,
> Borne with th'invisible and creeping wind,
> Draw the huge bottoms through the furrowed sea,
> Breasting the lofty surge. O do but think
> You stand upon the rivage and behold
> A city on th'inconstant billows dancing,
> For so appears this fleet majestical.
>
> (3.Cho.7–16)

Olivier, in an updated version of the pictorial Shakespeare productions of the nineteenth century, gives us literal ship-boys, 'silken streamers' (l. 6), sound effects, and ships cleaving the wave on their way to a brightly coloured, story-book France.

Another function of the Chorus, especially apparent in the Choruses of Acts 2 and 3, is to encourage identification of the theatrical audience with the 'youth of England' in King Harry's day, burning with patriotic zeal and a desire to participate in the great adventure. The verb 'follow' has at least two meanings in these Choral addresses. The audience is urged to participate vicariously, to 'behold' the departure of the fleet as if they were actually present. But the spectators in the playhouse are merged with those who, for reasons of 'honour', glory, or self-interest, 'follow' King Harry to France, joining his army: 'For who is he . . . that will not follow / These culled and choice-drawn cavaliers to France?' (3.Cho.22–4). 'Your England' is simultaneously the England of the action of the play and the England of the audience, and the passage suggests dangers as well as opportunities in an England left behind 'at dead midnight', 'guarded with grandsires' and striplings (3.Cho.19–21).

Critical commentary on the Choruses has generally emphasized the element of patriotism – 'martial music', as one critic puts it. By its title, *The Famous Victories of Henry V*, an earlier play that is one of Shakespeare's sources, pro-vides the kind of uncomplicated, morale-boosting patriotism, the 'unequivocal celebration of Henry and his war in France', that *Henry V* generally eschews.[29] Even in the Chorus to Act 2, the assertion that 'honour's thought / Reigns solely in the breast of every man' is qualified by the comment, several lines later, that Harry's 'followers' are motivated partly by the hope of gain, 'crowns imperial, crowns and coronets' (2 Cho.1, 3–4, 10–11). In a characteristic Shakespearean juxtaposition, the next scene introduces, by their military titles, Pistol, Bardolph, and Nym, who parody ideas of honour and a swordsman's heroism.

The Chorus to Act 4 serves several functions. It builds up suspense, with the outcome of the forthcoming battle kept in uncertainty, emphasizing the odds against 'the low-rated English', outnumbered by 'the confident and over-lusty French'. With vivid and evocative scene-painting, it encourages the theatrical audience to see and hear what the words of the Chorus describe:

> The hum of either army stilly sounds,
> That the fixed sentinels almost receive
> The secret whispers of each other's watch.
> Fire answers fire, and through their paly flames
> Each battle sees the other's umbered face.
> (4 Cho.4–9. 18–19)

The portrayal of King Harry in this Chorus is heroic: he is depicted as the ideal prince, doing exactly what a military leader and pattern of courtesy should do in such circumstances. Though passing among his men like a god disguised, he treats all men alike: 'mean and gentle' are the same to him, as he speaks to his soldiers as 'brothers, friends and countrymen':

> With cheerful semblance and sweet majesty,
> That every wretch, pining and pale before,
> Beholding him plucks comfort from his looks.
> A largess universal, like the sun,
> His liberal eye doth give to every one,
> Thawing cold fear, that mean and gentle all
> Behold.   (4 Cho.34, 40–6)

Yet the scene that follows deliberately confounds expectation.[30] As with the earlier scene with the four quarrelling captains, each speaking a different dialect, the encounter of King and common soldier ends not with solidarity, courage trickling down from above to the happy plebeians, but with disharmony – a quarrel, a challenge, a box on the ear.

The Quarto version of *Henry V* (Q1, 1600) was evidently shortened for performance by Shakespeare's company. Andrew Gurr, in his recent edition of the Quarto text, argues that the cuts were made for early performances at the Globe, and that Q1 'was a carefully planned adaptation, designed to make a viable two-hour script for acting'. With the Chorus and eleven other speaking parts omitted, this version of the play could easily be performed, with some doubling, by nine to eleven adult male actors and two boys. One effect of the revision is to remove much of the ambivalence with which the King and the war with France are treated in the play: 'the underlying emphasis of the changes is to intensify Henry's heroism, and to play down the setbacks to his campaign.'[31] If the Chorus is eliminated, then the many passages of ironic juxtaposition, where the account of the Chorus clashes in some way with the action that follows, also disappear.

Brotherhood and hierarchy

In many of the Chorus's addresses to the audience, as in the King's two speeches to his troops before Harfleur and Agincourt, a dominant theme is unity: disparate elements are seen as enrolled in a common cause. According to Terry Hands, his production sought to bring out the 'unity . . . of individuals . . . voluntarily accepting some abdication of that individuality in a final non-hierarchic interdependence – a real brotherhood'.[32] In depicting the London crowd celebrating the victorious return of King Harry and his army, the Chorus to Act 5 collapses distinctions of time, place, and rank in society:

> But now behold,
> In the quick forge and working-house of thought,
> How London doth pour out her citizens.
> The Mayor and all his brethren in best sort,
> Like to the senators of th'antique Rome
> With the plebeians swarming at their heels,
> Go forth and fetch their conquering Caesar in.
>   (5.Cho.22–8)

Shapiro and Patterson present evidence that in the specific circumstances of 1599 England was far from unified. The principal cause of these 'deep anxieties' is hinted at in the lines immediately after those just quoted – the highly controversial expedition of the Earl of Essex to Ireland:

> Were now the General of our gracious Empress,
> As in good time he may, from Ireland coming,
> Bringing rebellion broached on his sword.
>   (5.Cho.30–2)

Though the overt meaning of these lines presents Essex as victorious over rebellion, it is possible to detect a latent suggestion that he is bringing home the sword of rebellion, threatening the harmony of the state.[33]

Where in *Coriolanus* Shakespeare shows Roman senators and plebeians as locked in bitter conflict, the Chorus to Act 5 presents the two groups as separate, by no means equal, and yet united – those of 'best sort' and those 'swarming' in an undifferentiated mass behind them. King Harry's two stirring addresses to the troops acknowledge distinctions in rank and birth. The 'noble English', those who can attest to their ancestry, their 'blood' among the aristocracy or gentry, a long line of warriors, are distinguished from 'men of grosser blood', the 'good yeomen' whose 'breeding' is compared to that of the cattle they herd (with a pun on 'pasture'):

> And you, good yeomen,
> Whose limbs were made in England, show us here
> The mettle of your pasture; let us swear
> That you are worth your breeding – which I doubt not,
> For there is none of you so mean and base
> That hath not noble lustre in your eyes.
>
>   (3.1.17–20, 24–30)

The lines both assert and deny hierarchy, redefining 'mean and base' in terms of moral character rather than the accident of 'noble' birth. In the St Crispin's Day oration, King Harry goes a step further, saying that all who join with him in the forthcoming battle will by that action turn into gentlemen, sealed as one in the bond of brotherhood, united in blood.

> We few, we happy few, we band of brothers.
> For he today that sheds his blood with me
> Shall be my brother; be he ne'er so vile,
> This day shall gentle his condition.
>
>   (4.3.60–3)

Yet when, after the battle, the King reads out the names of the French and English dead, hierarchy is re-established, as only 'princes, barons, lords, knights, squires / And gentlemen of blood and quality' are allowed names, carefully arranged in descending order of rank, with those 'of good sort' carefully kept distinct from 'common men':

> KING
> Edward the Duke of York; the Earl of Suffolk;
> Sir Richard Keighley; Davy Gam, esquire;
> None else of name, and of all other men
> But five-and-twenty.
>
>   (4.8.76, 80, 90–1, 104–7)

Hierarchy and brotherhood are problematized in the disguised King's encounter with Williams and in the soliloquy 'Upon the King' in 4.1. King Harry's 'I think the King is but a man, as I am; the violet smells to him as it does to me' (a variant on Shylock's 'Hath not a Jew eyes?') claims equality, or at least equivalence, among men of differing social status – though distinctions are readmitted by the concession that 'his affections are higher mounted than' those of ordinary men (4.1.102–3, 106–7). Here and in the soliloquy King Harry presents 'ceremony', the trappings of power – 'the sword, the mace, the crown imperial, / The intertissued robe of gold and pearl' – as the only thing separating a King from a commoner: 'his ceremonies laid by, in his nakedness he appears but a man' (4.1.105–6, 258–9, 263). Yet of course the King's assertions in the dialogue with Williams are pretence, a momentary carnivalesque 'playing holidays' (*1 Henry IV*, 1.2.192), since he can remove the cloak disguising him and resume his proper position as monarch and commander of the army at any point. Williams, thinking that the stranger is, like him, a common soldier, is bitingly sceptical about the promises of kings and noblemen, protected by their status in a hierarchical society:

> WILLIAMS
> Ay, he said so to make us fight cheerfully; but when our throats are cut he may be ransomed and we never the wiser.   (4.1.191–3)

When, in a later scene, Williams takes up the challenge to the King ('Let it be a quarrel between us'), the difference in rank makes it impossible for either man to fight the other. The King cannot enter into combat with a commoner over 'a private displeasure', and for Williams to strike the King, or even his designated representative, would, as Fluellen says, constitute 'treason'. At the same time, honour requires that the 'soldier keep his oath' (4.1.196, 203; 4.7.129–30; 4.8.22). When the King, now in full regalia, chastises Williams for his behaviour in their earlier encounter, Williams's answer is dignified, recognizing distinctions of rank yet asserting his independence. In defending his actions and words, Williams invokes the Tudor doctrine of the King's two bodies, by which a King both is and is not like a 'private man':

> KING
> It was our self thou didst abuse.
>
> WILLIAMS
> Your majesty came not like your self: you appeared to me but as a common man – witness the night, your garments, your lowliness; and what your highness suffered under that shape, I beseech you take it for your own fault and not mine, for had you been as I took you for, I made no offence; therefore I beseech your highness pardon me.
>
> (4.1.234; 4.8.50–57)

 When the King offers him a sum of money and Fluellen adds a tip of a shilling, Williams's response – not quite insubordinate but surly and unwilling to be treated patronisingly – is 'I will none of your money' (4.8.69).

The King's speech on ceremony resembles Henry VI's soliloquy at the battle of Towton in its emphasis on the double nature of kingship, in which a monarch, encased in his ceremonial robes, is simultaneously akin to and estranged from ordinary men. Henry VI, unhappy at the collapse of the kingdom into a destructive civil war that he is powerless to avert, imagines an alternative life for himself; 'O God, methinks it were a happy life / To be no better than a homely swain.' As he presents it here, the lot of a humble shepherd, in harmony with nature and able to sleep at night, is in all respects preferable to worldly greatness:

> Gives not the hawthorn bush a sweeter shade
> To shepherds looking on their silly sheep
> Than doth a rich embroidered canopy
> To kings that fear their subjects' treachery?
>
> (*3 Henry VI*, 2.5.21–2, 42–5)

Later in this scene, Henry VI expresses feelings of solidarity with the sufferings of his subjects, mourning 'for subjects' woe' (l. 111) as they mourn. Henry V in his soliloquy rejects 'thrice-gorgeous ceremony' as a false god, unworthy of 'adoration': the hypocritical obeisance of courtiers cannot keep off sickness and sorrow (4.1.242, 250–2, 263). But in comparing the sleeplessness of monarchs with the peaceful sleep of the humble peasant, King Harry's language takes on a distinct note of snobbery. Kings may be less happy, but, it is implied, they are superior beings, on a different plane of existence from the 'wretch' or 'lackey' whose 'gross brain' makes him little better than an animal.

> Not all these, laid in bed majestical,
> Can sleep so soundly as the wretched slave,
> Who with a body filled and vacant mind
> Gets him to rest, crammed with . . . bread.
>
> (4.1.264–7, 269, 275, 279)

Since a moment ago we have seen Bates and Williams, fully articulate rational beings, with voices that refuse to be silenced, the King's characterization of such men as slaves, deserving their subjection because of their mental incapacity, appears self-serving, morally obtuse.[34] Here as elsewhere in *Henry V*, Shakespeare's text shows a puzzling ambivalence.

Chapter 9

Epilogue: *Henry VIII*

Pomp and glory

Henry VIII is an anomaly among Shakespeare's history plays. Written in 1613 at the end of Shakespeare's career, two decades after his other history plays, *Henry VIII* is rarely discussed in books on the histories.[1] Though frequently performed in the eighteenth and nineteenth centuries, in sumptuous, elaborate productions, there have been very few twentieth-century productions: 1931, 1949, 1969, 1983, and 1996, with wide intervals between. As a play of joint authorship with John Fletcher (and thus an early Fletcher as well as a late Shakespeare play), *Henry VIII* is relatively unusual in the Shakespeare oeuvre. Generically, the play appears to be a hybrid, and critics have commented on affinities with Shakespeare's late romances and with the Jacobean court masque.[2] The extremely detailed stage directions in such scenes as 2.4 and 4.1 are like nothing else in the Shakespeare canon, and suggest a pronounced element of spectacle in *Henry VIII*.

Johnson, writing in 1765, described the play as 'one of those which still keeps possession of the stage, by the splendour of its pageantry'. Victorian and Edwardian productions by Charles Kean, Henry Irving, and Herbert Beerbohm Tree featured elaborate scenic effects. Irving, for example, by a 'careful study of every possible archaeological authority', guaranteeing 'correctness of every ruff, head-dress, swordbelt, shoe', sought to make his production 'the most perfect reproduction of court life in the days of Henry VIII, that this stage or indeed the stage of any country, has ever seen'.[3] Tree's banquet scene in 1.4 included 235 separate props, 'all exact copies taken from originals in museums or from paintings in the National Gallery'. This production, with its cast of 172 and 26 separate scene changes (necessitating cuts of nearly half the text) was extraordinarily popular, running for 254 performances, seen by over 375,000 people.[4]

Early productions, especially that of John Philip Kemble in 1789, often built up the role of Queen Katherine, a part in which Sarah Siddons found 'continued popularity' for many years. Johnson thought 'the meek sorrows and virtuous distress' of the Queen, resolute in her integrity, were the best thing in the play.[5] The tradition of treating Katherine as a tragic heroine and the play's dominant figure continued into the twentieth century, especially in Trevor Nunn's 1969 production, with Peggy Ashcroft as the wronged Queen, in a performance notable for its 'moral strength' and 'dignity'. According to Nunn, the actress

> had become obsessed with Katherine of Aragon to the point where she brought into rehearsals every kind of defence of the character . . . She would turn up with extra lines from the historical trial or from Katherine's letters and try to put them into the text . . . I don't think I ever argued Peggy out of her conviction that she was not playing Katherine but that she *was* Katherine.[6]

In the productions of Irving and Tree, full of pageantry, Wolsey was the star role, and Cardinal Wolsey's rise and fall became the play's principal action (with Act 5 cut entirely by Tree).

Twentieth-century productions have tended to react against the tradition of grand spectacle and noble sentiments. Terence Gray in 1931 approached the play as caricature, dressing the characters as playing cards and having them act like automata, 'depersonalized playthings'. Tyrone Guthrie's 1949 production, though aiming more at psychological realism, filled the play with comic business, to keep the audience from becoming bored.

> In the scene where the scriveners take down Queen Katherine's plea for leniency, priests scribbling away on their parchment are rolled about the floor like bowls by careless courtiers.

In this production in which 'the main spirit . . . is comedic', Harold Hobson said tartly, 'any resemblance to Shakespeare [was] purely accidental'.[7] Howard Davies's RSC production in 1983 was consistently ironic in its approach, described by one reviewer as 'the most thoroughgoing Brechtianisation of Shakespeare' he had ever seen. The sets were cut-outs, resembling a toy theatre, the costumes were 'oatmeal-coloured', the music was pastiche Weill, a jaunty tango and 'squawks and howls from a stage orchestra'.[8] The performances were resolutely anti-heroic, resisting empathy: Richard Griffith, who saw his character as 'an early version of Stalin, quite ruthless', played Henry VIII as though 'under an instruction to avoid being kinglike'. Nearly all the characters were presented as bureaucrats and careerists, in a production emphasizing 'affinities with Thatcher's Britain'.[9]

Greg Doran's 1996 RSC production, on the other hand, sought to reinstate 'discreet spectacle', balancing the ceremonial and the ironic – in Doran's words, 'reclaiming the fullness of spectacle at the same time as demonstrating . . . its emptiness'. At his first entrance, the King appeared 'dressed in gold, wearing the crown, sitting on a golden horse'. Paul Jesson, who played the King, saw him as 'a man who may not be sure of himself, but is certainly sure of his position and his ability to terrorize'.[10] Several reviewers commented on the combination of ceremony and 'brutal *realpolitik*' in the production, dominated by Jesson's tough, commanding monarch. Jesson brought out the 'unpredictable, volatile' nature of the monarch in a play where each scene was 'a separate entity' that 'isolates and illustrates particular aspects of his personality'. In this production, King Henry VIII 'has no qualms about self-contradiction: putting his humiliated Queen in the dock and then applauding her spirited exit'.[11]

Farewell to greatness

More than any other Shakespeare history play, *Henry VIII* consists of a series of discrete episodes, each following the same general pattern. The repeated pattern is that of *de casibus* tragedy, a fall from worldly prosperity and greatness. In each of the successive episodes, the King plays a significant part, though a second character is the main focus of interest. The first episode (taking up 1.1–1.3 and 2.1) is the fall of the Duke of Buckingham, Wolsey's enemy, accused of treason by a false witness suborned by Wolsey. The second is the fall from royal favour of Queen Katherine, with four extended scenes (2.2, 2.4, 3.1, and 4.2), interwoven with two scenes (1.4 and 2.3) devoted to the rise of Anne Bullen. In nearly all productions, Queen Katherine is treated as a tragic figure. The fall of Katherine represents the height of Wolsey's power: though in 2.4 and 3.1 she mounts a spirited defence against the Cardinal's accusations, these scenes help to establish him as a formidable adversary, an over-mighty favourite exulting in the trappings of earthly greatness.

> KATHERINE
> You have, by fortune and his highness' favours,
> Gone slightly o'er low steps, and now are mounted
> Where powers are your retainers, and your words,
> Domestics to you, serve your will as't please
> Yourself pronounce their office. I must tell you,
> You tender more your person's honour than
> Your high profession spiritual.   (2.4.109–15)

But in 3.2, the King suddenly turns against him, seemingly made aware for the first time of the Cardinal's arrogance and greed, the 'piles of wealth' he has accumulated (3.2.107). Wolsey's fall is precipitous, and he is able to moralize, in 'a long farewell to all my greatness', about the instability of fortune.

> Nay then, farewell.
> I have touched the highest point of all my greatness,
> And from that full meridian of my glory
> I haste now to my setting. I shall fall
> Like a bright exhalation in the evening,
> And no man see me more.   (3.2.222–7, 351–2)

Each of these episodes ends with a homiletic moral, pronounced by the victim of fortune. Buckingham, on his way to the block, forgives his enemies, praises the King who has condemned him, and reflects on the insecurity of the court world:

> For those you make friends
> And give your hearts to, when they once perceive
> The least rub in your fortunes, fall away
> Like water from ye, never found again.
>   (2.1.127–30)

Wolsey, in the play's best-known lines, reflects on worldliness as against 'integrity to heaven', renouncing ambition and 'the ways of glory':

> Had I but served my God with half the zeal
> I served my King, he would not in mine age
> Have left me naked to mine enemies.
>   (3.2.435, 440, 453, 455–7)[12]

Katherine, in an extended farewell to the world, dies at peace with her conscience, able charitably to forgive Wolsey, the man 'whom I most hated living' (4.2.73), blesses the King who rejected her, and expresses concern for the welfare of her poor servants, male and female. The pattern is varied in the fourth episode, where the virtuous Cranmer, threatened by the machinations of the wily, bigoted Gardiner, is suddenly reprieved by the intervention of the King. In this instance, the fall is an interrupted one, and the innocent Cranmer, falsely accused, is left to pronounce a prophecy of the reign of Queen Elizabeth, with its 'thousand blessings, / Which time shall bring to ripeness' (5.4.19–20).

What is problematical in all this is the role of the King, whose behaviour, as several critics have noted, is frequently opaque. There are no soliloquies to let the audience know the King's true feelings towards Queen Katherine or Anne Bullen, and the play is tantalizingly silent about the motivations of its principal character. As Lord Herbert of Cherbury said in his *Life and Raigne of King Henry the Eight* (1649):

> It is not easie to write that Princes History, of whom no one thing may constantly be affirmed . . . It is impossible to draw his Picture well who hath several countenances.[13]

Though the King speaks unconvincingly about his 'conscience' several times – 'But conscience, conscience –/ O, 'tis a tender place, and I must leave her' – the comments of courtiers are bracingly cynical about such claims.

> CHAMBERLAIN
> It seems the marriage with his brother's wife
> Has crept too near his conscience.
>
> SUFFOLK
>   No, his conscience
> Has crept too near another lady.
>
> NORFOLK
>   'Tis so,
> This is the Cardinal's doing.
>   (2.2.15–18, 141–2)

Again and again, the audience is presented with 'dilemmas of interpretation', conflicting versions of events or behaviour from observers with differing perspectives, creating an atmosphere of radical uncertainty. The play's subtitle, 'All is True', may refer not to a claim of fidelity to historical sources but the impression that virtually anything may be considered true: 'the impossibility of certain knowledge of truth in this mutable, politic world'.[14]

The atmosphere of uncertainty is established from the outset. Buckingham is treated sympathetically, Wolsey is ambitious and ruthless, but we are given no indication whether the charges against Buckingham are justified. The narration of Buckingham's trial by two anonymous Gentlemen is carefully neutral, telling 'what has happened' (2.1.6), without expressing any opinion as to whether the trial exemplified justice or injustice. Shakespeare follows Holinshed in not taking sides for or against Buckingham:

> But how trulie, or in what sort prooved, I have not further to say, either in accusing or excusing him, other than as I found in *Hall* and *Polydor*, whose words in effect, I have thought to impart to the reader, and without anie partial wresting of the same either to or fro.[15]

A delicate balancing act is apparent in the treatment of Katherine and Anne. Katherine (though a devout Roman Catholic and an obstacle to the Elizabethan settlement) is portrayed sympathetically throughout, defending herself against unjust accusations with courage and dignity, in a manner similar to Hermione in *The Winter's Tale*. Nothing in her behaviour as 'a true and humble wife', she tells the King, could justify his 'displeasure' or sudden 'dislike' (2.4.16–25).[16] Later, in the trial scene, aware that in Henry VIII's court 'virtue finds no friends', she contrasts divine and earthly justice. Her innocence and exemplary behaviour as a wife cannot protect her in a society where the arbitrary will of the monarch rules unchecked.

> Can you think, lords,
> That any Englishman dare give me counsel?
> Or be a known friend 'gainst his highness' pleasure? –
> Though he be grown so desperate to be honest –
> And live a subject?
>   . . .
> Heaven is above all yet: there sits a judge
> That no king can corrupt.   (3.1.84–7, 100–1, 126)

By inserting a banquet scene early in the play, in which the King, as masquer, meets and flirts with Anne Bullen ('By heaven, she is a dainty one'), Shakespeare and Fletcher hint that the King's motivation for the divorce is something other than 'conscience'. This scene, probably by Fletcher, was presented in the Doran and Davies productions as a phallic, bacchanalian romp. Anne is treated with some irony, with consistent emphasis on her outward appearance, 'the beauty of her person', as a tasty morsel, 'the goodliest woman / That ever lay by man'. An anonymous Gentleman, viewing her pass by in the coronation procession, praises 'the sweetest face I ever looked upon'.

> Our King has all the Indies in his arms,
> And more, and richer, when he strains that lady.
> I cannot blame his conscience.
>   (4.1.43, 45–7, 68–70)

In a dialogue with a worldly, cynical Old Lady, Anne professes to disavow ambition, expressing 'pity' for Katherine, now out of favour. The scene, with its wry comic realism, is similar to the exchange between Desdemona and Emilia in *Othello*, 4.3.59–84, though without the pathos of that scene:

> ANNE
>   By my troth and maidenhead,
> I would not be a queen.

OLD LADY
                    Beshrew me, I would,
And venture maidenhead for 't; and so would you,
For all this spice of your hypocrisy.
    . . .
                    You would not be a queen?

ANNE
No, not for all the riches under heaven.

OLD LADY
'Tis strange: a threepence bowed would hire me,
Old as I am, to queen it. But I pray you,
What think you of a duchess?
                            (2.3.18, 23–6, 34–8)

In the court world depicted in *Henry VIII*, some rise and some fall, without particular distinction of merit.

Kings as gods

One traditional view of *Henry VIII* sees it as a celebration of royal power. Frank Kermode, seeing the King as 'the agent of . . . divine retribution' and a man with 'a proper kingly concern over the health of the state', finds a Tillyardian pattern of order affirmed, in the portrayal of 'a King who, though human, is *ex officio* the deputy of God, and the agent of divine punishment and mercy'. R. A. Foakes, emphasizing similarities with Shakespeare's late romances, argues that Henry VIII, like Prospero, is 'a representative of benevolent power acting upon others', in a play where 'the dramatic effect is to enhance the stature of Henry as God's deputy'.[17] John Cox, finding parallels with the Jacobean masque, sees *Henry VIII* as exemplifying 'a favorite tenet of Jacobean kingship: the godlike power of the king'. To Cox as to other critics arguing a similar position, King Henry grows in moral stature in the course of the play, becoming educated in kingship: 'from dependence on his ministers, Henry moves to firm control of them.'[18]

These critics place particular emphasis on the prophecy of a Tudor golden age which ends the play. Cranmer, rescued from the malice of the heresy-hunting, villainous Gardiner, Wolsey's ally and successor as malign influence, in 5.4 celebrates the birth of Princess Elizabeth with a long, extravagant speech. Though he introduces his panegyric by calling his words 'truth' rather than 'flattery', the speech is full of hyperbole, presenting the reign of Elizabeth as heaven on earth, an image of perfection.

> She shall be
>
> . . .
>
> A pattern to all princes living with her
> And all that shall succeed.
>
> . . .
>
> All princely graces
> That mould up such a mighty piece as this is,
> With all the virtues that attend the good,
> Shall still be doubled on her. Truth shall nurse her;
> Holy and heavenly thoughts still counsel her.
>
> (5.4.16, 20–9)

Her reign will bring the blessings of peace, and after the death of this 'maiden phoenix', a successor (the reigning monarch, James I) will rise from her 'sacred ashes', bringing continued prosperity and glory to the nation.

> In her days, every man shall eat in safety
> Under his own vine what he plants, and sing
> The merry songs of peace to all his neighbours.
>
> (5.4.33–5, 40, 45)

The problem with passages like this, and with interpretations that see such passages as the key to the play, embodying 'Shakespeare's equation between royalty and order', is that it is hard not to see them as flattery, and as wholly conventional. *Richard III* ends with a similar prophecy of 'smooth-fac'd peace' and 'smiling plenty' in 'the time to come', but contrasted with a brutal, chaotic civil war that has made 'poor England weep in streams of blood'.[19] One reviewer of Greg Doran's production described Cranmer's speech as 'horribly toadying', another as 'excruciatingly sycophantic', and Davies's production satirized its patriotic sentiments. Felperin, though he finds a 'pervasive providential cast' in *Henry VIII*, with its action watched over 'by the Christian God', considers the play 'a failure' and Cranmer's prophecy 'hardly more than glorified propaganda', in keeping with the play's 'exclusion of the nastier aspects of a reign littered with corpses'.[20]

No clear providential pattern or equation of earthly and heavenly justice is discernible in the play, even in the escape of the virtuous Cranmer from the clutches of his persecutors. The source for the interview between Cranmer and the King in 5.1 and for the trial of Cranmer in 5.2, followed closely in the text, is Foxe's *Acts and Monuments* (1563).[21] In these two scenes and in the equivalent scenes in Samuel Rowley's play, *When you see me, you know me. Or the famous Chronicle Historie of king Henry the eight* (1605), the reign of Henry VIII is portrayed as a key episode in the English Reformation. Cranmer and his ally Thomas Cromwell are explicitly depicted as Protestant reformers, Gardiner as an intolerant Catholic, accusing his enemy as 'a most arch heretic, a pestilence / That doth infect the land' (5.1.45–6). This element of religious polemic is much more prominent in Rowley's play, which is unequivocally anti-Catholic in its stance. In several scenes in that play, Gardiner and his associate Bonner, Papist conspirators ('Let them untimely dye, / That scorne the Pope and *Romes* supremacie'), inveigh against 'false Luthers doctrins'. Their main intended victim is not Cranmer, but Queen Katherine Parr, who is saved by the intervention of the thoroughly Protestant Prince Edward.[22]

Rowley's play presents Henry VIII not as any kind of divinity, actual or potential, but as fallible, a mixture of virtues and weaknesses. He nearly succumbs to the plotting of Gardiner and Bonner, acting like the archetypal tyrant in initially refusing to let Queen Katherine Parr speak in her own defence:

> Mother a God, tis time to sturre I see,
> When traitors creepes so nere our majestie:
> Now in old age, must I feare my life,
> By hatefull treason of my Queene and wife
>   . . .
> Bend all your Holbeards points against the dore,
> If she presume to enter strike her through,
> Dare she presume againe to looke on me.
>   (2573–7, 2607–9)

Rowley's Henry VIII is hot-tempered and rash, a 'good fellow', able to mix on equal terms with rogues and thieves and to appreciate the wit of the fool Will Summers, and, though impetuous, is able to forgive as quickly as to condemn when the impulse strikes him.

> Give me thy hand, come kisse me *Kate*, so now ime friends againe,
> hurson knaves, crafty varlets, make thee a traytor to oulde *Harries*
> life . . . Mother a god he that says th'art false to me by Englands crowne
> ile hang him presently.   (2687–92)[23]

Shakespeare and Fletcher's Henry VIII is a more complex, enigmatic figure than Rowley's, but he is presented neither as an ideal monarch nor as God's instrument in Act 5. Though Cranmer's trial ends in his exoneration rather than his downfall, the '"justice" he receives bears a strong resemblance to the political manipulation' apparent in the earlier trials of Buckingham and Katherine. The court of Henry VIII is a place where 'power, not integrity, governs life and death'.[24] Katherine, like Cranmer, is a figure of unspotted integrity, surrounded by 'corrupt minds' able easily to 'procure knaves as corrupt / To swear against' the innocent (5.1.132–3). Both attempt to defend themselves against judges who are also their accusers, hoping to 'stand on . . . truth and honesty' as their defence (5.1.123). With Katherine, Buckingham, and Wolsey, the King's arbitrary power brings about their condemnation, where with Cranmer that same arbitrary power is exercised on his behalf. Wolsey in his fall recognizes that the smiles of princes are no more reliable than their frowns:

> O, how wretched
> Is that poor man that hangs on princes' favours!
> There is betwixt that smile we would aspire to,
> That sweet aspect of princes, and their ruin
> More pangs and frowns than wars . . .
>
> (3.2.366–70)

Following Foxe, Shakespeare and Fletcher have the King warn Cranmer of the accusations against him by powerful enemies, and then, recognizing that 'the justice and the truth o'th'question' rarely 'carries the due o'th'verdict with it', give him a means of defending himself, by producing the King's ring to confound his accusers (5.1.130–1, 149–52).[25] The courtiers humiliate Cranmer by making him 'wait like a lousy footboy / At chamber door' (5.2.173–4) and then order his imprisonment, 'like a traitor', 'till the King's further pleasure / Be known to us' (5.2.124–5, 130). When he produces the King's ring, the courtiers immediately recognize that he, not they, now bears the King's favour, and that their own positions within the court are suddenly put at risk.

> SUFFOLK
> 'Tis the right ring. By heaven. I told ye all,
> When we first put this dangerous stone a-rolling,
> 'Twould fall upon ourselves
>
> . . .
>
> CHAMBERLAIN
> Would I were fairly out on't.   (5.2.138–40, 143)

Arbitrary monarchy is no less arbitrary in reprieving Cranmer than in suddenly condemning Katherine, Buckingham, and Wolsey. Katherine's defiant response to her accusers when they advise her 'Put your main cause into the King's protection' sharply distinguishes between human and divine justice, as Isabella does in *Measure for Measure* in reminding Angelo of the presumption of 'proud man, / Dress'd in a little brief authority':

Ye tell me what ye wish for both – my ruin.
Is this your Christian counsel? Out upon ye!
Heaven is above all yet: there sits a judge
That no king can corrupt.[26]

The view of monarchy and of political authority in *Henry VIII*, as in all of Shakespeare's histories, then, is deeply ambivalent and susceptible of a variety of interpretations.

Notes

Abbreviations

ELR   *English Literary Renaissance*
SQ   *Shakespeare Quarterly*
SS   *Shakespeare Survey*

1 The uses of history

1 North, 'Amiot to the Reader', *Plutarch's Lives* (1595), Sig. *iii^v–*iiii.
2 Ralegh, *History of the World*, p. 48.
3 Johnson, *Preface to Shakespeare* (1765), *Works*, VII. 72.
4 Heywood, *Apology for Actors* (1612), Sig. F3v.
5 *King Henry V*, 4.3.56–60; sonnet 55, line 9.
6 Sidney, *Selected Writings*, pp. 107, 113; Aristotle, *Poetics*, ch. 9, in *Basic Works*, p. 1463.
7 White, *Metahistory*, pp. 6–7; Sidney, *Selected Writings*, p. 113.
8 Levy, *Tudor Historical Thought*, pp. ix, 167; Holinshed, Preface to the Reader, *The Third volume of Chronicles* (1587), in Patterson, *Reading Holinshed's Chronicles*, pp. 15, 40–41.
9 Ralegh, *History of the World*, pp. 213–14. On 'politic history', see Levy, *Tudor Historical Thought*, pp. 237–8, 249–52.
10 Arthur B. Ferguson, *Clio Unbound*, pp. 50–6, 80–9.
11 Leonard Krieger, *Ranke: The Meaning of History*, pp. 4–5.
12 White, *Tropics of Discourse*, pp. 55, 85.
13 Holinshed, *The Historie of England* (1587), p. 202, quoted in Ferguson, *Clio Unbound*, p. 14.
14 Bullough, *Narrative and Dramatic Sources*, III.16; Tillyard, *Shakespeare's History Plays*, pp. 42–5.
15 *3 Henry VI*, 1.1.1; *Richard III*, 1.1.9; *1 Henry IV*, 1.1.14.
16 On the generic instability of the history play, see Paulina Kewes, 'The Elizabethan History Play: A True Genre?', in Dutton and Howard, *Companion to Shakespeare's*

Works, vol. II, pp. 170–93, esp. 170–2; and Richard Helgerson, 'Shakespeare and Contemporary Dramatists of History', ibid., pp. 26–7.

17 Kewes, 'The Elizabethan History Play', p. 175.

18 *Julius Caesar*, ed. Daniell, p. 7.

19 Ralegh, *History of the World*, p. 61.

20 McMillin and MacLean, *The Queen's Men*, pp. 33, 89–90.

21 According to Harbage's *Annals of English Drama 975–1700*, five such plays can be dated between 1586 and 1590, and five others in 1591–5, after the *Henry VI* plays. On the authorship of *Edward III*, see the editions by Giorgio Melchiori (1998) and by Eric Sams (1996).

22 Ford, *Perkin Warbeck*, Prologue, 2; Levy, *Tudor Historical Thought*, p. 233; Rackin, *Stages of History*, p. 31. Ribner (*The English History Play*) lists fifty history plays before 1606, as against seventeen after that date.

23 In a recent essay, Paulina Kewes has questioned 'the preoccupation with the so-called "English" histories' in studies of the history play as genre, arguing that 'such an insularity of approach . . . elides important distinctions among the various kinds of native past', as well as 'the close affinity between the native and the foreign' in Elizabethan and Jacobean plays (Kewes, 'The Elizabethan History Play', pp. 172, 175).

24 Nashe, *Works*, II.212. The passage is quoted and discussed in Rackin, *Stages of History*, pp. 113–17.

25 See the editor's introduction, *King Henry VI, part 1*, ed. Burns, pp. 8–9.

26 *King Richard II*, ed. Forker, pp. 5, 14.

27 Kastan, 'Proud Majesty Made a Subject', *SQ*, 37 (1986), 459–75, esp. 462. On the deposition scene, see Clare, '*Art made tongue-tied*', pp. 68–72.

28 On the familiarity of Elizabethan audiences with the Roman past, see Kewes, 'The Elizabethan History Play', p. 180.

29 Coleridge, *Shakespeare Criticism*, I.125; Smith, *Production*, p. 51.

30 Rabkin, *Meaning*, p. 34; Smith, *Production*, p. 4.

31 Clare, '*Art made tongue-tied*', pp. 85–7. Worden, 'Which play', pp. 22–4, argues that the play commissioned by Essex's supporters was not Shakespeare's *Richard II*, but another play on the same subject.

32 Campbell, *Shakespeare's "Histories"*, pp. 125, 136, 211; Ralegh, *History of the World*, p. 80.

33 Jonathan Dollimore and Alan Sinfield, 'History and Ideology: The Instance of *Henry V*', in *Alternative Shakespeares*, pp. 216, 220, 225; Leah Marcus, 'Elizabeth', in Smith, *Histories*, pp. 149, 168. For *Coriolanus* and grain shortages, see Richard Wilson, 'Against the grain: Representing the market in *Coriolanus*', in *Will Power*, pp. 83–117; and David George, 'Plutarch, Insurrection, and Dearth in *Coriolanus*', in *Shakespeare and Politics*, ed. Alexander, pp. 110–29.

34 Miller, *The Crucible in History and other essays*, pp. 35, 49, 50; Arthur Miller, *The Crucible*, p. 11.

2 The wars of the critics

1 Bullough, *Narrative and Dramatic Sources*, III.17, 42.

2 Tillyard, *History Plays*, pp. 51, 320–1; cf. Campbell, *Shakespeare's "Histories"*, pp. 67–70.

3 See for example Reese, *The Cease of Majesty*, p. 91, and Ribner, *English History Play*, p. 254.

4 *An Homily against Disobedience and Wilful Rebellion* (1570), in *Sermons or Homilies*, pp. 384, 386, 408. Cf. Tillyard, *History Plays*, p. 320; and Campbell, *Shakespeare's "Histories"*, pp. 214–18.

5 Rackin, *Stages of History*, p. 43; Wilders, *Lost Garden*, p. 48.

6 Machiavelli, *The Prince*, XVIII, pp. 99–100; *3 Henry VI*, 3.2.193; *Richard III*, 1.1.37.

7 Ornstein, *Kingdom*, pp. 12–14; Kelly, *Divine Providence*, pp. 140–5, 304–5; Bullough, *Narrative and Dramatic Sources*, III. 408–9.

8 Kelly, *Divine Providence*, p. 36; Wilders, *Lost Garden*, p. 69; Ornstein, *Kingdom*, pp. 18–21.

9 Rossiter, *Angel with Horns*, pp. 51, 62; cf. Wilders, *Lost Garden*, p. 9; and Hazlitt, *Characters*, pp. 246–7.

10 Rossiter, *Angel with Horns*, p. 15. This is still the standard view of *Richard II* and to some extent of *Richard III*. The introduction to the recent Arden edition of *Richard II* includes the terms 'ambivalent responses to both antagonists' (*King Richard II*, ed. Forker, p. 30), 'doubleness of perspective' (p. 35), and 'mixed reactions to Richard' (p. 39).

11 *King Henry IV, Part 1*, ed. Kastan, p. 14; Bradshaw, *Misrepresentations*, p. 31. Like the Arden edition (pp. 19–23), the Oxford edition of *Henry IV, Part 1*, ed. Bevington, foregrounds 'the question of structural unity' and 'the pattern of opposites' in the play (pp. 39–52).

12 Jenkins, 'The Structural Problem', in Hunter, *Shakespeare: King Henry IV Parts 1 and 2*, pp. 155–172, esp. 171.

13 Rabkin, *Meaning*, pp. 34, 60–1.

14 Jean E. Howard, 'The New Historicism in Renaissance Studies', *ELR*, 16 (1986), 18; Dollimore and Sinfield, 'Foreword', *Political Shakespeare*, pp. vii–viii. Cf. Holderness, *Shakespeare Recycled*, pp. 32–5.

15 Bradshaw, *Misrepresentations*, p. 28; Dollimore, in *Political Shakespeare*, p. 10; Greenblatt, *Shakespearean Negotiations*, p. 3.

16 Rackin, *Stages of History*, pp. xi, 42. On this distinction, see Dollimore's introduction to *Political Shakespeare*, pp. 10–16.

17 Greenblatt, *Shakespearean Negotiations*, pp. 30, 52. Subsequent page references in text.

18 Dollimore and Sinfield, *Alternative Shakespeares*, pp. 216, 225, 227. Subsequent page references in text.

19 This scene has been discussed frequently by recent critics. David J. Baker, in "'Wildehirisshman': Colonialist Representation in Shakespeare's *Henry V*", *ELR*, 22 (1992), 37–61, sees Macmorris's repeated, belligerent 'What ish my nation?' as 'a demonstration of the disruptive multiplicity which cannot be eradicated from even the most powerfully "contained" and organized discourse' (p. 50).

20 Kiernan Ryan, *Shakespeare*, pp. 33, 36; Rackin, *Stages of History*, pp. xi, 234–5.

21 Holderness, *Shakespeare Recycled*, pp. 130–77, esp. 135–9; Bristol, *Carnival and Theater*, pp. 204–6; *King Henry IV, Part 1*, ed. Kastan, p. 49.

22 Rackin, *Stages of History*, pp. 148, 158, 204; Howard and Rackin, *Engendering a Nation*, p. 29.

23 On the ambivalence of Shakespeare's Joan, see Gabrielle Bernhard Jackson, 'Topical Ideology: Witches, Amazons, and Shakespeare's Joan of Arc', *ELR*, 18 (1988), 40–65.

3 The paper crown: *1, 2,* and *3 Henry VI*

1 *King Henry VI, Part 1*, ed. J. Dover Wilson pp. xxi, l; *First Part*, ed. Cairncross, p. liii. More recently, arguments for collaborative authorship of *1 Henry VI* have been advanced by Gary Taylor in 'Shakespeare and Others: the Authorship of *Henry the Sixth, Part One*', *Medieval and Renaissance Drama in England*, 7 (1995), 145–86.

2 Tillyard, *History Plays*, p. 173.

3 Jones, *Origins*, pp. 35, 182.

4 Ibid., pp. 42–54; cf. Luke 23:4 and Matthew 27:19

5 Jones, *Origins*, p. 186; *3 Henry VI*, 1.4.70, 79–83.

6 Jones, *Origins*, pp. 54–6, 182–6; Brockbank, 'The Frame of Disorder', p. 95; Bullough, *Narrative and Dramatic Sources*, III. 210.

7 Bernard Levin, *Daily Mail*, 18 July 1963 and 21 August 1963; Hodgdon, '*Wars*', p. 170.

8 Peggy Ashcroft, 'Margaret of Anjou', 7–9; Alan Brien, *Sunday Telegraph*, 21 July 1963.

9 Harold Hobson, *Sunday Times*, 21 July 1963. The video can be seen at the Shakespeare Centre Memorial Library, Stratford-upon-Avon.

10 See Bernard Levin, *Daily Mail*, 18 July 1963; Hodgdon, '*Wars*', pp. 174–5; and Shaughnessy, *Representing Shakespeare*, pp. 42–51.

11 Hodgdon, '*Wars*', p. 170; John Barton and Peter Hall, *The Wars of the Roses*, p. xv.

12 Barton and Hall, *The Wars of the Roses*, pp. xvii, xxi.

13 See Ashcroft, 'Margaret of Anjou', pp. 7–8.

14 *Players 3*, p. 143; Dominique Goy-Blanquet, in *TLS*, 10 November 1988.

15 Michael Billington, *Guardian*, 24 October 1988; Shaughnessy, *Representing Shakespeare*, pp. 85–7; Michael Coveney, *Financial Times*, 24 October 1988.

16 Lois Potter, 'Recycling the Early Histories', p. 175; cf. Bogdanov and Pennington, *The English Shakespeare Company*.

17 Interview with Edward Hall, *Sunday Times*, 9 June 2002; Edward Hall and Roger Warren, *Rose Rage*, p. 8; Nicholas de Jongh, *Evening Standard*, 17 June 2002;

Dominic Cavendish, *Telegraph*, 18 June 2002; Michael Billington, *Guardian*, 17 June 2002.

18 See Dessen, 'Stagecraft and Imagery in Shakespeare's *Henry VI*', in Smith, *Histories*, pp. 272–288.

19 Michael Billington, *Guardian*, 15 July 1977, 16 April 1978; Homer D. Swander, 'The Rediscovery of *Henry VI*', *SQ*, 29 (1978), 146–63.

20 Russell Jackson, *SQ*, 52 (2001), 383; Joyce McMillan, *Scotsman*, 20 December 2000.

21 Michael Billington, *Guardian*, 16 December 2000; Russell Jackson, *SQ*, 52 (2001), 285–6; Michael Dobson, *SS*, 55 (2002), 288–9.

22 Joyce McMillan, *Scotsman*, 20 December 2000; Nicholas de Jongh, *Evening Standard*, 14 December 2000.

23 Joyce McMillan, *Scotsman*, 20 December 2000; Michael Dobson, *SS*, 55 (2002), 288. Oyelowo and Howard presented the King as a figure of great dignity and moral stature, as 'the only person who understands the hollowness of power' (*Guardian*, 16 December 2000), Warner as a Dostoyevskyan holy innocent, Fiennes as deeply spiritual.

24 On the doubling of Joan and Margaret in Michael Boyd's production, see the interview with Fiona Bell, *Players 6*, pp. 164–5, 171–5.

25 *First Part*, ed. Cairncross, pp. xlvi–vii. Cf. Saccio, *Shakespeare's English Kings*, pp. 92–3, 104–13; and Dominique Goy-Blanquet, *Shakespeare's Early History Plays*, p. 57.

26 Cf. Rackin, *Stages of History*, p. 153, on this passage.

27 Bullough, *Narrative and Dramatic Sources*, III. 41; Jackson, 'Topical Ideology', pp. 49–53.

28 1.5.12; 2.2.28; 3.2.38–9, 45; 3.3.78 (English); 1.6.4–5, 29; 3.2.18; 3.3.16, 49 (French); Bullough, *Narrative and Dramatic Sources*, III. 75–7.

29 See Howard and Rackin, pp. 44–5; and Jackson, 'Topical Ideology', pp. 56–65. In the 2000 and 2006 productions, three silent female spirits accompany Joan throughout the play, abandoning her here.

30 Bullough, *Narrative and Dramatic Sources*, III, 102; Howard and Rackin, *Engendering a Nation*, p. 71.

31 Bullough, *Narrative and Dramatic Sources*, III. 105.

32 Ibid., 106.

33 Howard and Rackin, *Engendering a Nation*, pp. 73–4, 82; Penny Downie, in *Players 3*, pp. 115, 126, 139.

34 Bullough, *Narrative and Dramatic Sources*, III.111; cf. Goy-Blanquet, *Shakespeare's Early History Plays*, pp. 34, 77–8.

35 4.1.71–5. On 'popular protest' against Suffolk's influence, see Patterson, *Popular Voice*, pp. 47–8; and Jones, *Origins*, pp. 167–9.

36 Kemp was a member of Strange's Men between 1590 and 1594. If the initial performances of the play in 1591–2 were by the rival company Pembroke's Men, then the part of Cade was played by Kemp only after the formation of the Chamberlain's Men in 1594. See Gurr, *The Shakespearian Playing Companies*, pp. 261–77.

37 Bullough, *Narrative and Dramatic Sources*, III.113–16. Cf, Brockbank, 'Frame of Disorder', pp. 87–9; and Goy-Blanquet, *Shakespeare's Early History Plays*, pp. 69–72.

38 See Cartelli, 'Jack Cade in the Garden', pp. 52–8; and Patterson, *Popular Voice*, pp. 46–51.

39 4.7.1–14. On Cade as emblem of disorder, see Jones, *Origins*, pp. 169–73.

40 See Cartelli, 'Jack Cade in the Garden', pp. 54–9, 62–5; and Rackin, *Stages of History*, pp. 208–11. In the chronicles, Lord Saye is a less admirable figure, a supporter of Suffolk: see Saccio, *Shakespeare's English Kings*, pp. 123–4.

41 See Hattaway's introduction, *Third Part*, pp. 14–15; and Marlowe, *Tamburlaine, Part One*, 2.7.18–29.

42 *Third Part*, ed. Hattaway, p. 14.

43 See *The Prince*, chapters IX and XVII.

4 Determined to prove a villain: *Richard III*

1 *3 Henry VI*, 3.2 182–5; *Richard III*, 1.1.28, 30. Olivier adds an even longer passage (forty-odd lines) from *3 Henry VI* to Richard's first soliloquy.

2 *Richard III*, 1.1.1, 7, 14. See McKellen, *William Shakespeare's Richard III, A Screenplay*.

3 *Richard III*, 1.4. 52, 63–4; McKellen, *Richard III, a Screenplay*, p. 17. Olivier retains these powerful lines, but cuts the extended dialogue between Clarence and the murderers, where guilt and conscience are again central issues.

4 Editor's introduction, *Richard III*, ed. Jowett, p. 3; Jones, *Origins*, p. 206. On the date of *Richard III*, see Stanley Wells and Gary Taylor, *William Shakespeare: A Textual Companion*, p. 115.

5 Colley Cibber, *The Tragical History of Richard III*, in *Five Restoration Adaptations of Shakespeare*, ed. Christopher Spencer, 3.1.164, 174–8, p. 308.

6 Ibid., 5.9.23–6, p. 343.

7 On the Sher/Alexander production, see R. Chris Hassel's 'Context and Charisma: the Sher/Alexander *Richard III* and its Reviewers', *SQ*, 36 (1985), 630–43; and Antony Sher, *The Year of the King*.

8 See McKellen, *Richard III, a Screenplay*, pp. 188, 206–7; Hassel, 'Context and Charisma', p. 637; and Roger Warren's review in *SQ*, 36 (1985), 82–3.

9 Anton Lesser, in *Players 3*, p. 141.

10 See Bullough, *Narrative and Dramatic Sources*, III.224–8; and *King Richard III*, ed. Hammond, pp. 74–80. Quotations from More's *History*, except as noted, are from *The History of King Richard III*, ed. Sylvester.

11 *Richard III*, 1.1.19–20; *History*, ed. Sylvester, pp. 6, 8; cf. Bullough, *Narrative and Dramatic Sources*, III.253. I have substituted Hall's 'familier' for More's 'coumpinable' (presumably 'companionable').

12 Cf. More, *History*, p. 76.

13 Ibid., p. 81.

14 More, *Utopia*, trans. Robinson, pp. 39–40, 49; cf. More, *History*, p. 81.

15 Introduction, More, *History*, pp. xciii–viii, esp. p. xcvii.

16 McKellen, *Richard III, a Screenplay*, p. 13.

17 More, *History*, p. 46.

18 Cf. ibid., p. 52.

19 *3 Henry VI*, 3.2.185, 192; *Richard III*, 1.2.221–2.

20 *History*, pp. 8–9. Recent historians tend to acquit Richard of the charge of plotting Clarence's death: see Saccio, *Shakespeare's English Kings*, pp. 167–9.

21 See Rossiter, *Angel with Horns*, pp. 16–17, 19.

22 Ibid., p. 15.

23 See Bernard Spivack, *Shakespeare and the Allegory of Evil*, p. 58; and Weimann, 'Performance', pp. 73–4, 80.

24 On Clarence's dream, see Jones, *Origins*, pp. 206–11.

25 *Richard III*, 1.4.98–105; *Macbeth*, 1.7.7–8. I have followed the Folio and most editions here in the speech prefixes.

26 McKellen, *Richard III, a Screenplay*, p. 74.

27 See Weimann, 'Performance', pp. 76–7; and Howard and Rackin, *Engendering a Nation*, pp. 110–12.

28 *3 Henry VI*, 3.2.159–62; 5.6.31; *Richard III*, 1.1.19–20.

29 *Paradise Lost*, IV.110; *Richard III*, 1.1.30.

30 Bacon, *Essays*, ed. Pitcher, p. 191. The passage in Bacon is discussed in Berry, *Patterns of Decay*, p. 70; and in Marjorie Garber, 'Descanting on Deformity: Richard III and the Shape of History', in Smith, *Histories*, pp. 41–66.

31 Reviews by Michael Billington, Michael Ratcliffe, and Michael Coveney, quoted in Hassel, 'Context and Charisma', pp. 631–2. Sher describes his researches into disability and prosthetics in *The Year of the King*.

32 'September 1, 1939', 21–2, in W. H. Auden, *Selected Poems*; Sigmund Freud, 'Some Character-types met with in psychoanalytic work', in *On Creativity and the Unconscious*, p. 89.

33 'Interview with Ian McKellen', http://www.r3.org/mckellen/film/mckel1.html.

34 See Jones, *Origins*, pp. 196–206; and Berry, *Patterns of Decay*, pp. 82–3, 88–92.

35 Penny Downie, in *Players 3*, pp. 135–7; Holland, *English Shakespeares*, pp. 116–17; Roger Warren, in *SQ*, 36 (1985), 83. Memorable Margarets include Peggy Ashcroft (1963), Patricia Routledge (1984), Penny Downie (1988), and Cherry Morris (1992).

36 *Macbeth*, 5.3.27; Tillyard, *History Plays*, pp. 205, 208, 212.

37 *Players 3*, p. 137.

38 Stephen Pimlott's 1995 RSC production, with David Troughton as Richard, makes Richard's relationship with his mother the key to its interpretation: see Holland, *English Shakespeares*, p. 241.

39 Bullough, *Narrative and Dramatic Sources*, III. 286–7. Recent productions tend to feature a strong and resolute Elizabeth: see Holland, *English Shakespeares*, p. 117; and Hassel, 'Context and Charisma', pp. 635–6.

40 Jones, *Origins*, pp. 220–27.
41 Tillyard, *History Plays*, p. 206.
42 Jones, *Origins*, p. 204; Rackin, *Stages of History*, pp. 63, 103.
43 For the comparison with *Macbeth*, see Berry, *Patterns of Decay*, p. 100; and Rabkin, *Meaning*, pp. 84, 101–2.

5 Gain, be my lord: *King John*

1 Arthur Colby Sprague, *Shakespeare's Histories: Plays for the Stage*, p. 4; Eugene Waith, '*King John* and the Drama of History', *SQ*, 29 (1978), 203–9.
2 Jones, *Origins*, pp. 233–5; cf. Waith, '*King John* and the Drama', p. 199.
3 See reviews of the 1988–9 production by Michael Coveney, *Financial Times*, 17 May 1988; Irving Wardle, *Times*, 3 May 1989; and Michael Billington, *Guardian*, 15 May 1988; reviews of the 2001 production by Michael Billington, *Guardian*, 30 March 2001; Benedict Nightingale, *Times*, 30 March 2001; and Paul Taylor, *Independent*, 31 March 2001; and reviews of the 2006 production by Dominic Cavendish, *Telegraph*, 7 August 2006; and Sam Marlowe, *Times*, 5 August 2006.
4 *Troublesome Raigne*, 1185–8, 1196–7, in Bullough, *Narrative and Dramatic Sources*, IV.151. Subsequently cited in text as Bullough.
5 Rackin, *Stages of History*, pp. 52, 184. For further discussion, see Guy Hamel, '*King John* and *The Troublesome Raigne*: A Reexamination', in Curren-Aquino, *King John: New Perspectives*, pp. 55–8; Virginia M. Vaughan, '*King John*: A Study in Subversion and Containment', ibid., pp. 73–4; and Sigurd Burckhardt, '*King John*: The Ordering of this Present Time', *ELH*, 33 (1966), 149–53.
6 Tillyard, *History Plays*, pp. 219, 225.
7 Rackin, *Stages of History*, p. 66.
8 For further discussion, see *King John*, ed. Braunmuller, pp. 4–12; Bullough, *Narrative and Dramatic Sources*, IV.5–22; and McMillin and MacLean, *The Queen's Men*, pp. 162–5.
9 On the character and dramatic function of the Bastard, see Jones, *Origins*, pp. 246–52; Weimann, 'Mingling', pp. 109–33; and David Womersley, 'The Politics of Shakespeare's *King John*', *Review of English Studies*, 40 (1989), 502–15.
10 I follow Braunmuller in the Oxford edition in assigning these speeches to an unnamed Citizen, as in the equivalent scene in *The Troublesome Raigne*. Other editions assign these speeches to Hubert: see *King John*, ed. R. L. Smallwood (Harmondsworth: Penguin, 1974).
11 *Players 6*, p. 32. Though Shakespeare generally follows *Troublesome Raigne* in this scene, there is no equivalent of this speech in that play.
12 See Rackin, *Stages of History*, pp. 177–82.
13 Michael Billington, *Guardian*, 30 March 2001; Paul Taylor, *Independent*, 31 March 2001; *Players 6*, p. 29.
14 Jones, *Origins*, pp. 251–2; Weimann, 'Mingling', pp. 116–18.

15 Benedict Nightingale, *Times*, 30 March 2001; Michael Billington, *Guardian*, 30 March 2001.

16 See Braunmuller's note to 3.1.173–9, *King John*, p. 179.

17 Rackin, *Stages of History*, pp. 181–2; Burckhardt, '*King John*', pp. 139–45.

18 John Milton, *The Tenure of Kings and Magistrates, Major Works*, ed. Orgel and Goldberg, p. 274. On the offer of 'corrupting gold' to the 'discontented gentleman' Tyrrell and his ready acceptance, see *Richard III*, 4.2.33–9, 66–83.

19 *Richard III*, 4.2.17. The two scenes also differ in the way Buckingham refuses to take up Richard's hints: 'Cousin, thou wert not wont to be so dull' (4.11.16).

20 *The Prince*, trans. Bull, chapter XIX, pp. 57, 59.

21 *Troublesome Raigne*, 1391–4, Bullough, *Narrative and Dramatic Sources*, IV.110. See Burckhardt, '*King John*', pp. 135–9; and Hamel, '*King John*', pp. 45–7.

22 *Players 6*, p. 13. The scene in *King John* is only 10 lines long, where the equivalent scene in *Troublesome Raigne* has 26 lines – with an 'I dye, I dye' perilously close to *Pyramus and Thisbe*.

23 *Players 6*, p. 29.

24 Bullough, *Narrative and Dramatic Sources*, IV.7, 28.

25 *Troublesome Raigne*, 85–9, 254–6, Bullough, *Narrative and Dramatic Sources*, IV.75, 79.

26 Jo Stone-Ewings, in *Players 6*, p. 58; cf. Jones, *Origins*, pp. 249–51; and Weimann, 'Mingling', pp. 118–22.

27 Weimann, 'Mingling', pp. 114–16.

28 See Jones, *Origins*, p. 250; Womersley, 'The Politics', p. 507; and Weimann, 'Mingling', pp. 117, 121–4.

29 The speech is not technically a soliloquy, since it is likely that Hubert remains on stage during this speech, bearing the body of Arthur (though the Folio has no stage directions).

30 Burckhardt, '*King John*', pp. 146–7.

31 *Players 6*, pp. 65–6.

32 Womersley, 'The Politics', p. 514; cf. Burckhardt, '*King John*', pp. 150, 152.

33 *Players 6*, p. 24.

34 Shaughnessy, *Representing Shakespeare*, p. 174.

6 The death of kings: *Richard II*

1 Tillyard, *History Plays*, p. 67; Kantorowicz, *The King's Two Bodies*, p. 34.

2 Ribner, *English History Play*, p. 129.

3 See *King Richard II*, ed. Gurr, p. 20; and Richard D. Altick, 'Symphonic Imagery in *Richard II*', in Brooke, *Shakespeare: Richard II*, pp. 101–30.

4 Marlowe, *Edward the Second*, 1.1.5, ed. Forker.

5 *Players 6*, p. 88; Altick, 'Symphonic Imagery', pp. 103–7.

6 Wootton, ed., *Divine Right and Democracy*, pp. 98, 104.

7 'An Horatian Ode upon Cromwell's Return from Ireland', 45–8, in Marvell, *Poems*, ed. Smith; Rackin, *Stages of History*, pp. 40–6.

8 Kantorowicz, *The King's Two Bodies*, pp. 7, 13.

9 Ibid., p. 21.

10 Ibid., pp. 35–6.

11 Worden, 'Which Play', p. 24; Evelyn Albright, 'Shakespeare's *Richard II* and the Essex Conspiracy', *PMLA*, 42 (1927), 691.

12 Clare, '*Art made tongue-tied*', pp. 83–6; cf. Worden, 'Which Play', pp. 22–4; and Albright, 'Shakespeare's *Richard II*', pp. 699–706.

13 Cyndia Susan Clegg, '*Richard II* and Elizabethan Press Censorship', *SQ*, 48 (1997), 437–43.

14 Janet Clare ('*Art made tongue-tied*', pp. 68–72) argues for censorship of performances by the Master of the Revels. Clegg ('*Richard II*', pp. 436–46) argues for press censorship on political grounds, while agreeing with Gurr's Cambridge edition that the play may have been performed uncut during Queen Elizabeth's lifetime. Gurr concedes that 'there is no clear indication whether the deposition scene stayed in the performed text when it was deleted from the printed versions' (p. 9).

15 W. B. Yeats, 'At Stratford-on-Avon', *Essays and Introductions*, pp. 105–6.

16 See Margaret Shewring, *Shakespeare in Performance: King Richard II*, pp. 133–4. Cf. *2 Henry IV*, 3.1.4–8.

17 *Players 6*, pp. 102–3. In this production, these lines were a motif repeated several times in the play, framing the action by being spoken by one monarch at the beginning and another at the end.

18 *The Prince*, XVII, p. 53.

19 On *Woodstock*, see Rossiter, *Angel with Horns*, pp. 29–32; and *Woodstock*, ed. Rossiter, esp. 4.1.146–7.

20 Saccio, *Shakespeare's English Kings*, pp. 20, 24; cf. Bullough, *Narrative and Dramatic Sources*, III.359–61.

21 *Woodstock*, 2.2.40–2; see Clare, '*Art made tongue-tied*', pp. 64–7.

22 Marie Axton, *The Queen's Two Bodies: Drama and the Elizabethan Succession*, pp. 97–9.

23 According to David Troughton, 'many of the audience will have no idea who this murdered man they keep talking about, this Gloucester, is. What they see are two men desperate to fight each other, and Richard desperate to avoid that' (*Players 6*, p. 105). Cf. Wilders, *The Lost Garden*, p. 107.

24 *Players 6*, p. 92; Peter Holland, *English Shakespeares*, pp. 249–50.

25 On West's performance, see Russell Jackson, *SQ*, 51 (2000), 114; and Nigel Saul, *TLS*, 12 May 2000. On Shaw's, see Michael Billington, *Guardian*, 5 June 1995; and Holland, *English Shakespeares*, pp. 249–50.

26 See Rabkin, *Understanding*, pp. 87–8; and Wilders, *The Lost Garden*, p. 109.

27 Kantorowicz, *The King's Two Bodies*, p. 32; cf. Altick, 'Symphonic Imagery', p. 106.

28 Bullough, *Narrative and Dramatic Sources*, III.408.

29 'Shakespeare's English Kings' (1889), in Brooke, *Shakespeare: Richard II*, p. 58.

30 Altick, 'Symphonic Imagery', pp. 110–12.

31 Bullough, *Narrative and Dramatic Sources*, III.371, 377; Saccio, *Shakespeare's English Kings*, p. 27.

32 1.3.200–1; 2.1.63–4; 3.2.81; 4.1.235. See Altick, 'Symphonic Imagery', pp. 116–17.

33 Shewring, *Shakespeare in Performance*, p. 123; *SQ*, 51 (2000), 116.

34 See the commentaries on this soliloquy in Frank Kermode, *Shakespeare's Language*, pp. 43–5; and in Winifred Nowottny, *The Language Poets Use*, pp. 88–9.

7 Lord of Misrule: *1* and *2 Henry IV*

1 Sidney, *Selected Writings*, p. 141.

2 Bullough, *Narrative and Dramatic Sources*, IV.181.

3 Tillyard, *History Plays*, p. 264; Wilson, *Fortunes of Falstaff*, p. 4.

4 Marlowe, *Complete Plays*, p. 183.

5 Jenkins in Hunter, *Henry IV Parts 1 and 2*, p. 165.

6 *Famous Victories*, 455–6, 581, in Bullough, *Narrative and Dramatic Sources*, IV.312, 316. See McMillin and MacLean, *The Queen's Men*, pp. 132–3.

7 Hunter, *Henry IV Parts 1 and 2*, p. 16: McMillin, *Performance*, p. 2; *1 Henry IV*, ed. Kastan, p. 80.

8 Schlegel (1809) and Guthrie (1747), quoted in New Variorum Edition, ed. Hemingway, pp. 404, 418. Subsequent page references in text.

9 Hunter, *Henry IV Parts 1 and 2*, pp. 59–60, 65, 74.

10 Goddard, *Meaning*, pp. 172, 179.

11 Bloom, *Shakespeare: The Invention of the Human*, pp. 288, 289.

12 Wilson, *Fortunes of Falstaff*, pp. 20, 22.

13 Barber, *Shakespeare's Festive Art*, pp. 23–5.

14 *1 Henry IV*, 2.4.138, 434–5, 492; 3.3.170; *2 Henry IV*, 2.3.61–2. Cf. Wilson, *Fortunes of Falstaff*, pp. 27–31.

15 See François Laroque, 'Shakespeare's "Battle of Carnival and Lent"', in Knowles, ed., *Shakespeare and Carnival*, pp. 87–8; and Michael Bristol, *Carnival and Theater*, pp. 204–7.

16 Greenblatt, *Shakespearean Negotiations*, pp. 42, 43; Barber, *Shakespeare's Festive Art*, p. 199.

17 Tillyard, *History Plays*, pp. 21, 320; Greenblatt, *Shakespearean Negotiations*, p. 65.

18 Bristol, *Carnival and Theater*, pp. 22, 200; Holderness, p. 138; Rackin, p. 203.

19 Weimann, *Shakespeare and the Popular Tradition*, p. 244; cf. Rackin, *Stages of History*, pp. 206–7.

20 David Scott Kastan, '"The King Hath Many Marching in His Coats"', in Kamps, *Shakespeare Left and Right*, p. 248.

21 McMillin, *Performance*, pp. 77, 83.

22 Welles, *Chimes at Midnight*, ed. Bridget Gellert Lyons, pp. 5–8, 261; subsequent page references in text; McMillin, *Performance*, pp. 93, 97–8.

23 McMillin, *Performance*, pp. 109, 114.

24 Desmond Barrit, in *Players 6*, p. 133.

25 Russell Jackson, *SQ*, 52 (2001), 118–19; Charles Spencer, *Telegraph*, 23 February 2001.

26 *Players 6*, p. 129.

27 Paul Taylor, *Independent*, 5 May 2005; Michael Billington, *Guardian*, 5 May 2005.

28 *Players 6*, p. 135.

29 See Saccio, *Shakespeare's English Kings*, pp. 39–43.

30 Annibale Romei, *The Courtiers Academie*, quoted in Council, *When Honour's at the Stake*, p. 40.

31 Bullough, *Narrative and Dramatic Sources*, IV.258–9: Greenblatt, *Shakespearean Negotiations*, pp. 47–8.

32 See Welles, *Chimes at Midnight*, pp. 13–15.

33 *1 Henry IV*, ed. Bevington, p. 274; Wilson, p. 85

34 Tillyard, p. 267; cf. Council, pp. 38–9; and Wilson, *Fortunes of Falstaff*, pp. 90–3.

35 Barrit in *Players 6*, pp. 137–8.

36 On the role of the Lord Chief Justice, see Wilson, *Fortunes of Falstaff*, pp. 98–103.

37 Sonnet 60, 12; see L. C. Knights, 'Time's Subjects: *2 Henry IV*', in Hunter, *Henry IV Parts 1 and 2*, pp. 174–86.

38 See Bullough, *Narrative and Dramatic Sources*, IV.227; and, for *Famous Victories*, ibid., IV.317–18.

39 *Players 6*, pp. 114–16.

40 *Famous Victories* makes a similar point more crudely, having the Prince say 'Howsoever you came by it, I know not, / But now I have it from you, and from you, I will keepe it' (Bullough, *Narrative and Dramatic Sources*, IV.319).

8 Band of brothers: *Henry V*

1 William Empson, *Some Versions of Pastoral*, p. 26; cf. Anne Barton, 'The king disguised: Shakespeare's *Henry V* and the comical history', *Essays, Mainly Shakespearean*, p. 217.

2 *Henry V*, ed. Taylor, pp. 9–12.

3 Hazlitt (1817), Masefield (1911), and Van Doren (1939), in Quinn, ed., *Shakespeare: Henry V*, pp. 36–7, 61, 116, 119.

4 Tillyard, *History Plays*, pp. 305, 306, 308.

5 Barton, *Essays, Mainly Shakespearean*, pp. 217–18; *Henry V*, ed. Taylor, p. 55.

6 Gerald Gould, 'A New Reading of Henry V', in Quinn, *Shakespeare: Henry V*, pp. 83, 91; Goddard, *Meaning*, pp. 216, 268.

7 Gould, 'New Reading', p. 70; Goddard, *Meaning*, p. 218.

8 Greenblatt, *Shakespearean Negotiations*, 57–8, 63.

9 Dollimore and Sinfield, 'History and ideology', *Alternative Shakespeares*, pp. 217–18, 222; 2.Cho.19–22; 4.3.17–18, 60.

10 Holderness, *Shakespeare Recycled*, pp. 22, 178, 185. Subsequent page references in text.

11 Patterson, *Popular Voice*, pp. 72–3, 87, 90. Subsequent page references in text.

12 Rabkin, *Meaning*, pp. 34, 48, 55, 60.

13 Shapiro, *Year in the Life*, pp. 104–5.

14 Holderness, *Shakespeare Recycled*, p. 184; Peter S. Donaldson, 'Taking on Shakespeare: Kenneth Branagh's *Henry V*', *SQ*, 42 (1991), 60, 61. On the popularity of Olivier's film in 1944–5, see Smith, *Production*, pp. 53–4.

15 *SQ*, 52 (2001), 121–2.

16 Michael Billington, *Guardian*, 14 May 2003; National Theatre Platform Papers, 20 June 2003 (www.nationaltheatre.org.uk).

17 Michael Dobson, *SS*, 57 (2004), 279, 281.

18 NT Platform Papers, p. 3.

19 The death of Bardolph on stage first occurred in the RSC production of 1984, directed by Adrian Noble, with Branagh as King Harry. Hytner's production has the King shoot Bardolph with a pistol, showing no regrets.

20 Branagh, *Henry V*, *A screen adaptation*, p. 12.

21 In Branagh's film, Robert Stephens as Pistol and Ian Holm as Fluellen, like Paul Scofield, are notable Shakespearean tragic actors: all three were memorable Lears.

22 Branagh, *Henry V, a Screen Adaptation*, p. 12.

23 Ibid., p. 59.

24 Alan Howard in Terry Hands's 1975 production also showed 'tears of relief' at the end of this scene (Beauman, *RSC Production of Henry V*, pp. 23, 151).

25 Several critics object to Branagh's emphasis on the King's reaction here as illegitimately 'tilting the movie away from' involvement with Henry's victims and towards admiration of the King: see Chris Fitter, 'A Tale of Two Branaghs', pp. 266, 268; and, an even more hostile account, Curtis Breight, 'Branagh and the Prince', pp. 95–111.

26 Rabkin is one of many critics who have found the King's argument here unconvincing (*Meaning*, p. 51).

27 See the account of the critical reception of Olivier's film in Anthony Davies, 'The Shakespeare films of Laurence Olivier', *The Cambridge Companion to Shakespeare on Film*, ed. Jackson, pp. 163–82.

28 Beauman, *The RSC Henry V*, p. 62.

29 Goddard, *Meaning*, p. 217; Barton, *Essays, Mainly Shakespearean*, p. 215. Cf. Shapiro, *Year in the Life*, pp. 98–100.

30 See Barton, *Essays, Mainly Shakespearean*, pp. 212–15; and Patterson, *Popular Voice*, pp. 88–91.

31 *First Quarto*, ed. Gurr, pp. 5, 9–11, 22. Cf. Shapiro, *Year in the Life*, p. 103; Patterson, *Popular Voice*, pp. 72–77; and *Henry V*, ed. Taylor, pp. 20–6.

32 Beauman, *The RSC Henry V*, p. 15.

33 Shapiro, *Year in the Life*, pp. 91–2, 101–3; Patterson, *Popular Voice*, pp. 83, 86.

34 See Patterson, *Popular Voice*, pp. 90–1. Like other passages that raise awkward questions, it has been excised from Q1.

9 Epilogue: *Henry VIII*

1 The play is not discussed by Tillyard, Campbell, Holderness, Rabkin, Rossiter, Greenblatt, or Smith, *Histories*, and is treated dismissively in brief accounts by Ornstein and Ribner.

2 See John D. Cox, '*Henry VIII* and the Masque', *ELH*, 45 (1980), 390–409; Howard Felperin, *Shakespearean Romance*; and *King Henry VIII*, ed. Foakes, pp. xliii–xlv, lxi–ii.

3 Johnson, *Works*, VIII. 657; Hugh Richmond, *Shakespeare in Performance: King Henry VIII*, p. 56.

4 Richmond, *Shakespeare in Performance*, pp. 61–2, 65–6; *King Henry VIII*, ed. McMullan, pp. 33–7.

5 Johnson, *Works*, VIII, 657; Richmond, *Shakespeare in Performance*, pp. 43, 51–2.

6 Richmond, *Shakespeare in Performance*, pp. 98–9.

7 *King Henry VIII*, ed. McMullan, pp. 44–8; Richmond, *Shakespeare in Performance*, p. 83; *Sunday Times*, 24 July 1949.

8 Shaughnessy, *Representing Shakespeare*, p. 159; Richmond, *Shakespeare in Performance*, pp. 121, 129, 132.

9 Shaughnessy, *Representing Shakespeare*, pp. 155, 160; Richmond, *Shakespeare in Performance*, pp, 122, 127.

10 *King Henry VIII*, ed. McMullan, p. 54; *Players 4*, pp. 119, 123.

11 *Players 4*, pp. 117, 120; Irving Wardle, *Sunday Telegraph*, 1 December 1996; Michael Billington, *Guardian*, 29 November 1996.

12 The lines are derived from Cavendish's *Life of Wolsey* and Holinshed: see *King Henry VIII*, ed. McMullan, p. 362.

13 Quoted in Peter Rudnytsky, '*Henry VIII* and the Deconstruction of History', in Alexander, *Shakespeare and Politics*, p. 58. Cf. Barton, *Essays, Mainly Shakespearean*, pp. 184–5.

14 Rudnytsky, '*Henry VIII* and the Deconstruction', pp. 47–9; Bliss, 'The Wheel of Fortune and the Maiden Phoenix', p. 5. Cf. Anderson, *Biographical Truth*, pp. 126–40.

15 Bullough, *Narrative and Dramatic Sources*, IV.461; cf. Bliss, 'Wheel of Fortune', pp. 4–6.

16 Cf. *Winter's Tale*, 3.2.27–53; and *King Henry VIII*, ed. McMullan, pp. 125–9.

17 Kermode, 'What Is Shakespeare's *Henry VIII* About?', p. 54; *King Henry VIII*, ed. Foakes, pp. lii, lxi.

18 Cox, '*Henry VIII* and the Masque', pp. 395–6; cf. *King Henry VIII*, ed. Foakes, pp. lix–lx.

19 Cox, '*Henry VIII* and the Masque', p. 395; *Richard III*, 5.5.33–4, 37.

20 Felperin, *Shakespearean Romance*, pp. 197, 207, 209; reviews in *Daily Telegraph*, 28 November 1996; and *Time Out*, 4 December 1996.

21 See Bullough, *Narrative and Dramatic Sources*, IV.485–9. If 5.1 is by Shakespeare and 5.2 by Fletcher, then the collaboration must have been unusually close, since both scenes follow Foxe's account in detail.

22 Samuel Rowley, *When you see me, you know me*, ed. F. P. Wilson (Oxford: Malone Society, 1952), lines 523, 2568–9.

23 On Rowley's Henry VIII, see Barton, *Essays*, pp. 184, 236–7.

24 Bliss, 'Wheel of Fortune', pp. 14–15; cf. Rudnytsky, '*Henry VIII* and the Deconstruction', p. 56.

25 Cf. Foxe in Bullough, *Narrative and Dramatic Sources*, IV.487; and *King Henry VIII*, ed. McMullan, p. 399.

26 3.1.93, 98–101; *Measure for Measure*, 2.2.118–23.

Bibliography

Plays by Shakespeare are quoted from the following editions, except where noted:

King Henry IV, Part 1, ed. David Bevington (Oxford Shakespeare, 1987).
King Henry IV, Part 2, ed. A. R. Humphreys (Arden Shakespeare 2, 1966).
Henry V, ed. T. W. Craik (Arden Shakespeare 3, 1995).
The First Part of King Henry VI, ed. Andrew Cairncross (Arden Shakespeare 2, 1962).
Henry VI, Part Two, ed. Roger Warren (Oxford Shakespeare, 2003).
The Third Part of King Henry VI, ed. Michael Hattaway (New Cambridge Shakespeare, 1993).
King Henry VIII, ed. Gordon McMullan (Arden Shakespeare 3, 2000).
Julius Caesar, ed. David Daniell (Arden Shakespeare 3, 1998).
The Life and Death of King John, ed. A. R. Braunmuller (Oxford Shakespeare, 1989).
King Richard II, ed. Andrew Gurr (New Cambridge Shakespeare, 1984).
The Tragedy of King Richard III, ed. John Jowett (Oxford Shakespeare, 2000).

All other Shakespeare plays and poems are quoted from the Arden editions. All books and essays cited in the notes to this volume are listed here in full, as well as a selection of works that may be found useful for further study.

Albright, Evelyn, 'Shakespeare's *Richard II* and the Essex Conspiracy', *PMLA*, 42 (1927), 686–720.
Alexander, Catherine M. S., ed., *Shakespeare and Politics* (Cambridge: Cambridge University Press, 2004).
Alternative Shakespeares, ed. John Drakakis (London and New York: Routledge, 1985).
Altick, Richard, 'Symphonic Imagery in *Richard II*', in Brooke, *Shakespeare: Richard II*, pp. 101–30.
Anderson, Judith, *Biographical Truth: The Representation of Historical Persons in Tudor-Stuart Writing* (New Haven and London: Yale University Press, 1984).
Aristotle, *Poetics*, in *Basic Works*, ed. Richard McKeon (New York: Random House, 1968).

Ashcroft, Peggy, 'Margaret of Anjou', *Shakespeare Jahrbuch (West)*, 103 (1973), 7–9.

Auden, W. H., *Selected Poems*, ed. Edward Mendelson (New York: Vintage Books, 1979).

Axton, Marie, *The Queen's Two Bodies: Drama and the Elizabethan Succession* (London: Royal Historical Society, 1977).

Bacon, Francis, *The Essays*, ed. John Pitcher (Harmondsworth: Penguin, 1985).

Baker, David J., '"Wildehirisshman": Colonialist Representation in Shakespeare's *Henry V*', *ELR* , 22 (1992), 37–61.

Barber, C. L., *Shakespeare's Festive Art* (Princeton: Princeton University Press, 1972).

Barton, Anne, *Essays, Mainly Shakespearean* (Cambridge: Cambridge University Press, 1994).

Barton, John and Peter Hall, *The Wars of the Roses* (London: British Broadcasting Corporation, 1970).

Bate, Jonathan, ed., *The Romantics on Shakespeare* (Harmondsworth: Penguin, 1992).

Beauman, Sally, *The Royal Shakespeare Company's Production of **Henry V*** (Oxford: Pergamon Press, 1976).

Berry, Edward, *Patterns of Decay: Shakespeare's Early Histories* (Charlottesville: University of Virginia Press, 1975).

Bliss, Lee, 'The Wheel of Fortune and the Maiden Phoenix of Shakespeare's *King Henry the Eighth*', *ELH* 42 (1975), 1–25.

Bloom, Harold, *Shakespeare: The Invention of the Human* (London: Fourth Estate, 1999).

Bogdanov, Michael and Michael Pennington, *The English Shakespeare Company* (London: Nick Hern Books, 1990).

Bradley, A. C., 'The Rejection of Falstaff' (1909), in Hunter, *Shakespeare: King Henry IV Parts 1 and 2*, pp. 56–78.

Bradshaw, Graham, *Misrepresentations: Shakespeare and the Materialists* (Ithaca, N. Y., and London: Cornell University Press, 1993).

Branagh, Kenneth, *Henry V, a Screen Adaptation* (London: Chatto & Windus, 1989).

Braunmuller, A. R., '*King John* and Historiography', *ELH*, 55 (1988), 309–32.

Breight, Curtis, 'Branagh and the Prince, or a "royal fellowship of death"', *Critical Quarterly*, 33 (1991), 95–111.

Bristol, Michael D., *Carnival and Theater: Plebeian Culture and the Structure of Authority in Renaissance England* (New York and London: Methuen, 1985).

Brockbank, J. P., 'The Frame of Disorder: *Henry VI*', in *Early Shakespeare*, ed. John Russell Brown and Bernard Harris (London: Edward Arnold, 1961), pp. 72–99.

Brooke, Nicholas, ed., *Shakespeare: Richard II* (London: Macmillan Casebooks, 1973).

Bullough, Geoffrey, *Narrative and Dramatic Sources of Shakespeare*, vols. III and
    IV (London: Routledge & Kegan Paul, 1960–2).
Burckhardt, Sigurd, '*King John:* The Ordering of this Present Time', *ELH*, 33
    (1966), 133–53.
Campbell, Lily B., *Shakespeare's "Histories": Mirrors of Elizabethan Policy* (San
    Marino, Calif.: Huntington Library, 1947).
Cartelli, Thomas, 'Jack Cade in the Garden: Class Consciousness and Class
    Conflict in *2 Henry VI*', in *Enclosure Acts*, ed. Richard Burt and John
    Michael Archer (Ithaca, N. Y.: Cornell University Press, 1994), pp. 48–67.
Cespedes, Frank V., '"We are one in fortunes": The Sense of History in *Henry
    VIII*', *ELR*, 10 (1980), 413–38.
Cibber, Colley, *The Tragical History of Richard III*, in *Five Restoration Adaptations
    of Shakespeare*, ed. Christopher Spencer (Urbana: University of Illinois
    Press, 1965).
Clare, Janet, '*Art made tongue-tied by authority*': *Elizabethan Dramatic Censorship*,
    2nd edn (Manchester: Manchester University Press, 1999).
Clegg, Cyndia Susan, '*Richard II* and Elizabethan Press Censorship'. *SQ*, 48
    (1997), 432–48.
Coleridge, Samuel Taylor, *Shakespeare Criticism*, ed. T. M. Raysor, 2 vols.
    (London: Everyman, 1960).
Council, Norman, *When Honour's at the Stake* (London: George Allen and
    Unwin, 1973).
Coursen, H. R., 'Filming Shakespeare's history: three films of *Richard III*', in
    Jackson, *Cambridge Companion to Shakespeare on Film*, pp. 99–116.
Cox, John D., '*Henry VIII* and the Masque', *ELH*, 45 (1980), 390–409.
Curren-Aquino, Deborah T., ed., *King John: New Perspectives* (London and
    Toronto: Associated University Presses, 1989).
Daniel, Samuel, *The Civile Wares betweene the Houses of Lancaster and Yorke*
    (London, 1609).
Davies, Anthony, 'The Shakespeare films of Laurence Olivier', in Jackson,
    Cambridge Companion to Shakespeare on Film, pp.163–82.
Dessen, Alan, 'Stagecraft and Imagery in Shakespeare's *Henry VI*', in Smith,
    Histories, pp. 272–88.
Dollimore, Jonathan, 'Introduction: Shakespeare, Cultural Materialism and the
    New Historicism', in *Political Shakespeare*, ed. Dollimore and Sinfield,
    pp. 2–17.
Dollimore, Jonathan, and Alan Sinfield, 'History and Ideology: The Instance of
    Henry V', in *Alternative Shakespeares*, ed. Drakakis, pp. 206–27.
Donaldson, Peter S., 'Taking on Shakespeare: Kenneth Branagh's *Henry V*', *SQ*,
    42 (1991), 60–71.
Dutton, Richard, and Jean E. Howard, *A Companion to Shakespeare's Works*,
    Vol. II: *The Histories* (Oxford: Blackwell, 2003).
Empson, William, *Some Versions of Pastoral* (New York: New Directions, 1960).
Felperin, Howard, *Shakespearean Romance* (Princeton: Princeton University
    Press, 1972).

Ferguson, Arthur B., *Clio Unbound: Perception of the social and cultural past in Renaissance England* (Durham: Duke University Press, 1979).

Fitter, Chris, 'A Tale of Two Branaghs: *Henry V*, Ideology, and the Mekong Agincourt', in Kamps, *Shakespeare Left and Right*, pp. 259 75.

Ford, John, *Perkin Warbeck*, ed. Donald K. Anderson (London: Edward Arnold, 1966).

Freud, Sigmund, *On Creativity and the Unconscious* (New York: Harper & Row, 1965).

Garber, Marjorie, 'Descanting on Deformity: Richard III and the Shape of History', in Smith, *Shakespeare's Histories*, pp. 42–66.

George, David, 'Plutarch, Insurrection, and Dearth in *Coriolanus*', in Alexander, *Shakespeare and Politics*, pp. 110–29.

Goddard, Harold, *The Meaning of Shakespeare* (Chicago: University of Chicago Press, 1951).

Gould, Gerald, 'A New Reading of *Henry V*', in Quinn, *Shakespeare: Henry V*, pp. 81–94.

Goy-Blanquet, Dominique, *Shakespeare's Early History Plays: From Chronicle to Stage* (Oxford: Oxford University Press, 2003).

Greenblatt, Stephen, *Shakespearean Negotiations* (Oxford: Clarendon Press, 1990).

Gurr, Andrew, *The Shakespearean Playing Companies* (Oxford: Clarendon Press, 1996).

    ed., *The First Quarto of King Henry V* (Cambridge: Cambridge University Press, 2000).

Hall, Edward, *The Union of the two noble and illustre families of Lancaster and Yorke* (London, 1548).

Hall, Edward, and Roger Warren, *Rose Rage* (London: Oberon Books, 2001).

Hamel, Guy, '*King John* and *The Troublesome Raigne*: A Reexamination', in Curren-Aquino, *King John: New Perspectives*, pp. 41–61.

Harbage, Alfred, *Annals of English Drama 975–1700*, rev. S. Schoenbaum (London: Methuen, 1964).

Hassel, R. Chris, 'Context and Charisma: The Sher/Alexander *Richard III* and its Reviewers', *SQ*, 36 (1985), 630–43.

Hazlitt, William, *Characters of Shakespeare's Plays* (London: Everyman, 1915).

Helgerson, Richard, 'Shakespeare and Contemporary Dramatists of History', in Dutton and Howard, *A Companion to Shakespeare's Works*, vol. ii: *The Histories*, pp. 26–47.

Henry V, ed. Gary Taylor (Oxford Shakespeare, 1984).

Heywood, Thomas, *An Apology for Actors* (London, 1612).

Hodgdon, Barbara, '*The Wars of the Roses*: Scholarship Speaks on the Stage', *Shakespeare Jahrbuch (West)*, 102 (1972), 170–84.

    The End Crowns All: Closure and Contradiction in Shakespeare's History (Princeton: Princeton University Press, 1991).

Holderness, Graham, *Shakespeare Recycled: The Making of Historical Drama* (London: Harvester, 1992).

ed., *Shakespeare's History Plays: Richard II to Henry V* (London: Macmillan New Casebooks, 1992).

Holinshed, Raphael, *The Historie of England* (London, 1587).

Holland, Peter, *English Shakespeares* (Cambridge: Cambridge University Press, 1997).

An Homily against Disobedience and Wilful Rebellion (1570), in *Sermons or Homilies, Appointed to be read in Churches* (London, 1986).

Howard, Jean E., 'The New Historicism in Literary Studies', *ELR*, 16 (1986), 13–43.

and Rackin, Phyllis., *Engendering a Nation* (London and New York: Routledge, 1997).

Hunter, G. K., ed., *Shakespeare: King Henry IV Parts 1 and 2* (London: Macmillan Casebooks, 1970).

Jackson, Gabrielle Bernhard, 'Topical Ideology: Witches, Amazons, and Shakespeare's Joan of Arc', *ELR*, 18 (1988), 40–65.

Jackson, Russell, ed., *The Cambridge Companion to Shakespeare on Film* (Cambridge: Cambridge University Press, 2000).

Jenkins, Harold, 'The Structural Problem in Shakespeare's *Henry IV*' (1956), in Hunter, *Shakespeare: King Henry IV Parts 1 and 2*, pp. 155–72.

Johnson, Samuel, *Johnson on Shakespeare*, ed. Arthur Sherbo, *Works*, VII and VIII (New Haven and London: Yale University Press, 1965).

Jones, Emrys, *The Origins of Shakespeare* (Oxford: Clarendon Press, 1977).

Kamps, Ivo, ed., *Shakespeare Left and Right* (New York and London: Routledge, 1991).

Kantorowicz, Ernst H., *The King's Two Bodies* (Princeton: Princeton University Press, 1957).

Kastan, David Scott, 'Proud Majesty Made a Subject: Shakespeare and the Spectacle of Rule', *SQ*, 37 (1986), 459–75.

'"The King Hath Many Marching in His Coats", or What Did You Do in the War, Daddy?', in Kamps, ed., *Shakespeare Left and Right*, pp. 241–58.

Kelly, Henry Ansgar, *Divine Providence in the England of Shakespeare's Histories* (Cambridge, Mass.: Harvard University Press, 1970).

Kermode, Frank, 'What is Shakespeare's *Henry VIII* About?', *Durham University Journal*, 9 (1948), 48–55.

Shakespeare's Language (Harmondsworth: Penguin, 2000).

Kewes, Paulina, 'The Elizabethan History Play: A True Genre?', in Dutton and Howard, *A Companion to Shakespeare's Works*, vol II: *The Histories*, pp. 170–93.

King Edward III, ed. Giorgio Melchiori (Cambridge: Cambridge University Press, 1998).

King Edward III, ed. Eric Sams (New Haven and London: Yale University Press, 1996).

King Henry IV, Part 1, ed. David Scott Kastan (Arden Shakespeare 3, 2000).

King Henry IV, Part 1, ed. S. B. Hemingway (Philadelphia and London: New Variorum Edition, 1936).

King Henry VI, Part 1, ed. Edward Burns (Arden Shakespeare 3, 2000).

King Henry VI, Part 1, ed. J. Dover Wilson (Cambridge: Cambridge University Press, 1952).

King Henry VIII, ed. R. A. Foakes (Arden Shakespeare 2, 1957).

King John, ed. R. L. Smallwood (Harmondsworth: Penguin, 1974).

King Richard II, ed. Charles R. Forker (Arden Shakespeare 3, 2002).

King Richard III, ed. Antony Hammond (Arden Shakespeare 2, 1981).

Knight, G. Wilson, *The Crown of Life* (London: Methuen, 1948).

Knights, L. C., 'Time's Subjects: *2 Henry IV*', in Hunter, *Shakespeare: King Henry IV Parts 1 and 2*, pp. 174–86.

Knowles, Ronald, *Shakespeare and Carnival: After Bakhtin* (Basingstoke: Macmillan, 1998).

Krieger, Leonard, *Ranke: The Meaning of History* (Chicago: University of Chicago Press, 1977).

Laroque, François, 'Shakespeare's "Battle of Carnival and Lent": The Falstaff Scenes Reconsidered', in Knowles, *Shakespeare and Carnival*, pp. 83–96.

Levin, Richard, *The Multiple Plot in Renaissance Drama* (Chicago and London: University of Chicago Press, 1971).

Levy, F. J., *Tudor Historical Thought* (San Marino, Calif.: Huntington Library, 1967).

Machiavelli, Niccolò, *The Prince*, trans. George Bull (Harmondsworth: Penguin, 1986).

McKellen, Ian, *William Shakespeare's Richard III, a Screenplay written by Ian McKellen and Richard Loncraine* (London: Doubleday, 1996), with annotations by McKellen.

McMillin, Scott, *Shakespeare in Performance: Henry IV, Part One* (Manchester: Manchester University Press, 1991.

McMillin, Scott, and MacLean, Sally-Beth, *The Queen's Men and their Plays* (Cambridge: Cambridge University Press, 1998).

Marlowe, Christopher, *Complete Plays*, ed. J. B. Steane (Harmondsworth: Penguin, 1971).

Edward the Second, ed. Charles R. Forker (Manchester: Revels Plays, 1994).

Marvell, Andrew, *Poems*, ed. Nigel Smith (London: Longman, 2003).

Miller, Arthur, *The Crucible* (Harmondsworth: Penguin, 1974).

The Crucible in History and Other Essays (London: Methuen, 1974).

Milton, John, *Major Works*, ed. Stephen Orgel and Jonathan Goldberg (Oxford: Oxford University Press, 2003).

Montrose, Louis, 'Renaissance Literary Studies and the Subject of History', *ELR*, 16 (1986), 5–12.

More, Thomas, *The History of King Richard III*, ed. Richard S. Sylvester (New Haven: Yale University Press, 1963).

Utopia, trans. Richard Robinson (London: Everyman, 1965).

Nashe, Thomas, *Works*, ed. R. B. McKerrow and F. P. Wilson, 5 vols. (Oxford: Basil Blackwell, 1966).

North, Thomas, *The Lives of the Noble Grecians and Romans, Compared together by that grave learned Philosopher Plutarke* (London, 1595).

Nowottny, Winifred, *The Language Poets Use* (London: Athlone Press, 1962).

Ornstein, Robert, *A Kingdom for a Stage: The Achievement of Shakespeare's History Plays* (Cambridge, Mass.: Harvard University Press, 1972).

Patterson, Annabel, *Shakespeare and the Popular Voice* (Oxford: Basil Blackwell, 1989).

   Reading Holinshed's Chronicles (Chicago and London: University of Chicago Press, 1994).

Pechter, Edward, ed., *Textual and Theatrical Shakespeare* (Iowa City: University of Iowa Press, 1996).

Players of Shakespeare 3, ed. Russell Jackson and Robert Smallwood (Cambridge: Cambridge University Press, 1992).

Players of Shakespeare 4, ed. Robert Smallwood (Cambridge: Cambridge University Press, 1998).

Players of Shakespeare 6, ed. Robert Smallwood (Cambridge: Cambridge University Press, 2004).

Political Shakespeare, ed. Jonathan Dollimore and Alan Sinfield (Manchester: Manchester University Press, 1985).

Potter, Lois, 'Recycling the Early Histories', *SS*, 43 (1990), 171–81.

Quinn, Michael, ed., *Shakespeare: Henry V* (London: Macmillan Casebooks, 1969).

Rabkin, Norman, *Shakespeare and the Problem of Meaning* (Chicago: University of Chicago Press, 1981).

   Shakespeare and the Common Understanding (New York: Free Press, 1967).

Rackin, Phyllis, *Stages of History: Shakespeare's English Chronicles* (London and New York: Routledge, 1991).

Ralegh, Sir Walter, *The History of the World*, ed. C. A. Patrides (London: Macmillan, 1971).

Reese, M. M., *The Cease of Majesty: A Study of Shakespeare's History Plays* (London: Edward Arnold, 1961).

Ribner, Irving, *The English History Play in the Age of Shakespeare*, 2nd edn (London: Methuen, 1965).

Richmond, Hugh, ed., *Shakespeare in Performance: King Henry VIII* (Manchester: Manchester University Press, 1994).

Roe, John, *Shakespeare and Machiavelli* (Cambridge: D. S. Brewer, 2002).

Rossiter, A. R., *Angel with Horns: Fifteen Lectures on Shakespeare*, ed. Graham Storey (London: Longman, 1961).

Rowley, Samuel, *When you see me, you know me*, ed. F. P. Wilson (Oxford: Malone Society, 1952).

Rudnytsky, Peter, '*Henry VIII* and the Deconstruction of History', in Alexander, *Shakespeare and Politics*, pp. 44–66.

Ryan, Kiernan, *Shakespeare*, 3rd edn (Basingstoke: Palgrave, 2002).

Saccio, Peter, *Shakespeare's English Kings*, 2nd edn (Oxford: Oxford University Press, 2000).

Shapiro, James, *1599: A Year in the Life of William Shakespeare* (London: Faber, 2005).

Shaughnessy, Robert, *Representing Shakespeare: England, History and the RSC* (London: Harvester, 1994).

Sher, Antony, *The Year of the King*, 2nd edn (London, Nick Hern Books, 2004).

Shewring, Margaret, *Shakespeare in Performance: King Richard II* (Manchester: Manchester University Press, 1996).

Sidney, Sir Philip, *Selected Writings*, ed. Richard Dutton (Manchester: Carcanet, 1989).

Smith, Emma, ed., *Shakespeare in Production: King Henry V* (Cambridge: Cambridge University Press, 2002).

ed., *Shakespeare's Histories* (Oxford: Blackwell, 2004).

Spivack, Bernard, *Shakespeare and the Allegory of Evil* (New York: Columbia University Press, 1958).

Sprague, Arthur Colby, *Shakespeare's Histories: Plays for the Stage* (London: Society for Theatre Research, 1964).

Swander, Homer D., 'The Rediscovery of *Henry VI*', *SQ*, 29 (1978), 146–63.

Taylor, Gary, 'Shakespeare and Others: The Authorship of *Henry the Sixth. Part One*', *Medieval and Renaissance Drama in England*, 7 (1995), 145–186.

Tillyard, E. M. W., *Shakespeare's History Plays* (Harmondsworth: Penguin, 1964).

Vaughan, Virginia M., '*King John*: A Study in Subversion and Containment', in Curren-Aquino, *King John: New Perspectives*, pp. 62–75.

Waith, Eugene, '*King John* and the Drama of History', *SQ*, 29 (1978), 203–9.

Weimann, Robert, *Shakespeare and the Popular Tradition in the Theater* (Baltimore: Johns Hopkins Press, 1978).

'Performance-Game and Representation in *Richard III*', in *Textual and Theatrical Shakespeare*, ed. Edward Pechter (Iowa City: University of Iowa Press, 1996), pp. 66–85.

'Mingling Vice and "Worthiness" in *King John*', *Shakespeare Studies*, 27 (1999), 109–33.

Welles, Orson, *Chimes at Midnight*, ed. Bridget Gellert Lyons (New Brunswick, N.J.: Rutgers University Press, 1988).

Wells, Robin Headlam, 'The Fortunes of Tillyard: Twentieth-Century Critical Debate on Shakespeare's History Plays', *English Studies*, 66 (1985), 391–403.

Wells, Stanley, and Gary Taylor, *William Shakespeare: A Textual Companion* (Oxford: Clarendon Press, 1987).

White, Hayden, *Metahistory* (Baltimore and London: Johns Hopkins University Press, 1973).

Tropics of Discourse (Baltimore and London: Johns Hopkins University Press, 1978).

Wilders, John, *The Lost Garden: A View of Shakespeare's English and Roman History Plays* (London: Macmillan, 1978).

Wiles, David, *Shakespeare's Clown* (Cambridge: Cambridge University Press, 1987).

Wilson, J. Dover, *The Fortunes of Falstaff* (Cambridge: Cambridge University Press, 1943).

Wilson, Richard, *Will Power* (London: Harvester, 1993).

Womersley, David, 'The Politics of *King John*', *Review of English Studies*, 40 (1989), 497–515.

Woodstock, ed. A. P. Rossiter (London: Chatto & Windus, 1946).

Wootton, David, ed., *Divine Right and Democracy: An Anthology of Political Writing in Stuart England* (Harmondsworth: Penguin, 1986).

Worden, Blair, 'Which play was performed at the Globe Theatre on 7 February 1601?', *London Review of Books*, 10 July 2003, pp. 22–4.

Yeats, W. B., 'At Stratford-upon-Avon', *Essays and Introductions* (London: Macmillan, 1961), pp. 105–6.

Index